Sport in Australian National Identity

For many Australians, there are two great passions: sport and 'taking the piss'. This book is about national identity – and especially about Australia's image as a sporting country. Whether reverent or not, any successful national image has to reflect something about the reality of the country. But it is also influenced by the reasons that people have for encouraging particular images – and by the conflicts between differing views of national identity, and of sport.

Buffeted by these elements, both the extent of Australian sports madness and the level of stirring have varied considerably over time. While many refer to long-lasting factors, such as the amount of sunshine, this book argues that the ebb and flow of sporting images are strongly linked to current views of national identity. Starting from Archer's win in the first Melbourne Cup in 1861, it traces the importance of trade unions in the formation of Australian Rules, the success of a small rural town in holding one of the world's foremost running races, and the win-from-behind of a fat arsed wombat knocking off the official mascots of Sydney 2000.

This book was based on a special issue of *Soccer and Society.*

Tony Ward is a writer and researcher based in Melbourne. Apart from his interest in national identity and sports, he runs a small consulting firm specialising in economic and financial analysis. He lives with his wife Gail in Elwood, inner Melbourne, and enjoys several sports, including golf, tennis, swimming and walking.

Sport in Australian National Identity

Kicking Goals

Tony Ward

Routledge
Taylor & Francis Group
LONDON AND NEW YORK

First published 2010 by Routledge
2 Park Square, Milton Park, Abingdon, Oxon, OX14 4RN

Simultaneously published in the USA and Canada
by Routledge
270 Madison Avenue, New York, NY 10016

Routledge is an imprint of the Taylor & Francis Group, an informa business

This book is a reproduction of *Soccer and Society*, vol.10, issue 5. The Publisher requests to those authors who may be citing this book to state, also, the bibliographical details of the special issue on which the book was based

Typeset in Times New Roman by Value Chain, India
Printed and bound in Great Britain by TJI Digital Ltd, Padstow, Cornwall

British Library Cataloguing in Publication Data
A catalogue record for this book is available from the British Library

ISBN10: 0-415-56520-0 (h/b)
ISBN10: 0-415-57555-9 (p/b)
ISBN13: 978-0-415-56520-2 (h/b)
ISBN13: 978-0-415-57555-3 (p/b)

CONTENTS

Sport in the Global Society – Contemporary Perspectives

Series Editor: Boria Majumdar

Sport in Australian National Identity
Kicking Goals

The social, cultural (including media) and political study of sport is an expanding area of scholarship and related research. While this area has been well served by the Sport in the Global Society Series, the surge in quality scholarship over the last few years has necessitated the creation of *Sport in the Global Society: Contemporary Perspectives*. The series will publish the work of leading scholars in fields as diverse as sociology, cultural studies, media studies, gender studies, cultural geography and history, political science and political economy. If the social and cultural study of sport is to receive the scholarly attention and readership it warrants, a cross-disciplinary series dedicated to taking sport beyond the narrow confines of physical education and sport science academic domains is necessary. Sport in the Global Society: Contemporary Perspectives will answer this need.

Other Titles in the Series

Introduction

In early 2001, social commentator John Carroll went searching for iconic images of 'Australian Dreaming', and found himself at the Melbourne Cricket Ground. During the packed one-day cricket match:

> the Mexican wave gets going, circling the ground. As it reaches the Members' segment it stops, giving way to booing, before taking up again, in rhythm, on the far side. The booing is good-natured, even affectionate, a way of saying we know there is some sort of social hierarchy in this country – differences of wealth, position and status – but don't imagine that you are any better.[1]

If he visited the MCG a couple of years later, Carroll could have reported a surreal rejoinder. The old Members' Stand had been demolished for redevelopment – but when the Mexican wave reached the stark gap, the crowd still booed the members' ghosts for not joining in.[2]

Around the world, many commentators have chosen specific events as illustrating something typical about a national identity. And, like Carroll, many have visited sports stadiums looking for examples of a particular national spirit.

But Australia seems ahead of the pack in the frequency and importance of sport in descriptions of national character. When Melbourne hosted the Commonwealth Games in March 2006 many commentators, both Australian and overseas, agreed there was something especially 'Aussie' about the role of sports. One typical comment: 'The Australian psyche is bound in sports, as a passion and as an essential component of national identity.'[3]

The Australian team was certainly very successful at the 2006 Commonwealth Games, winning 221 medals. This was more than the combined effort of the second and third place getters (England, with 110, and Canada, 86), despite Australia's significantly smaller population than either competitor.[4]

Some commentators explained these successes as part of the national identity. New Zealand journalist Greg Ansley saw the sports passion stemming originally from desires to wipe the 'convict stain' by beating the mother country, reinforced by greater opportunities for participation in a society more egalitarian than England.[5] UK writer Nick Afka Thomas argued the Australian successes link to the 'outdoors culture' enabled by Australia averaging 3,000 hours of sunshine a year compared with southern England's 1,750 hours. For Thomas, however, the most telling factor was that athletes who had trained at the Australian Institute of Sports won half the Australian medals. He concluded that 'winning medals is more about how much countries invest in their talent than anything else'.[6]

Looking more broadly than Commonwealth Games success, a Google search in January 2006 also emphasized the role of sports in the Australian image. This search found a total 899 occurrences of the four phrases 'sports mad Australia', 'sports mad Australians', 'Australia is sports mad' and 'Australians are sports mad'. A similar search for 'America' and 'Americans' produced 56 matches, while the New Zealanders rated 36 matches (one of which was 'like Australia, New Zealand is sports mad'). England, despite the efforts of soccer fans only achieved 11 mentions, while Canada tailed the field with three.

Nor is this a recent occurrence. In 1964, social commentator Donald Horne argued in his path breaking *The Lucky Country*:

> Sport to many Australians is life and the rest a shadow. Sport has been the one national institution that has had no 'knockers'. To many it is considered a sign of degeneracy not to be interested in it. To play sport, or watch others and to read and talk about it is to uphold the nation and build its character. Australia's success at competitive international sport is considered an important part of its foreign policy.[7]

Indeed, historian Ian Jobling has documented more than 30 such comments, from 1880 to 1980[8] – and his list can be supplemented by many other examples discovered in the research for this collection.

So the image of sport as a key part of the Australian national identity is a very common one. But if we look in more detail at the image, surprises rapidly appear. The first surprise comes from looking behind the medal count at Melbourne 2006. Despite the archetypal image of the bronzed Aussie male athlete, Australian women were the real champions of the Commonwealth. Australian women won 42% of the gold medals open to them; their male counterparts only won one-quarter. Although these particular results were affected by the absence of two champion male swimmers, these statistics are part of a general pattern of better female performance, especially before 1980. In terms of the factors cited above, do Australian women benefit from the sunshine more than the men? Are they that much keener to wipe the convict stain? Neither seems likely.

The second surprise is considerable variation in the extent of sports passions amongst Australians – and in how they are expressed. For all those taking part in the Mexican wave at the MCG, there were many others, not least in the Members', sitting firmly in their seats. There have also long been differences between Australians in the sports they are mad about. Some follow a range of sports. Others concentrate their passion on particular sports – and in the case of football, since the 1950s the most popular spectator sport, different codes around Australia. Some have bitterly criticized any lure of money, especially gambling money, in sport and have militated to clip the hooves of sports such as racing.

And others have seemed immune to the whole virus. After all, even the renowned cricket madness of long time Prime Minister Sir Robert Menzies did not convert his wife, Dame Pattie Menzies:

> The only test match she saw in Australia was in 1924, with the hosts taking on England. According to Dame Menzies 'my husband suggested I go to at least one day of the match. When I arrived at the ground Hobbs and Sutcliffe were batting, and after watching for a couple of hours, I became bored, and went home.' The next time she attended the cricket was in 1926, when her husband suggested that she should see at least one match in England. Dame Menzies 'went to the Oval where England was again playing

Australia ... When I arrived at the ground, there they were again, Hobbs and Sutcliffe. They were still batting.'[9]

And despite the many references going back to 1880 to Australian sports obsessions, a third surprise is the extent to which the detail of the image has varied over that time. For one measure, the extent of sporting success has waxed and waned, with many Australians seeing a 'disaster' at the Montreal 1976 Olympics, when the country won no gold medals. For another, sports' interactions with other aspects of the national identity have varied too. When Australian writer Gideon Haigh previewed the 2001 Australian cricket tour of England, he used another common image: 'This being an Australian team, a degree of drinking is to be expected.'[10]

While they are of course not the only sportsmen renowned for their drinking, the linkage of Australians and drinking is a strong one. In 2005 Victoria Bitter beer used this image in an advertising campaign centred on 250,000 talking dolls in the likeness of cricket batsman David Boon. While successful both in test cricket and the one day game, Boon is most frequently remembered for his exploits on the Australian test team's trip to England in 1989. He set what many cite as an unofficial world record for the amount of beer consumed on a flight between the two countries – 52 cans.[11]

This widely-held association with drinking has, however, varied. Modern sport emphasizes fitness – evident in much higher standards of fielding in cricket for example. So the degree of drinking tolerated in 2001 was less than in the 1960s tours, when a more relaxed attitude to carousing prevailed.

The drinking reputation of Australian cricketers goes back a long way, to at least the first English side to tour Australia in 1861–62. English batsman Roger Iddison, commented, 'Well, O'I doant think mooch of their play, but they are a wonderful lot of drinking men'.[12] Australian teams took their drinking to the British Isles as well: in 1893, a drunken brawl among players left blood all over a railway compartment. In 1912, raucous Australians were refused service by stewards on a ferry to Ireland.

But it would be a mistake to draw a straight line from these early experiences to the Booney doll, and conclude an unchanging image of sports-mad drinkers. In marked contrast, the 1930 Australian team to England was celebrated by the temperance movement for fielding 12 abstainers including Don Bradman, captain Bill Woodfull, and 1931 Wisden's player of the year Clarrie Grimmett.[13]

An even bigger transition has occurred for smoking. Smokers' nights were a central part of sports culture for decades, and cigarette firms were some of the first businesses to put major finances into sports advertising and sponsorship. Both aspects have by 2008 completely disappeared.

So a little investigation indicates we don't have one constant image of sports and the Australian national identity, produced by the hours of sunlight or inspired by memories of the convict stain. Rather, we have a more diffuse and changing picture, with some elements, such as drinking and smoking, being more important at some times (and to some people) and less so at others.

So where does this image come from, and why does it change? These are the central questions of this collection.

In answering them, the key argument is that images of national identity do not just 'happen'. To gain acceptance, they have to reflect something of a country, and are clearly influenced by events such as, in Australia's case, the sporting success at Melbourne 2006. But they are also strongly affected by the agendas of different people and social groups and the images they *want* to see of Australia.

As is documented throughout this collection, there have often been differences between people and groups in their preferred images of Australia. Between 1900 and 1940 the strong temperance movement aimed at a wholesome image, emphasizing amateur sport and decrying both drinking and gambling on sports. But another subculture at the same time was disdainful of the puritanical 'wowsers', and celebrated a vision of national character in which anti-authoritarian larrikins gambled, drank, smoked and enjoyed professional sport.

As in other countries, there was considerable variation over time in the interaction between the different visions of Australia, and the social groups promoting them. At times different visions coexisted. At others social tensions ran high, and particular groups tried to impose their vision as the national identity.

On the more harmonious side, a long occurring element in the Australian image has been the egalitarian spirit of 'the fair go'. Internationally, many sports historically have confined themselves to particular turfs, particularly of social class and gender. Many Australian sports successes have appealed across such divides, building larger audiences (and stadiums) and widening the talent pool from which to develop champions. This has been a key factor underlying the successes of women athletes noted above.

But such tolerance has not always been a feature of Australian society. Around 1900, journalist John Norton in *Truth* lambasted the Sydney elite running the Australian Jockey Club for degrading horse racing 'by selfish, if not sinister interest, prompted and maintained by class caddishness and society snobbery'.[14] In the 1930s, the country banned some 5,000 books 'on the grounds that they would tend to offend morality or good order' – and when a journalist for *The Bulletin* tried to find out about these, he found even the list of banned books was itself restricted. As late as 1965, an opinion poll showed 42% support for banning the bikini.[15] At the same time, champion Dawn Fraser, who came from working-class Balmain but succeeded in the 'silvertail' sport of swimming complained: 'Enough remarks have been made at times about my "background" to indicate that officials think I ought to feel very grateful that they even let me into swimming.'[16]

Attitudes to tolerance, even to the 'fair go', played a strong part in the differing ways people saw sport, and the sorts of image they wanted to create of 'this sporting nation'. As with the attitudes to participation in sport noted above, there were many different visions – and the competition between those visions had a strong influence on the ways different sports developed.

Amidst such differing views, how does one national identity, including sports imagery, develop? As many marketing campaigns have found, efforts to create images are only successful if they resonate with the broad population. So we need to look not only at the people trying to create or reinforce an image, but also at how other people respond.

In the dynamic between the creation of, and responses to, particular images, jostling occurs between the different visions of what sport means to the national identity. The more powerful the social group backing particular images, the more likely those images will flavour the overall pattern. The sway of the temperance movement was much greater in 1930 than in 2000.

A starting point is to assess what truth lies behind the images. Donald Horne qualified his picture above of sports madness: 'Australians usually had an inflated idea of this success. They weren't as good as they thought they were, and they falsely assumed that others always had the same regard for their prowess as they had themselves.'[17]

Picking up this theme, the collection tries where it can to present good evidence on the realities of sports involvement and achievement. A second theme is to look at how and why particular national images are encouraged and responded to. Later papers bring these two themes together in tracing over time the varying patterns and attitudes towards sports and national images that have always characterized Australian society.

The jostling between social groups over images has a lot to do with Carroll's 'good-natured' booing in the Mexican wave at the MCG. Australia does seem unusual in the popularity of a particular brand of sports humour. The *Australian Dictionary of Biography* is surely unique in including an entry for 'the world's greatest barracker', Yabba (Stephen Gascoigne). Throughout the 1920s and 1930s his heckling echoed around the Sydney Cricket Ground, such as responding to a spell of wild bowling with, 'Your length's lousy but you bowl a good width!'[18]

Also unusual were recent top-selling CD sales by albums mimicking, and sending up, cricket commentators. Comedian Billy Birmingham reckoned, 'There are two great Australian pastimes: watching sport and taking the piss, and I stumbled across the magic combination of putting them together.'[19]

The 'taking the piss' in Australian sports humour has elements of both self-deprecation and mocking those in authority. The latter has not always nor universally been popular, especially amongst its targets in authority. The varying success of larrikin attitudes to authority is thus another facet of the conflicts between differing visions of Australian national identity.

As well as his pilgrimage to the MCG, John Carroll's images of Australian Dreaming included the Sydney Olympics in 2000. Carroll – and many others – saw symbols of 'notable, and admirable' features of the distinctive character of the Australian people. The UK *Guardian* commented: 'The mixture of efficiency, friendliness and boundless enthusiasm is uniquely Australian.'[20] As we will see in the 11th paper 'Heyday of the Amateur?', much less complimentary things were said about Australian sports organizing abilities in the lead up to the Melbourne Olympics in 1956.

Tracing the ups and downs of 'uniquely Australian' sports culture over the past 150 years poses interesting questions about both actual patterns in sports and the reasons particular images of Australian identity were developed and accepted. The search encounters some surprising twists – and can be in itself an enjoyable journey.

Organization of the collection

In discussing themes of sports and Australian identity, this collection has three broad parts. The first, in papers 2 to 4, measures sports involvement and discusses how this relates to national identity. It also demonstrates the changing nature of Australian national identity. Papers 5 and 6 form the second part of the collection, questioning how universal particular sporting images are across Australia, and tracing some of the factors contributing to differences. The third section, papers 7 to 14, looks at the varying images of sport and national identity over the past 150 years, tracing how and why those images have changed.

This collection has the benefit of a massive amount of material, both primary data and other accounts, on a wide range of sports.[21] In utilizing this abundant material, the discussion focuses on a succinct overview of the events and sports that have contributed to Australia's national sports image. It illustrates key patterns and developments by taking examples from those sports that have historically attracted the most involvement and the greatest national attention. Any such choice by necessity leaves out other important aspects of sports, and their interaction with social trends. In this collection, these include such topics as less well-attended sports, sporting involvement of different groups such as Aborigines and recent migrants, and to a large extent, predominantly female sports.[22] Good accounts exist on many of these topics – but there are limits to how much a broad treatment focussed on key elements of national imagery can take advantage of these contributions.

Focusing on key national measures, the second paper compares Australian and international stories, to see how unique the experience here is. It analyses the evidence from four frequently used measures of sporting activity: international sporting success, active participation, active attendance and passive involvement, such as following sports on television.

Where Australians do lead the sporting stakes, is this really a central part of the national psyche? Paper 3 examines some international examples of sports and national identity, considers some aspects of forming national images, and how these have affected, and been evident in, sport.

Paper 4 discusses several icons of Australian national identity whose paths are interwoven with sporting success. The Anzac spirit and the national anthem have often played sporting roles. However, there have been some remarkable differences in attitudes towards these icons, both between social groups and over time. The differing, sometimes conflicting, views give insight into Australia's development – and about the agendas observers have brought to their views of sports and national identity.

Building on the international comparisons in Paper 2, Paper 5 looks at Australian sporting crowds. Surveying the most popular spectator sports, it asks how much the archetypal sports-mad fan dominates crowds, or how significant other motivations are. The paper looks at how attendances have changed over time, with the implications for the overall sporting image.

Many observers have related international success to high rates of active sports participation in Australia. Paper 6 discusses participation rates for both adults and children, and notes how these patterns too have varied between groups, and over time.

If sporting interests have changed over time, why has Australia long been described as a sporting nation? Paper 7 considers the origins of this tag, and the early development of organized sport in Australia. Far from contemporary celebrations of sunshine, some nineteenth-century observers felt the British race was degenerating under the Australian sun – and were highly relieved at early sporting successes against England. But factors such as the high standard of living assisted Australians to excel in many fields, and the paper asks why the sporting image in particular was so compelling.

Within the overall sporting image, there were differences between sports. Paper 8 discusses the early years of horse racing, which long had the greatest attendances in Australia, as well as sculling, which was highly popular between 1880 and 1910 then all but disappeared. Unusually for a major country, the dominant football codes differ between the two major cities, and the paper traces this development, explaining why the early strength of trade unions was one factor in the success of Australian rules in Melbourne.

In 1908, Prime Minister Alfred Deakin delivered a rousing speech celebrating 'we are and always have been, a sporting people'. Paper 9 examines the differing sporting visions of various groups across Australia. One key feature was the worldwide tension between amateur and professional sport. The paper also asks why, for most of the twentieth century, a small town of 6,000 in Victoria had one of the world's richest professional foot races – the Stawell Gift.

One piece of evidence sometimes cited for a special role of sports is Australia's raising of Sportsmen's Battalions for the First World War. However, as Paper 10 documents, a gap existed between the vision of the recruiters and the response they received. Looking at other developments from 1900 to 1940, especially in horse racing and cricket, the paper notes the effects of interactions between the competing visions.

Australia celebrated some remarkable sporting successes in the 1950s and 1960s. Looking at the Melbourne Olympics of 1956, and Australia's dominance in amateur tennis, Paper 11 discusses some of the tensions in conflicting visions behind this over-all image. It also discusses how those visions affected how sport was organized.

But times change, and Paper 12 notes that the visions of sport in the 1950s – and their organizing bodies – were much less effective in any sort of grandstand by 1970. By the 1970s, and especially after the disastrous Montreal 1976 Olympics, one news-paper editorial lamented the tarnishing of the sporting image and 'the decline of the Sporting Super Race'. The trends are illustrated in a case study of the remarkable increase in popularity, and subsequent decline, of women's bowls from 1950 onwards.

Appeals to national images formed very specific parts of strategies to market sports to wider audiences in the late 1970s. Paper 13 discusses the two leading exam-ples of these: the Australia II campaign for the America's Cup, and World Series Cricket – although it notes for the latter that the difference between the crowds for World Series and traditional cricket was not as large as often portrayed. Appeals to national pride also played a big role in the formation of the Australian Institute of Sport, and the paper discusses this development.

In recent years, as across the world, Australian sport and its images have changed considerably with commercialization and particularly the financial boom from broad-casting rights. Sports responded in different ways to these forces, and Paper 14 traces the patterns in Australian Rules, rugby league and horse racing.

Looking at a range of sports, and patterns over the last 150 years, the collection suggests a number of reasons why Australia has gained its sporting reputation. Paper 15, in conclusion, brings these suggestions together, tying them into the broader patterns of Australian national character and identity, and the role of both social patterns and agendas.

That image is, as this introduction has shown, both a powerful one and well worth some discussion. While waxing and waning, and often taking surprising turns, it has been a strong Australian feature since before the 1890s, when poet Henry Lawson wrote disdainfully:

> In the land where sport is sacred, where the labourer is a god,
> You must pander to the people, make a hero of a clod![23]

Whether applauded or treated more sceptically, the 'sports madness' tag rests on Australian shoulders, like a laurel wreath on an Olympic champion. The central aim of this collection is to ask why and how this tag was bestowed. And, to the extent that sports madness is indeed a unique part of the Australian image, to discuss the key influences that have developed that image. In doing so, the collection's approach mirrors that of Melbourne author Shane Maloney, in a similar situation: 'I approach this question as I do my golf swing. An open stance, a comfortable grip, and a vague sense that you know where you're going. And knowing that if you try too hard, you're bound to bugger it up.'[24]

Notes

1. Carroll, 'Australian Dreaming' in Warhaft, *Well May We Say,* 512.
2. Personal experience of this collection's research assistant, also reported by Haigh, *All Out,* 216.
3. The 'typical comment' was from Greg Ansley, 'Aussies – Natural Born Winners'. *New Zealand Herald*, March 25, 2006.
4. These medal counts taken from www.melbourne2006.com.au/Schedule+and+Results/ Medals.
5. Ansley, 'Aussies – Natural Born Winners'.
6. Nick Afka Thomas, 'Why Australia Keeps Winning the Medals'. *The Guardian*, March 30, 2006.
7. Horne, *The Lucky Country*, 37.
8. On the frequency of comments referring to Australian sports obsession, cult or similar terms, see Jobling, 'Australian Sporting Heroes', 91–2, giving some 30 examples, dating from 1880 to 1980. Nauright noted that, while oft repeated, the term had not been studied in detail, and called for research (Nauright, 'Sports Mad Nations?', 30). One response came from Hay, comparing major sports stadia around the world and the size of crowds: 'Sports Mad Nations'.
9. Cashman, Headon, and Kinross-Smith, eds., *The Oxford Book of Australian Sporting Anecdotes*, 130.
10. Haigh, *Game for Anything,* 286.
11. On the development of the Booney doll, see Spangler, 'Brand Builder', and Maiden, 'Booney Tunes'. *The Age*, January 28, 2006 Business, 1. Late in 2007, business writer Mark Hawthorne described the Booney doll as 'possibly the nation's greatest advertising creation' in 50 years. In three summers, some 845,000 dolls were distributed (440,000 of Boon, others of former English player Ian Botham and Australian spinner Shane Warne). The campaign won a major award at the Cannes Advertising Festival in 2006, and has helped sponsor Victoria Bitter 'to keep a stranglehold on the full-strength beer market'. Mark Hawthorne. 'If you Hated the Booney, You've Been Warned'. *The Age*, December 7, 2007, Business, 4. For Boon's drinking feats, see McClure, 'Sports Notes Column', *The Age*, November 28, 2005, Sport, 16.
12. Smart, ed., *Penguin Book of Australian Sporting Anecdotes*, 45–6.
13. Haigh, *Game for Anything*, 286.
14. Norton's tirade against the AJC appeared in his weekly newspaper *Truth* onAugust 20, 1899.
15. Molony, *Australia: Our Heritage*, 272, and Zogbaum, *Kisch in Australia*, 136. The 1965 opinion poll: Gallup poll summary February–March 1965.
16. Fraser, *Gold Medal Girl*, 101, cited by Stell, *Half the Race*, 117.
17. Horne, *The Lucky Country*, 37.
18. Yabba's details from the on-line *Australian Dictionary of Biography*: http:// adb.anu.edu.au/.
19. Birmingham comments on ABC radio programme, 'Stop being serious, this is funny!' The Sports Factor ABC Radio National, August 1, 2003 (available from the ABC website).
20. Carroll, 'Australian Dreaming', 509.
21. For examples, Lemon and Freedman's *History of Australian Thoroughbred Racing Volume 2* runs to 500 pages covering only 'The Golden Years 1862 to 1939'; Harte's revised *History of Australian Cricket* weighs in at 830 pages; and Gordon's *Australia and the Olympic Games* reaches 540 pages.
22. One statistic supporting this choice is that while the female sport netball ranks very highly in sports participation statistics, it is very low down on attendance numbers, even amongst women. In 2006, the numbers of women who attended netball matches in the previous year (131,000) were dwarfed by the numbers of women attending Australian rules (1,011,000) or horse racing (912,000). See Australian Bureau of Statistics, (ABS, www.abs.gov.au) *Sports Participation Australia 2005–06* (catalogue 4174.0), Table 7.

23. Lawson, 'A Song of Southern Writers', *The Bulletin*, May 28, 1892.
24. Maloney's quip was at a seminar in March 2006 on 'What makes a City Creative?', reported by Perkin, 'So Melbourne' column, *The Age (Melbourne) Magazine* April 2006, 19.

References

Australian Bureau of Statistics. *Sports Participation Australia 2005–06* (catalogue 4174.0)
Carroll, John. 'Australian Dreaming'. In *Well May We Say... The Speeches that Made Australia,* ed. Sally Warhaft, 510–12. Melbourne: Black, 2004.
Cashman, Richard, David Headon, and Graeme Kinross-Smith, eds. *The Oxford Book of Australian Sporting Anecdotes*. Oxford: Oxford University Press, 1993.
Fraser, Dawn. *Gold Medal Girl*. Melbourne: Lansdowne, 1965.
Gordon, Harry. *Australia and the Olympic Games*. Brisbane: University of Queensland Press, 1994.
Haigh, Gideon. *Game for Anything: Writings on Cricket*. Melbourne: Black, 2004.
Haigh, Gideon. *All Out: The Ashes 2006–07*. Melbourne: Black, 2007.
Harte, Chris. *A History of Australian Cricket*. London: Andre Deutsch, 1993.
Hay, Roy. 'Sports Mad Nations: Some Research Already Done'. *Australian Society for Sports History Bulletin* 33 (February 2001): 18–24.
Horne, Donald. *The Lucky Country*. 3rd ed. Melbourne: Penguin, 1977.
Jobling, Ian. 'Australian Sporting Heroes'. In *Sport: Nationalism and Internationalism,* ed. Wray Vamplew, 91–118. Melbourne: Australian Society for Sports History. ASSH Studies, no. 2, 1987.
Lemon, Andrew, and Harold Freedman. *History of Australian Thoroughbred Racing Volume 2: The Golden Years 1862 to 1939*. Melbourne: Southbank Communications, 1990.
Molony, John. *Australia: Our Heritage*. Melbourne: Australian Scholarly Publishing, 2005.
Nauright, John. 'Sports Mad Nations? A Call for Research by Sports Historians'. *ASSH Bulletin* 32 (August 1990): 30–31.
Smart, Richard, ed. *The Penguin Book of Australian Sporting Anecdotes*. Ringwood, Vic: Penguin Books, 1996.
Spangler, Ian. 'Brand Builder'. *PanStadia* 13, no. 3 (Spring 2007): 48–51.
Stell, Marion. *Half the Race: a History of Australian Women in Sport*. North Ryde, NSW: Collins/Angus and Robertson, 1990.
Warhaft, Sally, ed. *Well May We Say ... The Speeches that Made Australia*. Melbourne: Black, 2004.
Zogbaum, Heidi. *Kirsch in Australia*. Melbourne: Scribe, 2004.

Measuring sports madness

Sports 'tragics' loom large in Australian folklore. Many nods of recognition met Beth Spencer's 2004 recollection of an ex-boyfriend

> In the 1970s, when I lived with him, he wrote 'Essendon Football Club' in the space for religion on the Census form ... I met my ex-boyfriend a few years ago and he told me how disastrous his year had been: he had failed his exams, his girlfriend had left him and Essendon had lost the Grand Final. The hardest thing to take, he said, the bitterest blow, was the Bombers. So close.[1]

A central concern of this collection is the interaction between the Australian sporting images and the underlying realities. How typical is Beth's ex, and how much do he and his mates really differ from sports fans around the world? This paper discusses various ways of measuring involvement in sports, and compares the Australian track record with the efforts of others.

The international competition is tough. In Oklahoma in November 2005, James Torpy put his hand up as a contender for the craziest sports fan of all time when, after being sentenced to 30 years in prison for armed robbery and shooting with intent to kill, he pleaded with the judge to make it 33 years because his favourite basketballer of all time was legendary Boston Celtic No 33, Larry Bird.

> 'He said if he was going to go down, he was going to go down in Larry Bird's jersey' a stunned Ray Elliott, Oklahoma County District Court Judge, said, adding 'We accommodated his request and he was just as happy as he could be'.[2]

Further back, in 1990, the poorly rated Cameroon soccer team with ageing star Roger Milla provided several dramatic upsets in the World Cup in Italy. By the time the team made it to the quarter finals, they had support throughout Africa, and in many other Third World countries as well. When England beat Cameroon 3–2 in the quarter final, a Bangladeshi woman hanged herself, leaving a note reading 'the elimination of Cameroon also means the end of my life'.[3]

Valiant contenders also come to the starting gates of the sports crazy team event, especially thanks to soccer. A British survey to mark National Children's Day in December 2005 asked 2,500 UK under 10-year-olds to name the world's most famous person. Young Manchester United and England star Wayne Rooney not only beat Jesus to take second place, he also pushed his national team captain, David Beckham, into fourth. It was left to God to restore some Christian pride, taking top spot.[4]

Faced with tough competition from such valiant efforts, how can we decide on the gold medal? Can we find some measures to judge whether sports do indeed play an especially big role in Australian life?

A starting illustration on the importance of sport in Australia might be the extensive sports programme that formed a key part of the country's bicentennial celebrations in 1988. In marked contrast, sport rated hardly a mention in the US bicentennial programme in 1976.[5] But this is a comparison with only one country – and not all countries have had similar celebrations.

A second possibility, from the above examples, is to look at Census forms under 'religion' for the numbers of football club adherents. However, the Australian Bureau of Statistics codes such responses as 'not defined' – and it appears the numbers are very much smaller than the 70,509 Australians returning 'Jedi' as their religion in the 2001 Census. International comparisons of sports fever are hard enough without in addition concerning ourselves with a galaxy far, far away.[6]

As noted in the previous paper, one measure that does show Australia well ahead is a Google search on Australians and 'sports madness'. But what people refer to when they talk of sports madness frequently varies. Many observers have used specific measures of Australian sporting madness, although often without detailed international comparison. The most common measures have fallen into four groups: international sporting success; active participation in sport; active interest in sport, such as attending sporting events or betting on them; and more passive interest in sport, such as following sports events on TV or radio, or in social discussions.

At first glance, Australia seems to excel in all four of these areas – but a detailed look at international evidence, and at performance over time, throws up some surprises. This paper looks at the evidence on the above four measures, seeing how Australia's track record really does compare.

Green and gold, gold, gold – international sporting success

For a country with a relatively small population, Australia has recently had extraordinary sporting success in a variety of sports.

> Australia pretty generally beats most people at most things. Truly never has there been a more sporting nation. At the 1996 Olympics in Atlanta, to take just one random but illustrative example, Australia, the fifty-second largest nation in the world, brought home more medals than all but four other countries, all of them much larger ... There are even forty Australians playing baseball at the professional level in the United States, including five in the major leagues – and Australians don't even *play* baseball ... It is a wonder in such a vigorous and active society that there is anyone left to form an audience.[7]

The year Bill Bryson published those words, 1999, was one of Australia's most successful international sporting years. Australia was crowned World Cup Rugby Champions, World Cup Cricket Champions, Netball World Champions and Davis Cup Champions, in addition to being reigning Rugby League World Cup Champions (from 1995) and Women's World Cup Cricket Champions (from 1997).[8]

And Australia has also had far more than its fair share of individual world champions. As well as a raft of tennis players, especially in the 1950s and 1960s, these include Greg Norman (ranked number one golfer in the world for over six years in 1980s and 1990s); Geoff Hunt (ranked number one male squash player from 1975 to 1980); Heather McKay (dominated world women's squash, holding the British Open title from 1962 to 1977); and Walter Lindrum (who dominated world billiards in the early 1930s to such an extent that the rules were changed to limit his scoring).

While acknowledging this diversity of achievement, the best starting point for comparisons of international success is Olympic medals. After the Athens Olympics in 2004, the Australian Bureau of Statistics (ABS) took Bryson's approach a step further, by adjusting medal counts for the populations of competing countries. The ABS analysis showed that Australia won a gold medal for every 1,186,000 of the population. This result put Australia third, behind only Norway (one gold for every 910,000 people) and the Bahamas (one gold for each 317,000).[9]

Australia ranked even higher at Athens if we count total medals, coming second with 2.4 medals per million, behind the Bahamas on 6.3, and similar to Cuba, also 2.4. The United States, which topped the total medals table, had 0.4 medals per million people.

Looking over the 50 years of Olympics since 1952, Australia's total medal count (averaging 1.8 medals per million) was well ahead of larger countries such as Germany (0.9 – including both East and West Germany when they competed separately); and USA and Great Britain (both 0.4).[10]

There are, however, two major problems with seeing Australia's success at the Olympics as proof of a unique sports culture. First, a comparison with smaller countries is not quite as flattering for Australia. Secondly, Australia's success has waxed and waned over time.

Despite Bryson's claim that Australia's medal haul at Atlanta relative to population was 'streets ahead' of anyone else, this tally at 2.3 was just ahead of Hungary's 2.1, with New Zealand fairly close at 1.6 medals per million population. These two strongly performing countries provide even tougher comparisons across the 50-year period. Since 1952, Hungary has in fact outscored Australia on the medals per million rating, averaging 2.6. New Zealand's 1.6 is only a little behind Australia's 1.8.

Each of these three countries has seen some significant changes in its success rate across this period. Australians are proud of their medal tallies at Melbourne in 1956 and Sydney in 2000, which registered at 3.7 and 3.0 on the medals per million metre. However, both lie behind the best performances of Hungary (4.5 at Helsinki in 1952) and New Zealand (3.8 at Seoul in 1988) – and neither of those countries had a home ground advantage.

Results at one Olympics can be affected by particular individual athletes, so to get a better, longer-term picture the following graph shows average medals per million for four periods, each with three Olympics. The periods are: the 1950s, the 1960s, the 1976 to 1992 period (excluding 1980 and 1984, when the results were affected by widespread boycotts), and since 1996.

In the comparison with Hungary and New Zealand, Australia does not look as impressive as it does in comparison with the three larger countries. Per capita, New Zealand had comparable results in the 1960s, and better results 1976 to 1992, while Hungary had significantly better average results from 1952 to 1992.

The graph also shows that Australian medal tallies have varied considerably. Impressive results in the 1950s and since the mid-1990s contrast with poorer performance in the middle years, which reached a low point in 1976. Australia failed to win any gold medals at Montreal in 1976, prompting UK journalist Ronald Kaye to write:

> Like a middle-aged athlete gone flabby, Australia has stumbled into a national identity crisis, stricken by self-doubt and torn by bitter recriminations over real or imagined failings. The crisis has been brought about by the sudden collapse of Australia's greatest claim to world esteem: its athletes, who are turning in their worst Olympic performance

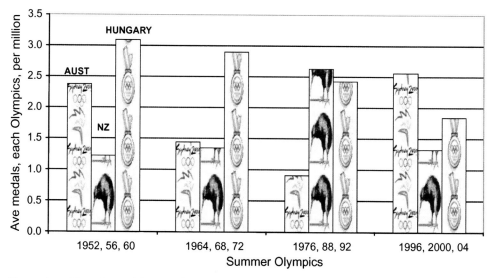

Figure 1.   Olympic medals per million population.

in 40 years ... Australians may [now] be the worst conditioned people on earth. The nation is fat and lazy, drinks too much beer, and suffers the highest rate of heart disease.[11]

An immediate reaction to Hungary's post-war performance might be to point to intensive government sporting programmes, especially from 1960 onwards. However, Hungary was doing well before that: its best year was 1952, and it also did reasonably in the interwar Olympics 1920 to 1936. In the interwar games, Australia managed a comparatively lacklustre 0.6 medals per million population, while Hungary was well ahead with an average of 1.5. Even Hungary's effort was itself put into the shade by remarkable Nordic performances: Sweden averaged 5.6 and Finland 8.5 medals per million at each Olympics in the interwar years.[12]

These medal tallies – and the variations they show – suggest some caution in trying to seek single explanations of sporting success. This caution is reinforced by a comparison of some explanations suggested for Australian and Finnish successes.

In 1962 *US Sports Illustrated* journalist Herbert Warren provided a succinct overview of reasons often suggested for Australian sporting success in the 1950s:

A fine climate, plenty of room, plenty of time, an inbred love of sports and the wish to excel at them, the lack of competing fields of interest, the worship of the physical which is part of a young country, the right pitch of support from one's family and friends, the splendid natural facilities, the relatively inexpensive cost of sport, the early orientation in school, the opportunity to develop in highly organised competition, and added to these good food for growing bodies and the natural desire of the people of a small nation to do famously in fields which command world attention and respect – these in combination are the amalgam which has made Australia the most vigorous sporting country of all time. It doesn't explain though the emergence of its super athletes. If you add two other factors on which Australia places strong emphasis it does. They are: able coaching and plain hard work.[13]

It seems plausible that such factors would indeed contribute to sporting success. However, many observers half a century ago also thought plausible various attempts to explain the remarkable Finnish Olympic success in the interwar years:

Table 1.   Comparison of explanations for Australian and Finnish sporting success.

	Australia 1960	Finland 1920–1940
Diet	good food for growing bodies	raw dried fish, rye bread 'hard as biscuit', and sour milk
Climate	fine climate	remote harshness
Wealth	splendid facilities, low cost of sport	relative poverty
Cultural heritage	young country 'worshipping the physical'	direct descendants of a physically tough 'wild Mongol strain'
Sport traditions	toughened by 'lots of competitive sport'	tough from hot saunas, birch whips and ice baths

Fascinating claims were made for native foods: raw, dried fish, rye bread 'hard as biscuit', and sour milk ... Another theory forwarded by the half-educated was that the Finns, distinctly different kinds of people from the neighbouring Swedes, were direct descendants of a physically tough 'wild Mongol strain'. The remote harshness of the land and the relative poverty of the people ... were proposed as reasons for Finland's superiority over softer, more technocratic, societies. Truth and fiction were intermingled in descriptions (by non-Finns) of the sauna baths. Some said it was an ice bath followed by a rolling in the snow that made them tough; others were sure that the peculiar heat of the sauna, accompanied by thrashing oneself with soft twigs and then the icy bath, couldn't help but breed tough men.[14]

Direct comparison of several factors gives us:

Such explanations may have important elements in them. However, apart from the inconsistency – if not direct conflicts – between the two lists, neither can explain variations in both Australian and Finnish performance over time.

More generally, the discussion of medal tallies asks some questions of Bryson's judgement 'Truly never has there been a more sporting nation.' Yes, the Australian performance has been impressive, at some times – but less so at others. And the picture from the Olympics is repeated across many other sports. So we need to look for explanations which can account for varying success over time.

Attention to detail also raises some further interesting questions about general explanations. A crucial example here is the markedly better performance at the Olympics up to the mid 1970s by Australia's women athletes compared to the men.

Table 2 shows the number of medals won by Australian men and women at each Olympics since 1948, compared with the numbers of men and women in the teams sent. There is a marked difference before and after 1976. Over the years up to 1972,

Table 2.   Olympic medals won by Australian men and women athletes compared to team numbers.

	Olympic Games Competitors			Total Medals Won		
	Men	Women	Women %	Men	Women	Women %
1948 to 1972	1,058	181	15%	76	52	41%
1980 to 2004	1,622	957	37%	134	86	39%

Source: ABS, 'A Sporting Nation' in *Australian Social Trends 1995* (catalogue 4102.0), which cites unpublished Australian Sports Commission data, and the sports commission website, www.ausport.gov.au/info/topics/olympics/olymtotals.asp.

the women's team (represented in the graph by Dawn Fraser) won an average of more than three medals for every ten team members. In contrast, Herb Elliott and other Australian male athletes won less than one medal for every ten team members. Since 1988, the performance has been more equal: Ian Thorpe and his male colleagues won an average 0.8 medals per ten team members, while Cathy Freeman and the women's team won 0.9. See Table 2 for the full figures.

The issue of better female performance was a matter of public discussion following the Melbourne Olympics in 1956, where the 'golden girls' dominated their track events. *Sydney Sun Herald* reporter Ray Robinson noted women athletes 'have broken or equalled Olympic and world records for women. Yet on the same track in similar breezes Australia's swiftest men have gasped into minor places.'[15]

In fact, Australia's swiftest men were not even competing in the Melbourne Olympics, because they were professional runners. In the 1949 Stawell Gift, Australian John Stoney ran a time equivalent to 10.1 seconds for the 100 metres – a time bettered in the Olympics only in 1968. But that's another discussion, one taken up in Paper 9.

Robinson sought answers for his question 'How Strong is our Weaker Sex?' He argued first that 'their successes are not because of any lack of femininity'. In some way, Robinson felt that femininity was vouchsafed by the fact that 'Betty Cuthbert's height is 5ft 6in – the same as Marilyn Monroe's least known dimension.' He then sought three expert opinions on his main question.

June Ferguson, Betty Cuthbert's coach contended: 'A sunny climate helps our girls … but that leaves us wondering why they should benefit, comparatively, more than the boys in the same country and raised on the same kind of food.' Ferguson also noted that the Australian women were part-timers, in contrast to their competitors from the United States (sports scholarships) or Soviet Union (state support). This image of the part-time and amateur athlete, relying on natural ability, was especially strong in Australian in the 1950s and 1960s. Actually, as is discussed in Paper 11 below, many of the successes of this period came from people who were effectively full-time athletes, and followed tough training regimes.

A second explanation came from an un-named member of the staff of the Department of Anatomy at the University of Sydney, who said the first essential for producing a champion, male or female, was luck in the fusion of the right kind of genes. 'A lot of lucky breeding must have been going on when the present generation of girls was born.' The academic did not comment on how or why such 'lucky breeding' had taken place – or why it affected mainly X chromosomes.

Dr Meyers, Director of the NSW School Medical Service, cited the outstanding physique of the female athletes. In contrast with 50 years earlier, when it had been fashionable to look anaemic, 'girls are dressing and eating more sensibly, benefiting from more sun and fresh air'. He noted that a schoolgirl of 15 in the 1950s was almost 2 inches taller and 18.5 pounds heavier than her counterpart 40 years earlier – but admitted being perplexed that the boys had not done better in the Olympics, given they were 4 inches taller and 26 pounds heavier than in 1916.

Champion swimmer Dawn Fraser had a typically down to earth response to the question: 'Australian women have always been gutsier than the men'.[16]

These comments followed many explanations of early Australian sporting success by trying to explain the 'natural ability' of the women athletes. In contrast, champion cricketer Don Bradman for one felt that the importance of natural ability was overestimated. In his 1958 coaching manual, Bradman emphasized the role of practice:

'Blessed is the boy who finds himself possessed of these abilities as a natural gift. But like the boy prodigy who at, say, five years of age, finds himself able to play the piano, practice and more practice is needed to perfect his talent.' Elsewhere in his manual, Bradman argued 'I don't care who the player is or how great his skill, there is no substitute for practice'; and 'nothing produces efficiency like practice'. Such an emphasis focuses attention more on the organization of sport, and how it encouraged practice and the development of skills.[17]

Paper 11 below discusses Australian successes in two sports in the 1950s: tennis and women's swimming. Contrary to the common image of 'natural ability', more important were intensive training regimes and the organization of the sport (both sports in fact stretched the boundaries of what was really 'amateur'). A further factor was the social context of the sports. Much of international competition in the 1950s was in amateur sports, which in many other countries were exclusive domains of the upper class. Athletes from poorer family backgrounds such as Dawn Fraser and Margaret Smith/Court rarely got a start in swimming or tennis in England or the United States in the 1950s.

Such social inclusion had boundaries historically. Despite early remarkable achievements by Aboriginal athletes such as runner Charlie Samuels (who broke the equivalent of the 10 seconds for 100 metres in 1888, 100 years before his time of 9.95 was bettered at the Olympics), there was little effort to develop that part of the talent pool until after 1950.[18] And, as discussed in Paper 11, both Fraser and Smith had run-ins with sports officialdom. But while there were such limitations, the boundaries were, for the times, wider in Australia than elsewhere.

So the extent of broader participation in sports is important in establishing an environment from which potential champions can be identified and encouraged. Which leads to the second area for comparing sports involvement – active participation in sport.

Kick it to me – sports participation

While Australia sent a team of almost 500 to Athens in 2004, wider measures are needed to test the sports involvement of a nation of 20 million people. This is especially so as a 2003 Australian Sports Commission report found that success in elite sports often has little impact on general participation in sport in Australia. Further, international research across 37 countries found no relationship between children's fitness and Olympic performance.[19]

The most recent comparative statistics show Australia does not have an especially high rate of participation in organized sport: 31% of Australians reported in 2002 that they had taken part in organized sport in the previous 12 months. This was almost the same as the 30% response to a similar question in the United States, and somewhat behind the 36% participation rate in New Zealand at the same time.[20]

In each country the usual 'sporty' image is of a fit young male, most probably in his 20s. In fact, the small differences in overall participation between these three countries owed nothing to differences in younger age groups. In all three, about 50% of 18–24 year olds took part in organized sport, with the rate falling to about 40% in the 25–34 age group. Differences occurred in older age groups: New Zealand had higher participation than Australia for all ages above 35, while the US outranked Australia for 35–54 year olds, but fell well behind in the older age groups above 55. The biggest gap between the three countries is in the 65+ age group, where both

Australia and New Zealand have considerable popular participation in golf (which is often socially exclusive in the US) and lawn bowls (which is not played in the US).

If activity levels are assessed by a broader measure, including other forms of exercise as well as organized sport, the percentage of Australians exercising doubles to 62%. However, this rate too is outstripped by our trans-Tasman neighbour. Apart from the age pattern, the other factor pushing New Zealand's rates up is the strong involvement in sports in the Maori and Polynesian communities.[21]

The previous section noted that Australian sporting success has varied over time. As Paper 6 discusses, there have also been changes in sports participation rates. Australian participation in organized sports was at its highest in the 1950s, and fell to a low point in the 1970s, but has since recovered somewhat, due especially to increased participation amongst women.

While such changes are significant, a comparison with other countries of sports participation in 2002 does not support a unique Australian sports culture. How do we go on the next of our four tests, attendances at sporting events?

C U @ the G: sport attendances

When in comes to active interest in sporting events, Mark Twain, visiting in 1895, found it hard to go past Australians on the first Tuesday in November:

> The Melbourne Cup is the Australasian National Day. It would be difficult to overstate its importance. It overshadows all other holidays and specialized days of whatever sort in … Cup Day is supreme – it has no rival. I can call to mind no specialized annual day, in any country which can be named by that large name – Supreme. I can call to mind no specialized annual day, in any country, whose approach fires the whole and with a conflagration of preparation and anticipation and jubilation.[22]

Big crowds have long been a feature of Australian sporting events: 100,000 people attended the Melbourne Cup in 1880; 34,000 turned up to watch South Melbourne play Geelong in Australian Rules Football in 1886; more than 170,000 attended the funeral of world sculling champion Henry Searle in 1888. Yet, as we will see in Paper 5, these numbers have not always been consistent, or equally representative of all sections of society.

But comparison with New Zealand and the US on this measure supports Twain's contention that there is something different here. Around 2000, about one third of both New Zealanders and Americans attended at least one sporting event. These figures were dwarfed by the close to half of Australians who attended. And while the gap was most pronounced for 18–24 year olds (two-thirds of Australians compared with slightly less than half in New Zealand and the US), Australian attendance figures are well ahead in every age group.[23]

Attendance at sporting events in all three countries generally declines with age, and is less amongst those in rural areas. In Australia and the United States, higher attendances correlate with higher income and more education, although this is less so in New Zealand, with high attendances amongst Maoris and Polynesians. In all three countries, women make up 40% of those attending sports.

The overall strength on this measure varies a little across Australia, for example from state to state. There are higher attendances in the traditionally Australian rules states of Victoria, South Australia and Western Australia (52% of the population) than in the states following rugby league and union: New South Wales and Queensland (45%).

Patterns have also varied between sports over time. Total attendances increased between 1995 and 2002, with strong growth in rugby union, Australian rules, soccer and horse racing, the latter especially in Victoria. However, these contrast with declines in cricket and basketball. These details, and the implications for the sports image, are discussed further in Paper 5.

Beyond attending sports matches, followers can demonstrate their sports madness in other, more passive, ways. This is the fourth of our tests.

Stopping the nation – passive interest

The Melbourne Cup is often described as 'the race that stops a nation'. A wide cross-section of Australians stop their normal activities for three minutes on the first Tuesday in November to watch or listen to the horse race. And certainly Australia is unusual internationally with each state holding public holidays for its leading Cup days.

Such examples indicate a high level of passive community interest in sport – beyond direct participation or attending sports events. Historian Wray Vamplew argued the Cup Day holidays and the numbers watching the televised counting of votes for the Brownlow Medal (the AFL annual award for the best and fairest player) as indicating sport is indeed a major ingredient in Australian lifestyle and culture.[24]

But measuring passive sports interest is complex. It covers a range of sins, including watching television, listening to radio, taking part in office sweeps or tipping competitions, playing sports games on computers or other high-tech entertainment systems, reading sports books or magazines.

In assessing the importance of sports in a nation's 'lifestyle and culture' how do you, for example, compare annual holidays for horse races with one-off events such as the enthusiasm which engulfed New Zealand during the ultimately successful campaign to win the America's Cup in 1995? Campaign finances for the yacht *Black Magic* were restored with massive sales of talisman red socks, which were proudly worn by many public figures including the Governor General and Prime Minister.

And there is other strong competition as well. In August 1995 a US academic teaching in Germany asked his class of 30 students (mostly aged 20–23) to name the members of the 1954 German World Cup championship team. While none of the women students came up with names, all the young men knew the names of at least three players – and two recited all 11 members of the team, 'just as if they had been the team's contemporaries rather than nearly two generations removed from it'.[25]

One possible measure of the broader influence of sports was suggested by journalist Greg Ansley in his article on the 2006 Commonwealth Games discussed in Paper 1: 'Since Aboriginal boxer Lionel Rose in 1967, 11 sportsmen and women have been Australians of the year, far more than those drawn from medicine, the arts or science.'[26]

But, once again, a detailed look at the 52 people who have received the 'Australian of the year' accolade since 1960 indicates a more complex picture. Table 3 lists the primary interest area of each winner, by decade.

There are indeed a good number of sportsmen and women recognized in this award, with 14 out of the total. However, that number is only just ahead of those in medicine/science (12) and the arts (12). The list includes five Nobel Laureates, and recognizes seven Aboriginal Australians, many for community leadership.

Table 3.　Primary interest areas of 'Australians of the year'.

	Total	Sport	Medicine/Science	Arts	Other
Since 1994	15	4	7	2	2
1980–92	13	3	1	4	5
1970–79	14	3	2	2	7
1960–69	10	4	2	3	1
Total	52	14	12	11	15

Source: The backgrounds of the winners were taken from the website: www.australianoftheyear.gov.au.
Notes:
a. Between 1975 and 1979, in addition to the formal process, the Canberra Australia Day Council also recognized an Australian of the Year. Both winners are listed on the website, and in the above statistics
b. Some winners excelled in more than one of the above categories – for example, Mandawuy Yunupingu was recognized in 1992 for both his work in Aboriginal education and for founding the rock band Yothu Yindi. The table uses the category for which they were most well-known.
c. Most of the winners in the 'Other' category were recognized for community, political or military service.

The pattern by decade is also of interest. If we judge the tempo of Australia solely by the category with the most winners each decade, this country's primary interest has moved from sport in the 1960s to community leadership for the next two decades (shared with arts in the 1980s), with most recently a celebration of science and medical research (especially in the field of immunology). Yet somehow we still think of ourselves as mad about sport, not about immunology!

Even on its own terms, the Australian of the year list is more complex than appears at first. And those complexities could well be exacerbated if we tried international comparisons of such a measure. Yes, it could well be true that more sports people have received the Australian of the Year accolade than have similar awards in other countries. But it also seems likely that, especially recently, more Australian medical researchers have been honoured. And, relative to population, the numbers of awards to indigenous people may also be high in international comparisons.

A more promising rigorous measure for international comparisons is sports television ratings. Major sporting events draw some of the biggest audiences for Australian TV. For example, the men's final of the Australian Tennis Open had the highest ratings of any programme on TV in 2005. Boosted by the presence of Australian player Lleyton Hewitt, the final attracted an average of 4 million viewers (20% of the country's population). Also in the top ten ratings for the year were the 2005 Australian Rules Grand Final (3.4 million) and the Melbourne Cup (2.5 million).[27]

With such viewer numbers for sport, high sums have been paid in recent deals for television rights. In 2005, the Australian Cricket Board entered a seven-year contract for television rights worth $300 million. At the end of that year, competition between television channels for five-year TV rights for Australian rules reached the $780 million mark.[28]

However, on both these measures, the Americans triumph over the Australians on a passive interest in sports. US sports broadcasts dwarf the Australian performance. Super Bowl football matches consistently top US TV ratings: the January 2003 television Super Bowl coverage attracted 138 million viewers, half of all American adults. In the same year, broadcaster CBS paid US$6 billion for 11 years' TV rights to the college basketball 'March madness' knockout competition.[29]

But one viewing statistic that does seem to mark Australia out is the popularity of television shows sending up sports.

Taking the piss

Prior to the Sydney Olympics in 2000, the Australian Broadcasting Corporation won solid ratings for a show called'The Games' which parodied the efforts of the organizing committee. During those Olympics, Channel 7, the host television channel, ran a late evening show 'The Dream', hosted by two comedians with remarkable sporting knowledge. Towards the end of the Olympics, 'The Dream' attracted remarkable numbers for its 11 p.m. starting time: 2.5 million viewers nationwide, and 30% of televisions in Sydney alone – and it still had 18% of Sydney TVs at 12.45 a.m. one morning.[30]

Compères of 'The Dream', Roy and HG, quizzed athletes for latest news on usage of the supposed 100,000 condoms supplied to the Olympic Village. Other parts of the show gave alternative commentaries for various sports, replacing technical terms for movements in male gymnastics with the more readily understandable 'hello boys' and 'battered sav'.

Apart from Roy and HG, the show also starred their creation Fatso, the fat-arsed wombat, who shared the victory dais for the men's 4 x 100 relay in the arms of the Australian swimmers. Fatso starred briefly in much international coverage of the Sydney Olympics, often as a quirky example of 'only in Australia'.

On the last night of 'The Dream', Roy and HG asked one guest, an American sprinter, what he would particularly remember about Sydney. His immediate reply was 'this show – there's nothing like it in the States'. He revealed that he had watched each episode, despite the late night timing – and, in a highlight of the show's spontaneity, blamed the show for the fact that he had not competed as well as he had hoped. HG commented, 'Even though they take their sport seriously in the US, people like the idea that adults are behaving childishly about sports.'[31]

The idea that there is something uniquely Australian about such off-the-wall humour like 'The Dream', or the biting satire of 'The Games', is reinforced by the success of comedian Billy Birmingham, aka the 12th Man. The 12th Man specializes in mimicking the voices of the cricket commentators on Channel Nine. One CD, *Wired World of Sports*, won the ARIA award for best selling album in Australia in 1995, and another, *The Final Dig*, sold well enough to be in the final five in 2002.[32]

Birmingham contends, 'There is something very unique about Australia and its sense of humour'. He conceded that skilled overseas comedians, 'far better than I will ever be' could well write send-ups of BBC sports coverage or US Monday Night Football. However, those send-ups wouldn't strike such a chord with the public: 'I just don't think spoken word comedy records, taking the mickey out of sports coverage, would ever be a No.1 single or album in any other country anywhere in the world.'[33]

Historian John Rickard argues:

> The Australian sense of humour can be raucous and aggressive as well as deadpan and underplayed, but it is usually characterised by irreverence and at times an almost surreal mordancy. 'Sardonic' is the adjective often used to characterise the favoured attitude. From the nineteenth century the art of the political cartoonist has flourished, and leaders have had to accustom themselves to the constant threat of public ridicule.[34]

Any sense of humour that can range from 'raucous and aggressive' to 'deadpan and underplayed' is covering a fair amount of territory. John Clarke, writer and co-star of 'The Games', cautions, 'If you look at the humour of each nation, every nation says "Of course, our humour is famously laconic and laid-back and deadpan". They all say this. It's the common feature in almost every nation's analysis of its own humour. It really is pretty much international.'[35]

Taking the discussion further is obviously a precarious venture. According to US writer E.B. White, 'Analysing humour is like dissecting a frog. Few people are interested, and the frog dies of it.' And Clarke reported speaking to people who had studied comedy: 'If you're ever fighting sleep, I'll give you their account. It's a numbing experience. It's not something that benefits from study.'[36]

Not everyone, and especially not some of the targets, have appreciated these efforts to 'take the piss' out of sporting officialdom. When Fatso emerged from his wombat hole to take on the three official 2000 Olympic mascots Olly, Syd and Millie (respectively a Kookaburra, a Platypus and an Echidna), many Sydney officials were not impressed. Some initially tried to ban members of the swimming team from sharing their victory dais with Fatso. Wiser heads avoided a confrontation with the Roy and HG creation, a confrontation which would only have added further pompous targets for stirring.[37]

John Clarke describes sport in New Zealand and Australia as having 'an overarching seriousness',

> run by people who take themselves incredibly seriously, and very often are sufficiently conceited and pompous to think that any of it matters, which is absurd ... What we might encourage is some people who think it's a lot of shit and taken far too seriously, and deserves to be sent up gutless.[38]

As illustrated in this paper, there are plenty of people worldwide who take sport very seriously. What gives Australian sporting humour its edge is not just this seriousness, but its additional readiness to be both self-deprecatory and to mock those in authority; to boo the members as the Mexican wave washes over them at the MCG.

But, as we will see later in this collection, humour and other efforts have not always been successful in battles with sporting officialdom. Like Australia's medal tallies, there have been swings and roundabouts. The battles, and their outcomes, can tell us much about the organization of sport, and about wider social patterns.

So, to sum up this paper, there do seem to be areas where Australia's sporting culture is ahead of the field – but this does not occur across the board. Current Australian participation levels in organized sport are similar to those of the US and New Zealand, and TV ratings for sport are lower than in the US. In international sports achievement, there have been impressive successes, but also quieter periods. There does however appear to be a difference, at least historically, in wider social involvement in sport. And Australia is definitely ahead in sports attendance levels, and in receptiveness to sports satire.

As we will find a number of times in this collection, the detailed evidence does not fully support the often-used national images of the Australian sporting culture. For just one example, despite the evidence of recent Australian of the Year awards, we are still much more likely to think of ourselves as obsessed with sports than with immunology. Looking at sports and other international examples, the next paper discusses some of the factors in the creation of national images.

Notes
1. Spencer, 'Playing the Man'. *Age Review*, September 25, 2004, 2.

2. Cited by Dwayne Russell, 'Sports Comments'. *The Sunday Age*, November 13, 2005, Sports, 24.
3. Kuper, *Football Against the Enemy*, 118–19.
4. ABC News online, 'The December 2005 British National Childrens' Day Survey'.
5. Spillman, *Nation and Commemoration*, 109.
6. Prior to the 2001 Australian Census, an email campaign encouraged Star Wars fans to respond as Jedis in the Census, claiming (erroneously) that if the numbers were sufficient the Government would have to recognize the group as an organized religion. The Australian Bureau of Statistics subsequently conducted a special count of those claiming to be Jedis in that Census, and its media release was reported in the *Sydney Morning Herald*, August 27, 2002. In this competition, Australian Jedis (0.35% of the population) were left far behind the 390,000 (0.7%) in the UK – see 'Counting People'. *The Economist*, December 22, 2007, 89.
7. Bryson, *Down Under*, 113.
8. Bloomfield, *Australia's Sporting Success*, 245–6.
9. Australian Bureau of Statistics media release 135/2004, August 30, 2004, www.abs.gov.au media releases.
10. The discussion and graph of Olympic medals per million population are calculated from the medal results from the International Olympic Committee website, and population numbers from United Nations Population Division, *World Population Ageing: 1950–2050*. The figures for Germany combine the results for East and West Germany prior to reunification in 1990 (the two Germanies competed as a joint team in the 1952 and 1956 Olympics).
11. Ronald Kaye, *The Guardian*, July 28, 1976, 1.
12. Data again calculated from the medal results from the International Olympic Committee website, and United Nations Population Division, *World Population Ageing*.
13. Cited in Bloomfield, *Australia's Sporting Success*, 30–1.
14. Lucas, *Modern Olympic Games*, cited by Guttmann, *The Olympics*, 42–3.
15. Ray Robinson, 'How Strong is our Weaker Sex?' *Sydney Sun Herald*, December 2, 1956, 31.
16. Phillips, 'Australian Women at the Olympics', 192; also cited in Kell, *Good Sports*, 124.
17. Hutchins, *Don Bradman*, 51.
18. Tatz, *Aborigines in Sport*, 18 on Charlie Samuels, and generally on the early barriers to Aborigines in sport.
19. Olds *et al.*, *Children and Sport*, 109–10.
20. Australian Bureau of Statistics (www.abs.gov.au), *Participation in Sport and Physical Activities* (4177.0) in 1996–97 and 2002, Sport and Recreation New Zealand, *SPARC Facts '97–'01*, (drawn from surveys conducted in 1997, 1998 and 2000) and *Statistical Abstract of the United States 2006*, 791, available from www.census.gov. All surveys asked respondents if they 'took part in at least one organised sporting activity in the last year'.
21. Maoris and Polynesians tend to be in the lower income groups in New Zealand. In Australia, and even more strongly in the US, lower income groups have lower rates of participation in organized sport.
22. Reprinted in Cashman *et al.*, eds. *The Oxford Book of Australian Sporting Anecdotes*, 50–1. The remarkable numbers attending early sporting events are discussed below in Paper 7.
23. Australian Bureau of Statistics, *Sports Attendance* (4174.0) 1995 and 2002, Sport and Recreation New Zealand, *SPARC Facts '97–'01*, and *Statistical Abstract of the United States 2006*, 791.
24. Vamplew, 'Australians and Sport', 13.
25. Markovits and Hellerman, *Offside*, 304, n.44.
26. Greg Ansley, 'Aussies – Natural Born Winners'. *New Zealand Herald*, March 25, 2006.
27. Wikipedia, 'List of Australian Television Roctings for 2005', http://en.wikipedia.org/wiki/List_of_Australian_television_ratings_for_2005 Some of the factors behind such numbers, especially for AFL Grand Finals, are discussed in Paper 5.
28. *The Age*, December 30, 2005, 1, Sport, 16.
29. Mandelbaum, *The Meaning of Sports*, 184.
30. Peter Wilmoth, 'Roy and HG Stoked by their Crazy Date with Viewers'. *The Age*, October 3, 2000, 2.

31. Interview with Australian Broadcasting Corporation reporter Warwick Hadfield in the radio programme 'Stop being serious, this is funny!' *The Sports Factor*, ABC Radio National, January 2, 2004. http://www.abc.net.au/rn/sportsfactor/stories/2004/1013393.htm.
32. Leading CD sales figures from the ARIA website, www.ariaawards.com.au.
33. ABC, 'Stop being serious, this is funny!'.
34. Rickard, *Australia: A Cultural History*, 258.
35. Interview with Peter Thompson, ABC 'Talking Heads', screened October 29, 2007, www.abc.net.au/talkingheads/txt/s2070547.htm.
36. Interview with Peter Thompson, ABC 'Talking Heads'.
37. Carroll, 'Australia Dreaming', 210.
38. Further interview on ABC, 'Stop being serious, this is funny!'.

References

ABC News Online. 'The December 2005 British National Childrens' Day Survey'. December 19, 2005. http://www.abc.net.au/news/archive/2005/12/19/default_2.htm.
Bloomfield, John. *Australia's Sporting Success: The Inside Story*. Sydney: UNSW Press, 2003.
Bryson, Bill. *Down Under*. London: Doubleday, 2000.
Carroll, John. 'Australian Dreaming'. In *Well May We Say ... The Speeches that Made Australia,* ed. Sally Warhaft, 510–2. Melbourne: Black, 2004.
Cashman, Richard, David Headon, and Graeme Kinross-Smith, eds. *The Oxford Book of Australian Sporting Anecdotes*. Oxford: Oxford University Press, 1993.
Guttmann, Allen. *The Olympics: A History of the Modern Games*. 2nd ed. Urbana, IL: University of Illinois Press, 2002.
Hutchins, Brett. *Don Bradman: Challenging the Myth*. Melbourne: Cambridge University Press, 2002.
Kell, Peter. Good Sports: Australian Sport and the Myth of the Fair Go. Sydney: Pluto Press, 2000.
Kuper, Simon. *Football Against the Enemy*. London: Orion, 1996.
Mandelbaum, Michael. *The Meaning of Sports: Why Americans Watch Baseball, Football and Basketball and What They See When They Do*. New York: Public Affairs, 2004.
Markovits, Andrei, and Steven Hellerman. *Offside: Soccer and American Exceptionalism*. Princeton, NJ: Princeton University Press, 2001.
Olds, T.S, Dollman, Ridley, Boshoff, Hartshorne, and Kennaugh. *Children and Sport Report for the Australian Sports Commission,* University of South Australia, September, 2004.
Phillips, Dennis. 'Australian Women at the Olympics: Achievement and Alienation'. *Sporting Traditions* 6, no. 2 (May 1990): 181–200.
Rickard, John. *Australia: A Cultural History*. 2nd ed. London: Longman, 1996.
Spillman, Lyn. *Nation and Commemoration: Creating National Identities in the United States and Australia*. Cambridge: Cambridge University Press, 1997.
Tatz, Colin. *Aborigines in Sport*. Adelaide: Australian Society for Sports History, ASSH studies in sport No. 3, 1987.
United Nations Population Division. *World Population Ageing: 1950–2050*. 2001.
Vamplew, Wray. 'Australians and Sport'. In *Sport in Australia: A Social History,* ed. Wray Vamplew and Brian Stoddart, 1–18. Melbourne: Cambridge University Press, 1994.

Sport and national identity

Long-time social stirrer Richard Neville enjoyed Sydney's 'vibrant culture' at the start of the 2000 Olympics:

> From the moment the stockwhips cracked I felt a burst of pride at being an Aussie, a sentiment later confirmed while mingling at the boxing venues: the good-natured piss-taking, the sense of fair play, the barracking for the underdog.[1]

One hundred years earlier, the *South Wales Daily News* also saw a unique national culture represented in sport. The paper celebrated the Welsh rugby union[2] team's win over the hitherto unbeaten New Zealand All Blacks in their 1905 tour of the British Isles:

> The men that represented Wales embodied the best manhood of the race ... the great quality of defence and attack in the Welsh race is to be traced to the training of the early period when powerful enemies drove them to their mountain fortresses. There was developed then those traits of character that find fruition today. 'Gallant little Wales' has produced sons strong of determination, invincible stamina, resolute, mentally keen, physically sound.[3]

As we will see in this paper, such entangling of sport and national images is common. But as the stories of variations in drinking prowess and in cricket interest discussed in the Introduction show, those images can be complex, and can change. This paper looks in detail at the idea of national identity. It starts by noting that changes have occurred in the national images linked to sport, drawing especially on examples from Europe. It then discusses recent research testing how accurate common images of national identity and character actually are. That research suggests there is some reality behind the images – but not as much as generally thought. And the 'typical' image can vary considerably between observers, and over time. There are often specific reasons why particular national images are touted at particular times, and why they meet with varying degrees of success. To demonstrate this, the paper surveys a range of changes in measures of national identity.

International sports enthusiasm

Australia is not alone in mass demonstrations of sporting enthusiasm. On 21 June 1988, the Dutch soccer team beat Germany 2–1 in a semi-final of the European soccer championships in Hamburg. Although it was a Tuesday night, nine million Dutch, 60% of the population, turned out onto the streets to celebrate. It was the largest public celebration since the liberation from German occupation in 1945, and a former Resistance fighter said on TV, 'It feels as though we've won the War at last'. In the Leidesplein square in Amsterdam, the celebrating crowd threw bicycles into the air and yelled 'we've got our bikes back!' (German troops had confiscated Dutch bikes during the occupation).[4]

At first glance, this seemed the outpouring of long-held frustrations left over from the war, celebrated through sport. However, the situation was more complicated than that. As indicated by an opinion poll five years later, Dutch teenagers (most of them two generations away from direct experience of the war) had more negative views about the Germans than their older compatriots. Further, the two soccer teams had met many times prior to 1988 – most famously in the 1974 final of the World Cup. Despite Germany winning a sometimes spiteful game, memories of the war were not restoked in public Dutch commiserations in anything like the same way as in 1988. And eight years before that, most Dutch players had barracked for Germany when it met England in the 1966 World Cup final. It seemed that memories of the war were stronger 40 years after the war than they were 20 or 30 years after – and also stronger among younger rather than older people.

Dutch bank ABN Amro has documented that the Dutch drink much more beer in years when their football team is doing well.[5] But it seems unlikely that alcohol was the sole influence on 60% of the Dutch population in 1988. Something else seems to have been happening as well in the 1980s, emphasizing those memories. What that something else might be is a central concern of this paper.

Two years after the Netherlands beat Germany in the European championships, the 1990 World Cup in Italy also led to outpourings of national enthusiasm. On this occasion, the fervour was especially strong in Dublin, where half a million people, or 15% of the population of the entire country, gathered to welcome the team back from Italy. It was the first time the Irish soccer team had reached the quarter-finals of the World Cup. To mark the occasion the national airline, Aer Lingus, temporarily christened the plane bringing the team home 'St Jack' in honour of the coach, Jack Charlton.[6]

But this Irish national euphoria over its soccer team was remarkable compared with attitudes only a few years before 1990. First, the Irish soccer team had only recently had any international success, with the 1988 European championships the first time they qualified for the finals of a major tournament. Soccer in Ireland had suffered from disdain from the country's sporting authorities. In the pursuit of 'pure' Gaelic sports, the Gaelic Athletic Association (GAA) had until 1972 banned its members from playing 'foreign' games such as soccer.

Second, as evidenced in the Aer Lingus naming of the celebratory flight, the team's success owed much to its coach. Jack Charlton, appointed in 1986, was English, and had himself played in England's World Cup team in 1966. The idea of a national Irish team having a foreign – let alone *English* – coach would have been anathema just a decade previously.

And thirdly, the team reflected a broader approach – and attitude – towards 'Irishness'. Charlton had made extensive use of an international soccer rule that allowed players to represent the country of their own, their parents' or their grandparents' birth. His successful Irish teams included a number of English, Welsh and Scottish accents. They also included black Irish players, such as defender Paul McGrath, perhaps the single most popular player with the fans in 1990. McGrath was the son of an Irish mother and a Nigerian father, born in London but taken to Dublin at the age of 2.

As one writer (himself of Czech-Irish parentage) wrote in *The Irish Times:*

> The Irish soccer team, with its extraordinary collection of polyglot Irish pedigrees, has given us a new pride in our multi-cultural Irishness, and put one more nail in the coffin of the old, exclusive ... GAA-supporting, Fianna Fail-voting definition of 'real' Irishness. I'm sure Leopold Bloom [the Jewish hero of James Joyce's *Ulysses*] is up there cheering along with the rest of us half-breeds.[7]

Forty years earlier, in Limerick in the late 1940s, Irish writer Frank McCourt recalled there were strong social barriers between different sports. Catholics played the GAA-approved sports of Gaelic football, hurling and camogie, a kind of field hockey. In contrast, there was no doubt that cricket and croquet were Protestant sports. McCourt remembered watching the croquet players, all in white, on the lawn next to St Michael's Anglican Church on Barrington Street, and thinking of 'the futility of it all'.

> Whatever the cries of 'Oh, good shot', 'we knew that unless they embraced the One, Holy, Roman, Catholic and Apostolic Church they were doomed for ever.'

> – 'What's the use of playing croquet when you're doomed?' said McCourt to his friend Billy Campbell.

> – 'What's the use of not playing croquet when you're doomed?' replied Campbell.[8]

But in looking at these examples, some caution is needed on how far sporting euphoria extends. Two years after the St Jack flight to Dublin, in the 1992 UK General Election, deputy-leader of the Scottish Nationalist Party Jim Sillars was unsuccessful in the seat he contested. After his defeat, Sillars chastised the Scottish electorate for not voting for the nationalist cause, maligning them for being '90 minute patriots' and saving their nationalist fervour solely for major sporting occasions.[9]

Paper 4 below looks at Australian patterns of interest in various national icons. As with these Irish and Scottish examples, it demonstrates that there are often wide variations in interest levels. This is reinforced in subsequent chapters for involvement in sports attendances and participation – and the differing motivations behind each.

But such variations are frequently pushed aside in the search for national sports that will reach across divides of religion, class and the rest. In Frank McCourt's childhood the uniting code was rugby union:

> There may have been Protestant clubs in Dublin but, in Limerick, we had Garryowen, Shannon, Bohemians and the one we idolised in the back lanes — Young Munster. When the international Irish rugby team won the Triple Crown in 1948 and the Grand Slam in 1949, we never asked if the scorers were Protestant or Catholic, and we knew Gaelic football players and hurlers cheered as loudly as we did.[10]

When such sports do unite a population, many comments follow the lead of the *South Wales Daily News* and its ilk in attributing success to timeless qualities of a people. This discussion has expressed some scepticism about such claims – as illustrated in the soccer successes of both the Dutch and the Irish, there were very specific and contemporary features in the way that nationality was celebrated.

This point is reinforced if we compare key national themes at different points in time. In 1988, sport played an important role in Australian celebrations of the bicentennial of white settlement, with a programme of international matches in various sports. One hundred years earlier, at the centennial celebrations in 1888, there was no such sports programme.[11] There were a couple of very practical reasons for this. The logistics of international travel were much more difficult in 1888 than 1988. And, as discussed in the final section below, there were very few international sports teams in 1888.

But the difference in recognizing sport accompanied other differences in the two celebrations. The four most important themes celebrated in the 1888 events were: the landing of the first fleet in 1788; social and economic progress; Australia's place in the world; and the country's achievements as a pioneer of democracy (for example with the secret ballot, first used in Victoria). Only one of these themes – Australia's place in the world – received as much recognition in 1988. The others had been replaced by: Australians' relationship with the land; diversity; and a more diffuse general history, which encouraged local communities to celebrate their own symbols.[12]

Such differences in key themes suggest problems with any 'timeless' descriptions of specific national characters. However, given the frequency of such descriptions, for a wide range of countries, it is necessary to have a more careful look at how much validity these descriptions really have. The next section considers this.

National stereotypes

> The redeeming feature of the Australian male, and the reason why, on balance, Aussie men are a cut above, is their wickedly dry sense of humour. That's something the English male tries to camouflage by quoting Shakespeare, but they seem to have delusions of grandeur … Give me an Aussie male any day over the cheap, inebriated, emotionally inarticulate and sexually repressed British version.[13]

This blog from the British *Guardian* website in November 2007 used common national images. Toning down the vitriol, such comments typically see Australians as outgoing and sports-loving, Americans as aggressive, while Germans are conscientious, and especially in the sporting context, methodical to the point of being described robotic. Indeed, in 2006, host country Germany explicitly tried to change its image to welcome visitors to the World Cup.[14]

English historian Peter Mandler has cautioned about the range of characteristics that can be employed in such descriptions:

> There is no necessary connection between the nature of Parliament, the boarding school, football hooliganism, fish and chips, snooker, the royal family, Monty Python and Admiral Nelson – except they are all thought to be 'characteristically' English.[15]

In 2005, US researchers Antonio Terracciano and Robert McCrae coordinated the most comprehensive international approach to this question. Their collaborative research project suggests that many common perceptions of quintessential character-istics are inaccurate.[16]

The research gathered and then compared two sets of data from 49 countries. The first set of data came from surveys in each country, asking 4,000 respondents what they thought was the typical character image of their own country. The second set of data came from averaging results of personality tests for a total of 27,000 people from the same countries. Unfortunately for our purposes, the researchers did not use a measure of sports madness, but concentrated rather on the five more standard personality measures of Neuroticism, Extraversion, Openness, Agreeableness and Conscientiousness.

The stereotypes were certainly there: Australians considered ourselves to be extrovert; Germans rated themselves as highly conscientious; and Canadians thought themselves to be more agreeable than most. But these projections of stereotype in most cases had little relationship with the actual personality profile of average citizens of each country.

Despite the Germans' self image as highly conscientious, they score just about the same on this trait as Turks, who consider themselves to be rather unreliable. Puerto Ricans consider themselves highly extrovert but they are apparently no more so than the French Swiss who consider themselves introverted. Despite Americans and Canadians seeing themselves on opposite ends of the spectrum in both agreeableness and assertiveness, the study found that actual personality traits in the later two countries are very similar. Both countries were close to average in terms of being agreeable and only slightly higher than the global average in assertiveness. The study found only four cultures, including Australians, where there was a reasonable correlation between the national image and the results of the personality tests.[17]

Table 1 compares the rankings among the 49 countries in the study for Australians and English on the personality test measures. For each country, the first column gives the perceived national characteristics – the national 'image', while the second column gives the actual results of the personality tests.[18]

Thus, Australians' image of ourselves on neuroticism gave a very low ranking, 48th out of the 49 countries. We gave ourselves a high ranking on extraversion – which came second out of the 49. Both of these were close to the actual rankings from the personality tests, where Australians ranked respectively 37th and second.

Overall, there is a reasonably close fit between image and reality for Australians on four of the five measures. Yet Australians faltered in one category, thinking we are about average on conscientiousness, when in fact we rank very low on this measure.

The marked contrast is with the English, with a self-image as introverted, low on openness and agreeableness, but conscientious. The results of the personality tests in the right hand column however reveal rankings very similar to those of the Australians – and indeed the English had the greatest disagreement between image and reality of any country in the study. Overall, the authors concluded:

> Perceptions of national character are not generalizations about personality traits based on accumulated observations of the people with whom one lives; instead, they appear to be social constructions ... in-group perceptions of national character may be informative about the culture, but they are not descriptive of the people themselves.[19]

Table 1.   Personality traits – rankings out of 49 countries.

	Australians		English	
	Self image	Actual	Self image	Actual
Neuroticism	48	37	25	20
Extraversion	2	2	39	3
Openness	22	15	35	4
Agreeableness	12	25	37	23
Conscientiousness	23	44	14	41

While Terracciano and McCrae's research throws doubt on the validity of most national stereotypes, it does suggest some soundness for the common Australian stereotype. Our 'sports mad' tag is perhaps especially linked to low levels of neuroticism and high extraversion. However, there were two very important further qualifications on these results.

The first is that the study compared national averages – and generally there is far more variation of personality types *within* countries than *between* national averages. There is also some variation in how people see their national character. While surveying a reasonable number of people in each culture gave fairly robust national pictures, the chances of any two people agreeing in their judgements of national character were actually fairly modest. Key factors likely to influence such variations include the personalities of the observers, and the way or context in which they were thinking about the national character.[20] This point is returned to below.

Secondly, and consistent with the above Irish examples, particular circumstances, and changes in those circumstances, can affect the way people view the national stereotype. Changes can occur over time that either emphasize or downplay particular elements in a national culture. But if, as Terracciano and McCrae argue, there is considerable variation within countries around the typical character, and if those variations change over time, who or what creates the widely held images of 'national character'?

US historian Peter Novick argues that the creation of such images has a lot to do with current agendas and issues:

> The most significant collective memories – memories that suffuse group consciousness – derive their power from their claim to express some permanent, enduring truth. Such memories are as much about the present as about the past, and are believed to tell us (and others) something fundamental about *who we are now*.[21]

The next section develops this theme further, starting with the range of attitudes towards the 'typical' Australian character.

Legends and identities

'Oz, Land of Sunshine, Sport and Sexism' read a headline in the British *Daily Telegraph* in November 2007. Describing a common image of the 'ocker' sports lover, the piece announced the publication of *The Ernies Book*. This 15-year collection of examples of Australian male chauvinism suggested 'many Australian men are still Neanderthals when it comes to their attitudes towards women'.[22]

Lee Glendinning, a columnist with the *Guardian*, riposted with a different image of Australian men:

> They are masculine and they like a drink, yes, but they are also emotionally literate, kind and engaging. Most of them are lively, well-read companions whose love of cricket or football doesn't dampen their interest in and knowledge on international affairs or domestic public policy. They would do anything for their male friends, but equally so, they enjoy and cherish the company of their female mates.[23]

A lively blogging interchange followed on the *Guardian's* Comment is Free website, with many of the diverse views apparently coloured by participants' good or bad luck in relationships with Australian men.

In the late 1970s, researcher Harry Oxley noted similar differences in standard Australian images. Fifty of his adult students described the 'ocker' sports lover in unflattering terms: 'a self-satisfied vulgarian' with a 'narrow outlook never rising to anything above mindless hedonism'. Oxley then compared this image with a more positive image of the 'Australian Legend' developed by writer Russell Ward 20 years earlier:

> There are some differences: the ocker-knockers do not talk about improvising ability, while Ward and his like are silent about male chauvinism. But on most points, these two accounts are of the same fellow, described respectively by those who do not like him and those who do.[24]

The distances between 'those who do not like him and those who do' indicate that the standard Australian character is not a great fit for the entire population. The images in 2007, and in Oxley's earlier discussion, draw on a number of character traits. But individuals rarely display all of these traits – in fact, there can be differences in the traits particular people show at different times. Terracciano and McCrae cite other research indicating that two observers can differ in their descriptions of a single person they both know well.[25] We all have a range of aspects to our individual characters, our identities, and people who know us in one context may well have different impressions from those seeing us in another.

In his recent book *Identity and Violence: The Illusion of Destiny*, Amartya Sen argues that there is generally little necessary connection between different aspects in our characters:

> The same person can be, without any contradiction, an American citizen, of Caribbean origin, with African ancestry, a Christian, a liberal, a woman, a vegetarian, a long-distance runner, a historian, a schoolteacher, a novelist, a feminist, a heterosexual, a believer in gay and lesbian rights, a theatre lover, an environmental activist, a tennis fan, a jazz musician … Each of these collectivities, to all of which this person simultaneously belongs, gives her a particular identity. None of them can be taken to be the person's only identity in a single membership category.[26]

Sen had personal experience of the damage done by those stressing just one aspect of identity. He was 11 years old during Independence and Partition of India in 1947, and remembers 'the speed at which the broad human beings of January were suddenly transformed into the ruthless Hindus and fierce Muslims of July'. Hundreds of thousands died in the Partition violence, one of them a Muslim day-labourer who risked an encounter with the mobs to try to find food for his hungry family. Knifed in the violence by Hindu rioters, the man sought shelter in the Sen family garden, but ended up dying in the ambulance on the way to hospital.[27]

Several reviewers of Sen's book, while conceding his point about multiple identities, have queried the equivalence he gives to different aspects of all this diversity. Historically, there are many more examples of people being susceptible to political militancy based on nation, or on religion, than on vegetarianism or theatre going.[28]

But even if people are more susceptible to appeals to nationality or religion, the strength of such appeals differs markedly over time. It is not just the latent potential at issue, but also the whys and hows of specific appeals to those traits. Researchers of nationalism argue that such appeals particularly occur at times of crisis. For but one example, a study of the growth of conservative French nationalism in the 1880s found that the central word in their political vocabulary was not 'family', 'order', 'tradition', 'religion', 'morality' or any similar term. It was 'menace'.[29] Such crises and menaces have been more common in times of economic, political, and social turmoil – and the strength of mobilization along national, religious or ethnic lines has similarly varied.[30]

This discussion has indicated some of the diversity which lies behind specific images of 'national identity' or 'character'. It has also noted that particular visions of identity have been mobilized at particular times, driven by particular agendas. Even while dwelling on fears and menaces, such mobilization emphasizes as rallying points key icons and symbols that especially inspire national feeling.

The next section discusses the varied history of such symbols, noting that many are of very recent development. It traces the reasons behind this.

National symbols

When the Welsh rugby union team – those 'sons strong of determination, invincible stamina' – met the New Zealand team in 1905, they did so under a new national symbol. The New Zealanders started the proceedings with a haka, a Maori war dance. The Welsh responded by singing the first notable public airing of what was to become the Welsh anthem – *Hen Wlad Fy Nhadau* (Land Of My Fathers).[31]

It is a key point that, despite the Welsh efforts supposedly representing 'that training of the early period when powerful enemies drove them to their mountain fortresses', the symbol of the national anthem was not adopted until after 1900. In fact, most such national symbols, while supposedly representing long-standing attributes, are also of fairly recent adoption.

This can be seen in the history of key American symbols. With the current ubiquity of the US flag and the image of Uncle Sam, it is surprising that Uncle Sam only became a common symbol around 1890 – at the same time that schools started to fly the US flag. The key national celebrations of the 4th July and Thanksgiving only became widespread after the Civil War of 1861–65 – and were promoted by some specifically to give unifying symbols for a bitterly divided country.[32]

Around the same time, key French symbols were adopted. La Marseillaise became the French national anthem only in 1879, a year before Bastille Day on 14 July was adopted as a national holiday. At the same time 'Marianne', another icon which started life in the French Revolution around 1789, was also cemented as a symbol of France.[33] There were specific reasons in France too for this timing. In the preceding 90 years, various French conservative governments had tried to suppress the three icons, which were in turn adopted as symbols by radical opponents. But by 1880 French conservatives, weakened by defeat in the Franco-Prussian war of 1871, were actively looking for images that would resonate with the general populace, many more of whom were now literate and, of the men, had the vote.[34]

But while there were specific circumstances in the US and France, such developments were by no means unique. Many countries with differing political dynamics started to popularize national images in these years. So why did such national symbols emerge in the 1870s and 1880s?

Our image of nation states – at least as far as they represent a popular nationalist identification – is a fairly recent phenomenon. Certainly there were examples of strong patriotic fervour in much earlier times. A line much used in the First World War (and bitterly attacked by poet Wilfred Owen) *'Dulce et decorum est pro patria mori'* ('It is sweet and fitting to die for one's country') was written by Roman poet Horace. And Shakespeare around 1600 had John of Gaunt utter the much quoted paen to 'This blessed plot, this earth, this realm, this England'.[35] But such references were mainly restricted to the literate, where most people in earlier societies were illiterate.[36] The very word 'nationalism' was little used before 1900,[37] and there is little evidence of mass enthusiasm for nationalism or national symbols prior to the 1870s. As historian Benedict Anderson has argued, nationalism involves 'imagined communities' of people who feel they have much in common despite never knowing, or even meeting, most of their fellow members.[38] The existence of such common feeling was highly unlikely to develop in feudal societies, not only because of the crystal clear class distinctions between lord and serf, but also because they often spoke different languages.[39]

A number of factors assisted the development of national symbols in the late nineteenth century. The first of these, stressed by Anderson, is the development of mass printing, especially of newspapers. The circulation boundaries of such newspapers themselves created communities of similar interest, and also encouraged particular preferred dialects. But while such newspapers had been present well before the 1850s (and had influenced the development of national identification amongst the middle class), it was the development of mass literacy in the later nineteenth century that extended their reach as vehicles of nationalism.[40]

A second important factor in the development of strong national images was the growth of the modern state in the later nineteenth century. Institutions such as regional administration, railways, the post office and especially mass education both encouraged, and were used as outlets for, nationalist messages. Prior to such institutions, there was little need for most people in a locally based peasant economy to change from a local dialect or see themselves as part of a wider group.

A third element was the extension of the franchise. As voting rights extended more broadly, political parties needed mechanisms and symbols to communicate with their expanding electorate. Related to this was the growth in developed countries of labour and socialist parties, with a strongly internationalist emphasis. Part of the increasing emphasis on nationalism and national symbols was a conscious conservative effort to repel this development.

But these factors encouraging the growth of national symbols in the late nineteenth century do not explain the form it took. Indeed, there is something of a paradox between the modern impetus for nationalism and the historical images and symbols – such as referring back to the French Revolution or Thanksgiving – that the nationalists stressed to gain support.

The impetus to create national symbols in the late nineteenth century can be viewed as a brand marketing exercise, of trying to get people to adopt or emphasize particular images. But there are plenty of examples of unsuccessful campaigns, where no connection was made with the target market. Appeals to images that already had some popular credence were often more successful in gaining the responses desired.[41]

Consistent with the above discussion of the complexity of identity, nationalist calls did not drown out all other aspects of personality and existence. For one example, at the start of the First World War in 1914, socialist organizers in Wales were aghast at the extent to which hitherto radical Welsh miners responded to the nationalistic call to arms. The conservatives beating the nationalist drum were dumbfounded a year later when, despite the War, those same miners staged a general strike.[42]

And there could be different types of calls to national symbols as well. Historian Peter Mandler has demonstrated that the context and usage of images of 'English national character' have varied considerably. In the late nineteenth century, the term was used predominantly by Liberals, who were in the forefront of moves to extend the franchise and supported this with descriptions of the common sense of the populace. Conservatives, for their part, used the term much less, stressing the importance of Imperial institutions which encompassed a range of national 'characters', including most notably in contemporary political discussions the Irish.[43]

In marked contrast, the 1920s saw the Conservatives make the most use of appeals to 'English national character'. Prime Minister Stanley Baldwin made explicit use of the term in trying to build a national consensus after the social schisms of the First World War, the secession of Ireland, and the 1926 General Strike.[44]

Such political usage of terms of national identity and character continues to the present day. For one example, a concern with national identity seems especially strong amongst conservative writers in the United States. Recent books on the topic have included Samuel Huntington's *Who are We? The Challenges to America's National Identity,* Allan Carlson's *The American Way: Family and Community in the Shaping of the American Identity,* and Michael Savage's *The Enemy Within: Saving America from the Liberal Assault on our Churches, Schools and Military.* Such books have little doubt that there is a strong American national identity – and that it is under threat.

This paper has stressed the complexity of identity. National and ethnic origins are important traits in identity, but they coexist with many others, and are emphasized and take particular forms at specific times. The raw material for the images draws from a variety of sources, especially historical sources, but the images at any time are also strongly influenced by the current agendas that proponents have, and responses from the target audience.

The examples of the raw material for nationalist symbols discussed thus far have been largely historical – appeals to images from the French revolution or the forerunners of 'Gallant little Wales' holed up in their mountain fortresses. But especially from the 1920s onwards proponents of nationalism started to use additional raw material – national teams on the sporting field. As we will see in later papers, Australia was well ahead of this international trend, with successful advertising of Australian 'world champions' from the 1880s. But prior to turning to the reasons for that precociousness, the next section looks at how sport became an important part of other countries' national images.

Impacts on sport

In April 1990, English Conservative MP (and later Lord) Tebbit, in an interview with the *LA Times,* announced his 'cricket test' for national identity, especially for migrants from India and Pakistan living in Britain: 'A large proportion of Britain's Asian population fail to pass the cricket test. Which side do they cheer for? It's an interesting test. Are you still harking back to where you came from or where you are?'[45] Amartya Sen disputed the validity of this cricket test, seeing a number of varying factors involved, including national loyalty and residential identity, but also the quality of play, and the overall interest of a match, and a series.[46]

Despite the force of Sen's argument, many more people have used Tebbit's approach over the years, seeing national sporting teams as indeed symbolizing something of the national identity. The above discussion has emphasized that in looking at the spread of national symbols we need to consider both the agendas of the proponents and the way others in the population respond. Consistent with this, this section looks at examples from both sides.

Predating Tebbit, the phrase 'national identity' has frequently been used in sporting contexts in the UK – at least, as judged from a search of *The Times* newspaper.
The Index recorded 85 articles mentioning national identity between 1945 and 1955,
71 articles in the following decade, and only 70 in the decade 1965 to 1975. Although
this is not a high level of mentions, a striking fact of this list was its relationship to
sport. Just under 80% of the mentions across these years were in articles about rugby
union.[47]

The discussion above also noted the importance of newspapers in encouraging the
'imagined communities' of nations. Once those newspapers started developing mass
markets, they quickly realized the importance of sport in attracting an audience.

Despite the levels of both popular and newspaper interest, competitive sport at an
international level lagged behind the developments within individual countries –
largely because of the logistics involved. While soccer matches between neighbours
England and Scotland were well established by 1900, the first soccer World Cup was
not held until 1930 (and England itself did not send a team until 1950). And while the
modern Olympics date back to 1896, the IOC website notes that early games attracted
only small numbers of athletes and little media interest. The structure of the games
themselves was a problem: often held in conjunction with World Fairs, competitions
took place over some three months. The 1932 Los Angeles Games were the first to
establish the modern format, more competitor and viewer friendly, of lasting a
concentrated two to three weeks. Only eight years earlier, the 1924 Paris Games were
the first that could be considered a major event. Forty-four nations sent athletes (the
previous best was 30), and 1,000 journalists accompanied them.[48]

It was not just journalists who showed an increased interest in such sporting
events. Dictators Mussolini and Hitler took full advantage of the respective World
Cup in Italy in 1934 and the Olympics in Berlin in 1936 as propaganda opportunities
for their regimes – both within the country and internationally. Italy won the 1934 and
1938 World Cups, and German athletes did well in Berlin in 1936. However, Hitler's
goal of these Games as a total triumph for Aryan supremacy was confounded by the
successes of black American athlete Jesse Owens.

The military junta running Argentina in 1978 was equally determined to make their
World Cup that year a political and propaganda success for their regime. Fifteen years
later, one general remembered Argentina's win over the Netherlands in the final: 'There
was an explosion of ecstasy and hysteria. All the country was on the streets. Radicals
embraced with Peronists, Catholics with Protestants and Jews, and all had only one
flag: the flag of Argentina.'[49] The military, which had seized power in 1976, were at
the time involved in a bloody repression of dissidents in Argentina. Their hosting of
the World Cup was a conscious effort to build a unifying national success, both inter-
nally and for worldwide media consumption. And they went much further than just
building expensive stadiums and other infrastructure. There were widespread rumours
that Argentina's 6–0 win over Peru to go into the finals stage of the competition was
strongly assisted by extensive and well-documented Argentinean Government financial aid to Peru.[50]

But the Government's hopes that its massive investment in the World Cup would
lead to an extended 'explosion of ecstasy and hysteria' in its favour were not realized.
Despite considerable duchessing, much of the international media gave extensive
coverage to stories of those who had 'disappeared' at the military's hands. And within
the country the exuberance did not last long in a climate of military repression,
economic downturn and massive inflation. The junta's slogan '25 million Argentineans

will play in the World Cup' soon morphed into a cynical '25 million Argentineans will pay for the World Cup'.[51]

So conscious efforts to use sports as part of nation-building by governments do not always get the results that they seek. In looking at such efforts, it is critical to consider how others respond – and in these reactions as well a range of agendas can be in play.

Similar diversity and contingency complicate more general efforts to see sport as mirroring some intrinsic aspect of national identity. Examples can be seen in Americans' passion for baseball, which some commentators have seen as symbolizing a yearning to maintain contact with a purer agrarian way of life.[52] Rather than such grand schemes, confirmed baseball fan Steven Jay Gould saw his 'serious and lifelong commitment to baseball … purely as a contingent circumstance of numerous, albeit not entirely capricious, accidents'. The first of two key accidents was being Jewish when both his father and grandfather viewed a dedication to a distinctively American sport as a major tactic for assimilation.[53] The second was time and place. From 1947 to 1957, Gould's formative years, New York City had the three best teams in major league baseball. In seven of those eleven years, the championship play-off World Series was a 'subway series' between two New York teams. The successes encouraged a mass local following for the sport.[54]

Gould's mixed motivations, and the interaction of contingent circumstances, bring us back to the central themes of this paper. Despite the many attempts to see sports as representing particular national identities, those national identities themselves are neither as clear nor as static as often claimed. Rather, they are complex, as most identities are, and morph as social and other changes affect a country. The way that identities present themselves also change, influenced amongst other things by political agendas among those helping shape the image and by the response of the audience to the images being created.

Using these insights, the next paper looks at key icons of Australian identity. The differing ways in which these icons have been promoted and responded to provides a good context for understanding in subsequent papers the unfolding patterns of our 'sporting nation'.

Notes

1. Richard Neville, 'Grandchildren of the Revolution', *The Age*, November 5, 2005, A2, 5.
2. Each of the five major codes of football refers to their own game as 'football', often denigrating the other pretenders to this title. As a sidestep to avoid confusion, this book uses the generic terms for each code: Australian Rules (notwithstanding the official title is Australian football); grid iron (aka American football); rugby league; rugby union ('rugby' being one game prior to splits into league and union in the 1890s and 1907); and soccer.
3. *South Wales Daily News*, December 18, 1905, cited by Andrews, 'Welsh Rugby', 339.
4. Kuper, *Football Against the Enemy*, 4–8.
5. ABN Amro, *Soccernomics*.
6. This and the following discussion of the Irish celebrations and team are from Ticher, 'Notional Englishmen', 82–5.
7. *The Irish Times*, June 30, 1990, cited by Ticher, 'Notional Englishmen', 85.
8. Frank McCourt, 'With God on their Team'. *The Age*, February 3, 2007 (reprinted from *The Observer*).
9. Bairner, 'Football and the Idea of Scotland', 19–20.
10. McCourt, 'With God on their Team'.
11. Spillman, *Nation and Commemoration*, 108–10.

12. Ibid., 111–32, 139.
13. Comment from DannyRyan, *Guardian* CiF website, Comments following Lee Glendinning, 'Aussie Males', November 6, 2007.
14. See Hay and Joel, 'The Football World Cup and its Fans'.
15. Mandler, *English National Character*, 2.
16. Terracciano, McCrae *et al.*, 'National Character'; Terracciano, McCrae *et al.*, 'Personality Profiles of Cultures'; and McCrae *et al.*, 'Consensual Validation', 179. The text (for ease of expression) refers to 49 countries – the analysis used 47 countries but in two of those (Britain and Switzerland) two cultural groups were studied: English and Northern Irish in Britain, and French-Swiss and German-Swiss.
17. The four countries where the image was close to the reality were Australia, Lebanon, New Zealand and Poland. Not all of these self-images were complimentary.
18. Dr Terracciano kindly provided the author with the detailed statistics in a data appendix to the above papers.
19. Terracciano, McCrae *et al.*, 'National Character', 99.
20. Ibid., 97.
21. Novick, *Holocaust and Collective Memory,* 202; emphasis in original.
22. Nick Squires, 'Oz, Land of Sunshine, Sport and Sexism', *Daily Telegraph* (UK), November 6, 2007.
23. Lee Glendinning, 'Aussie Males'. *Guardian*, November 6, 2007.
24. Oxley, 'Ockerism, the Cultural Rabbit', 195.
25. Terracciano, McCrae *et al.*, 'National Character', 97.
26. Sen, *Identity and Violence*, 4–5. Sen's 2006 book is an explicit rejoinder to works such as Huntington's two books *Clash of Civilizations* (1996), and *Who are We? The Challenges to America's National Identity* (2004).
27. Sen, *Identity and Violence*, 4, and elsewhere in his book. Sen developed his ideas further in a joint report *Civil Paths to Peace: Report of the Commonwealth Commission on Respect and Understanding*. See article in *The Economist*, November 10, 2007, 75.
28. For example, the review of Sen's book in *The Economist*, May 11, 2006.
29. Hobsbawm, *Nations and Nationalism*, 121; and see McCrone, *Sociology of Nationalism*, 31.
30. See Friedman, *Moral Consequences of Economic Growth,* which emphasizes the importance of differences in economic conditions.
31. Andrews, 'Welsh Rugby'.
32. Spillman, *Nation and Commemoration*, 24–5.
33. McCrone, *Sociology of Nationalism*, 45–6.
34. Hobsbawm, *Nations and Nationalism*, 121; McCrone, *Sociology of Nationalism*, 46.
35. John of Gaunt's speech was in Shakespeare's *Richard II*, Act 2, Scene I.
36. Hobsbawm, *Nations and Nationalism*, 51.
37. Anderson. *Imagined Communities*, 4, n.7. Prior to this time the word 'nation' simply meant 'society' or 'state', not a group coalescing state, cultural and self-identifying aspects.
38. Ibid., 6.
39. Mandler, *English National Character*, 8; and see examples in McCrone, *Sociology of Nationalism*, 45 and Hobsbawm, *Nations and Nationalism*, 37, 60.
40. Anderson, *Imagined Communities*, especially 44 and 61.
41. Hobsbawm, *Nations and Nationalism*, 92.
42. Ibid., 124.
43. Mandler, *English National Character*, 125.
44. Ibid., 152.
45. Tebbit's 'cricket test' has been widely cited, for example, by John Carvel, social affairs editor, *Guardian*, January 8, 2004.
46. Sen, *Identity and Violence*, 155.
47. Maguire and Tuck, 'Global Sports and Patriot Games', 115.
48. International Olympic Committee website: www.ioc.org.
49. Kuper, *Football Against the Enemy*, 173.
50. Ibid., 175.
51. Ibid., 177, 174.
52. Mandelbaum, *The Meaning of Sports*.
53. For more on this theme, see Hay, 'Approaches to Sports History', 74.
54. Gould, *Triumph and Tragedy in Mudville*, 29–32.

References

ABN Amro. *Soccernomics: Soccer and the World Economy 2006.* March. http://www.abnamro.com/pressroom/releases/media/pdf/abnamro_soccernomics_2006_en.pdf.

Anderson, Benedict. Imagined Communities: Reflections on the Origin and Spread of Nationalism. Revised ed. London: Verso, 2006.

Andrews, David. 'Welsh Indigenous! and British Imperial? – Welsh Rugby, Culture, and Society 1890–1914'. *Journal of Sport History* 18, no. 3 (1991): 335–49.

Bairner, Alan. 'Football and the Idea of Scotland'. In *Scottish Sport in the Making of the Nation,* ed. Grant Jarvie and Graham Walker, 9–26. Leicester: Leicester University Press, 1994.

Friedman, Benjamin. *The Moral Consequences of Economic Growth.* New York: Knopf, 2005.

Gould, Steven Jay. *Triumph and Tragedy in Mudville.* New York: W.W. Norton, 2003.

Hay, Roy. 'Approaches to Sports History: Theory and Practice'. *Sporting Traditions* 22, no. 2 (May 2006): 70–81.

Hay, Roy, and Tony Joel. 'The Football World Cup and its Fans: Reflections on National Styles'. Paper presented at the ASSH Conference, Canberra, June 2007.

Hobsbawm, Eric. *Nations and Nationalism since 1780: Programme, Myth, Reality.* 2nd ed. Cambridge: Cambridge University Press, 1994.

Huntington, Samuel. *Clash of Civilizations.* New York: Simon & Schuster, 1996.

Huntington, Samuel. *Who Are We: The Challenges to America's National Identity.* New York: Simon & Schuster, 2004.

Kuper, Simon. *Football Against the Enemy.* London: Orion, 1996.

McCrae, R.R., P.T. Costa Jr., T.A. Martin, V.E.A.A. Rukavishnikov, I.G. Senin, *et al.* 'Consensual Validation of Personality Traits Across Cultures'. *Journal of Research in Personality* 38 (2004): 179–201.

McCrone, David. *Sociology of Nationalism.* New York: Routledge, 1998.

Maguire, Joseph, and Jason Tuck. 'Global Sports and Patriot Games: Rugby Union and National Identity in a United Sporting Kingdom since 1945'. In *Sporting Nationalisms,* ed. Mike Cronin and David Mayall, 103–26. London: Frank Cass, 1998.

Mandelbaum, Michael. *The Meaning of Sports: Why Americans Watch Baseball, Football and Basketball and What They See When They Do.* New York: Public Affairs, 2004.

Mandler, Peter. *The English National Character.* New Haven, CT and London: Yale University Press, 2006.

Novick, Peter. *The Holocaust and Collective Memory: The American Experience.* London: Bloomsbury, 1999.

Oxley, Harry. 'Ockerism, the Cultural Rabbit'. In *Australian Popular Culture,* ed. Peter Spearitt and David Walker, 190–209. Sydney: Allen & Unwin, 1979.

Sen, Amartya. *Identity and Violence: The Illusion of Destiny.* New York: W.W. Norton, 2006.

Spillman, Lyn. *Nation and Commemoration: Creating National Identities in the United States and Australia.* Cambridge: Cambridge University Press, 1997.

Terracciano, A, R.R., McCrae *et al.* 'National Character Does Not Reflect Mean Personality Trait Levels in 49 Cultures'. *Science* 7 (October 2005): 96–100 (see also the Supporting Online Material for this article, available at www.sciencemag.org/cgi/content/full/310/5745/96/DC1)

Terracciano, A; R.R., McCrae *et al.* 'Personality Profiles of Cultures: Aggregate Personality Traits'. *Journal of Personality and Social Psychology* 89, no. 3 (2005): 407–25.

Ticher, Mike. 'Notional Englishmen, Black Irishmen and Multicultural Australians: Ambiguities of National Sporting Identity'. *Sporting Traditions* 11, no. 1 (November 1994): 82–5.

'The heart of what it means to be Australian'

February 1933, a hot day at the Sydney Cricket Ground, the final cricket test in the controversial bodyline series. Douglas Jardine, the English captain and architect of bodyline, flicked a fly away from his face. A barracker yelled out, 'Leave our bloody flies alone Jardine, they're the only mates you've got.'[1]

Bill 'Tiger' O'Reilly was the Australian spin bowler in that series. Some 20 years later at a dinner in London, O'Reilly found himself sitting next to Jardine, listening to guest speaker Australian Prime Minister Bob Menzies. Menzies contrasted the welcome he received from his English hosts with the views of some of his countrymen: 'I'm certain that there are very many Australians who think I'm the greatest bastard that ever stood in their country.' Jardine elbowed O'Reilly in the ribs 'The honourable member is misinformed. He could never possibly be more than number two.'[2] It is not surprising that people differ in their choice of 'the greatest bastard that ever stood' in Australia. It is considerably more surprising that there have been considerable variations in support for more revered Australian symbols.

Whether or not he won the 'greatest bastard' accolade, Bob Menzies, Prime Minister in the 1950s and early 1960s, was a good example of the unevenness of Australian nationalism. He was a fervent supporter of the Australian cricket team, especially in test matches against England. He also proudly described himself as 'British to the bootstraps', even suggesting that when Australia adopted decimal currency in 1965, the new unit should be the 'royal', rather than the dollar.[3]

While Menzies was unusual by the 1960s in the strength of his imperial sentiments, he illustrates a common complexity in feelings about nationality. Dual feelings are often felt by recent migrants settling into Australia, but were clearly also true of an earlier generation. There was strongest identification as 'Australian' for sporting events, with a medium identification in political terms, and, at least for the better-off until the 1960s, a widespread acceptance of 'Britishness' in cultural terms.

Paper 3 discussed Amartya Sen's argument that nationality is only one part of a person's identity, and, depending on the situation, not necessarily the dominant part. How national feelings are expressed – and in the above cases, *which* feelings are expressed – depends very much on the specific situation at hand. The way in which nationalistic feelings are being appealed to and the ways that people respond to those appeals are also significant.

Paper 3 also noted many international examples of how apparently enduring national symbols often reflect current agendas and issues. This paper demonstrates the same point for Australia, in discussing three national symbols that are often linked to sport and sports achievement. The national anthem has long been played at premier sporting events. Many a sporting hero has been applauded for showing the 'Anzac spirit'. But, as this paper shows, there has been considerable variation in attitudes towards these symbols.

The first part of the paper contrasts uses at different times of two key symbols: Simpson and his donkey, and the bush call 'cooee'. Looking at some of the factors that affect such changes, the paper then discusses adherence to the national anthem. The final part of the paper returns to Anzac, discussing the differing agendas that have affected the way the symbols have been presented and viewed.

A central point of the discussion is that changes in how symbols are used do not simply reflect the passage of time, nor follow a straight path, as Australian nationalism 'came of age' (to use a much overworked phrase).[4] Changes occurred in various ways, very much affected by both particular situations and the working out of differing visions of nationality.

Changing national symbols

In August 2005 Brendan Nelson, the Federal Minister for Education, joined many others in seeing the symbol that best represented 'everything at the heart of what it means to be Australian' coming from the First World War: Simpson and his donkey.[5] Simpson served in the battles at Anzac Cove at Gallipoli in 1915, guiding his donkey to bring wounded soldiers down from the front to treatment.[6]

Simpson is commemorated in a statue on the front steps of the Australian War Memorial in Canberra. The Australian Dictionary of Biography cites him as 'the symbol of all that was pure, selfless and heroic on Gallipoli'. And the stamps to commemorate the 50th anniversary of Gallipoli in 1965 also featured Simpson and his donkey.

But, if we go back further in time, there was much less recognition of Simpson as an icon. A book on Gallipoli published in 1956 had no mention of him at all. In the early 1930s, the military hierarchy did not support an appeal for a proposed Simpson memorial in Melbourne – they were fund raising at the same time for a memorial to General Monash, the commander of the Australian forces on the Western Front in 1917–18.[7] And when returned soldiers lobbied the government for a stamp in 1935 to commemorate the 20th anniversary of the Gallipoli landing, there was no suggestion that Simpson and his donkey should be on the stamp. Indeed, Gallipoli itself was not chosen. The Postmaster General felt that the War generally should be commemorated, and that the stamp should reflect the Imperial, not just Australian, forces. The stamp has a picture of the Cenotaph in Whitehall, London.[8]

Even the image of Simpson himself changed over time. Some six weeks after his death in May 1915, a photo with the donkey was published in the *Sydney Morning Herald*, and became widely used in recruitment propaganda. One newspaper report described him as 'a six-foot Australian' with 'a woman's hands' who said in a British Australian accent, 'I'll take this fellow next'. In fact, Simmo (as his mates called him) was five-foot-eight, had arrived in Australia from Newcastle in north-east England only in 1910, had a stoker's hands, and spoke in Geordie dialect.[9]

So the symbol that now represents 'everything at the heart of what it means to be Australian', was not officially recognized as such in the first 40 years after Gallipoli. As the discussions in Paper 3 noted, the strength of a symbol comes from both its origins and the contemporary ways people present and use the symbol. This point is reinforced by the story of what had been seen as a strong Australian symbol in 1900 – the 'cooee' call, which almost completely disappeared by the 1950s.

In 1873 W.G. Grace led an English cricket team to Australia. In a match in Melbourne, Harry Boyle, who lived in Bendigo, bowled the English star. In the crowd some '1500 Bendigo men, who had come because Boyle was their champion, went fairly mad and cooeed with true Australian fervour'.[10]

This key Australian symbol also helped detective Sherlock Holmes solve a murder in *The Boscombe Valley Mystery*, written in 1891. Charles McCarthy, renting an English farm in Hereford after returning from the Victorian gold fields, met his death after keeping an appointment near Boscombe Pool. At the appointed time, McCarthy's son James overheard his father cry 'Cooee'. Holmes deduced:

> The 'Cooee!' was meant to attract the attention of whoever it was that he had the appointment with. But 'Cooee' is a distinctly Australian cry … There is a strong presumption that the person whom McCarthy expected to meet him at Boscombe Pool was someone who had been in Australia.[11]

The cooee was originally an Aboriginal call, used to contact people across distance: on a still night the cry might carry as far as three kilometres. It was adopted by early white settlers in the bush, and used as an all-purpose call to signify a range of messages. Above all it established contact, with the agreed etiquette to always return a cooee.[12] Beyond being a useful tool in the bush, the cooee became a symbol of Australian identity after 1850. Several stories (some of which were probably urban myths) attest to Australians using the cooee in London to reconnect with lost members of their party.

Many Australian literary efforts in the latter part of the 1800s joined Conan Doyle in using the cooee, and between 1880 and 1920 the word was also used as a brand-name for products as diverse as dairy foods, wine and spirits, matches and galvanised iron. Here, the effort was to establish Australianness, an effort taken further by a number of social leaders. In 1902, when opera singer Nellie Melba returned in triumph to Melbourne, she was welcomed at the railway station by a crowd from her old school, Presbyterian Ladies' College, calling cooee in unison.[13] The cooee was also employed in an enlistment drive in the First World War, as a group of volunteers marched from Gilgandra, in country NSW, to Sydney.

The wider social use of the cooee fell away markedly after 1920, and by the 1960s even the purely functional call was little heard in the bush. But the demise of the cooee was more than simply one rustic symbol going out of favour. In fact, the demise reflected a considerable realignment of national symbols, away from primarily Australian images. For several decades from the middle of the First World War, conservatives were appealing to a 'British people', and emphasizing imperial symbols. During that war, the South Australian government introduced a new oath of loyalty in public schools, which lasted until the 1950s: 'I love my country the British Empire, I salute her flag the Union Jack'.[14]

Similarly, in 1921 the NSW government set rules requiring schoolchildren to salute the British flag, and recite the pledge, 'I honour my God, I serve my King, I salute the flag'. From the early 1920s, God Save the King was used for annual Empire Day celebrations on 24 May. The ceremony was opposed by the NSW Trades and Labour Council, and by Catholic schools who saluted the Australian, not British, flag, and sang Advance Australia Fair on 24 May.[15]

The reasons for this shift in the aftermath of the First World War are discussed in more detail in Paper 10. The key point for our current discussion is the impacts that differing agendas can have on symbols of national identity. These can be traced in more detail by looking at the changing views of the Australian national anthem.

Song of Australia

Australian sprinter Cathy Freeman won the 400 metres in the Sydney 2000 Olympics. Watching the medal ceremony on television, commentator Ross Warneke didn't mind confessing, 'I got a bit teary when the 100,000 or so spectators at the Stadium burst into a spirited rendition of Advance Australia Fair after our Cath was presented with her gold medal.'[16]

National flags and anthems have long played a role in Olympic medal ceremonies, though rarely with the crowd fervour that made Warneke teary. But when Shirley Strickland won the Olympics 80 metres hurdles in Helsinki in 1952, her pride at being Australian accompanied some confusion amongst the hosts. The ceremony played two national anthems: Advance Australia Fair and God Save the Queen. Strickland remembered 'It took forever, but I loved every minute of it'.[17]

The previous day, when runner Marjorie Jackson won the 100 metres, the Finns had played Advance Australia Fair at the medal ceremony. It seems the organizers expected that as Australia marched as a separate nation, its national anthem would be different from the British anthem. This led to an uproar amongst team officials, as Australia's official national anthem was indeed God Save the Queen. The next day, the Finns took the unprecedented step of playing both songs for Strickland's victory, and then changed again after further discussions with Australian officials. Marjorie Jackson's second trip to the winner's podium, for the 200 metres, was celebrated with only one anthem, God Save the Queen.

Both the anthem played at medal ceremonies, and attitudes towards that anthem, have changed since the Second World War. Over these years, support grew for 'Advance Australia Fair', which formally became Australia's anthem in 1984. But the path to this change was uneven, and marked by divergent opinions on the issue.

At its first performance in 1878, Advance Australia Fair was not as antagonistic to British ties in Australia as it later came to symbolize. Songwriter Peter Dodds McCormack honoured Australians as a British people, with the (now rarely performed) fifth stanza of the song proclaiming:

> Britannia then shall surely know
> Beyond wide oceans' rolls
> Her sons in fair Australia's land
> Still keep a British soul. [18]

By 1943, the song was widely seen as 'giving the Australian touch', and a margin of 2 to 1 supported playing the anthem alongside God Save the King (the opinion poll did not ask whether people wanted just the Australian anthem). However, opinions differed by political affiliation: Labor voters were 3 to 1 in favour, while Non-Labor voters were evenly divided.[19]

This divergence influenced the Australian Broadcasting Commission (ABC) in its choice of news theme. From February 1942, under a Labor government, the ABC used Advance Australia Fair. On 1 January 1952, two years after the conservative Menzies government was elected, the ABC changed to the more imperial 'Majestic Fanfare', by an English composer, and performed by a London light orchestra.[20] In 1965, the ABC considered using something more modern and Australian than Majestic Fanfare, but decided that any possible gain would be outweighed by negative reactions from its established (and generally conservative) audience.[21]

Sensitivity to the audience's tastes also seems to have influenced the ABC in its choice in 1954 of music to start each day's broadcasting. The higher brow network started in most states with Advance Australia Fair, while the light network began each day with the strains of Waltzing Matilda.

But such Australian songs still ranked well behind the official national anthem. By late 1952, support for God Save the Queen as the single anthem had strengthened to half the population, up from one third in 1943. This was probably influenced by the publicity given to the accession of the young and popular Elizabeth II, and also a more conservative national mood under the Menzies government.[22]

The lead up to the 1956 Melbourne Olympics saw some support for a distinctive Australian anthem at the medal ceremonies. However any proposal had to contend with Wilfred Kent Hughes, the chairman of the organizing committee and a strong supporter of imperial ties. It was also initially expected that the Queen would open the games, so God Save the Queen was cemented as the anthem. Perhaps as consolation prize, the Games did have an Australian 'song' – set to the tune of Waltzing Matilda.[23]

Immediately after the 1956 Olympics, a new Gallup survey asked for a preference between God Save the Queen and 'something Australian'. The vote was even higher for the established anthem, with 60% support. Once again, Labor voters were more likely to support the Australian song, as was a majority of younger people, while women and non-Labor voters heavily supported God Save the Queen.

Views on the official national anthem in 1965 were almost identical to those in 1956 – a 3 to 2 vote for God Save the Queen. But this support depended a little on context. A year earlier, Gallup polls asked for people's preference for the song to be played when Australian athletes won gold at the 1964 Tokyo Olympics. Comparing the two results, two out of five differed in their choice, wanting Advance Australia Fair for sporting events but God Save the Queen for formal national occasions.[24]

However, the support for God Save the Queen crumbled dramatically in the next seven years. By 1972, the one in five supporting the anthem as 'She is our Queen', were heavily outnumbered by the three-quarters arguing 'we are no longer part of England'.[25] A change also occurred in the post-war years in attitudes to nationality. In July 1946, 60% considered themselves British compared to 37% Australian, while by late 1968 only 11% considered themselves British, and 76% Australian.[26]

These changes were affected by changes in the composition of Australians. In 1947, 90% of the population had been born in Australia – and more than half of the overseas-born hailed from the United Kingdom. By 2006, after 50 years of strong immigration, now 76% are Australian-born, and the British contingent is less than one quarter of those born overseas.[27]

Origins certainly affected attitudes towards the national anthem. In the 1965 poll, when two-thirds supported God Save the Queen, a strong majority of Democratic Labor Party voters wanted Advance Australia Fair. The DLP was generally socially conservative, but many supporters also had strong Irish backgrounds which influenced views towards the British anthem.[28]

The changing origins of Australians had a long-term effect on a wide variety of social patterns, including national symbols. However, such gradual changes by themselves are hard put to explain the dramatic drop in support for God Save the Queen in the late 1960s, from 60% in 1965 to 21% in 1972. Probably more important were a raft of social changes at this time, discussed in more detail in Paper 12 below.

Responding to these changes in popular attitudes, the new Labor Prime Minister, Gough Whitlam, announced in 1973 a search for a distinctive Australian anthem. Following an unsuccessful national competition for a new song, the Australian Bureau of Census and Statistics polled 60,000 people in 1974 on four possibilities (Advance Australia Fair, God Save the Queen, Waltzing Matilda and Song of Australia). Half those polled preferred Advance Australia Fair, and the Government selected this as the national anthem in April 1974.[29]

The subsequent conservative Fraser Government, elected in late 1975, clearly much preferred God Save the Queen, although it approved Waltzing Matilda as the official song for the Montreal Olympics in 1976.[30] The following year, in a National Song Poll, 6.5 million voters preferred Advance Australia Fair to Waltzing Matilda, with God Save the Queen third on 19%. Despite these results, the Government kept God Save the Queen as the national anthem, with Advance Australia Fair as the 'national song'.

In April 1984, the Prime Minister of the next Labor government, Bob Hawke, decided that Advance Australia Fair was finally and permanently the official anthem. There was general support for the move, although the Melbourne *Herald-Sun* reported some complaints of the slowness of the song. Many also would have supported the laid-back attitude of 21-year-old Middle Park resident Peter Brown: 'I don't like flag-waving songs. "Click go the Shears" would be just as good – at least sheep can identify with it.'[31]

The 1977 poll results indicate a range of views about at least this national symbol. Many commentators have seen the Whitlam Government as representing a move towards an independent Australian identity. However, still one fifth of the population wanted to keep the British national anthem. Further, while 28% wanted Waltzing Matilda recognized as the 'dinky-di' national anthem, many voting for other songs clearly considered a ballad about a swagman rustling a jumbuck as highly unsuitable for such an accolade.[32]

Over time, there was growing support for an Australian song as the national anthem, and this was formally recognized in 1984. However, that trend was not even, and was affected by the political climate of the times. Support for the British anthem was stronger in the early 1950s and early 1960s, when the conservative Menzies government was in power, than in the mid 1940s, under Labor. And the conservative Fraser government in the late 1970s clearly felt it could restore God Save the Queen as the anthem without too much political fall-out.

These political and social agendas have also affected the ways that Australians have remembered and responded to probably the most significant national symbol – that of Anzac.

Reliving the ANZAC myth

At the Athens Olympics in 2004, a softball team member enjoined the others to 'think of the Anzacs'. 'It lifted us', commented another. 'It really lifted us.'[33] Twenty years earlier, when yacht Australia II was 1–3 down in match races for the America's Cup, team head Alan Bond urged journalists: 'don't write us off, we will win and win gloriously, just like our boys did at Gallipoli'. Image salesman that he was, Bond was little fazed when journalists pointed out that Gallipoli had actually been a defeat.[34]

Apart from such sports motivation, most thinking of the Anzacs occurs on 25 April each year. Anzac Day in Australia and New Zealand commemorates landings at

Gallipoli, western Turkey, in the First World War. One ceremony is held at dawn at the site of the 1915 landings, Anzac Cove. In 2002, after dawn had broken:

> The ceremony ended, but almost no one moved. Tom's friend Kate was weeping and the boys were clearing their thoughts. Tom admitted he was 'a bit shaky' and Chris volunteered that he had discovered a tear in his eye … Ben, usually slow to display any emotion blurted out 'I've been fighting back the tears for ten minutes. I found it amazing. I've never felt so proud to be Australian'.[35]

Some 16,000 mainly young people shared the 2002 Anzac Cove service with Tom, Kate, Chris and Ben – but such numbers in the pilgrimage are a recent phenomenon, starting from the 75th anniversary in 1990. Only 300 people attended the 50th anniversary in 1965 – and in 1961 Betty Roland was the sole Australian at Anzac Cove on Anzac Day.[36]

Changes such as the remarkable growth in attendances at the dawn service at Anzac Cove are often influenced by several factors. One central factor for Tom, Kate, Chris and Ben was the onset of cheap airfares transporting backpackers to Gallipoli each year. Others, which we will look at in this section, include a changing image of Australian identity, and changes in the commemoration of Anzac Day, from a more military orientation prior to the 1960s to the more recent acknowledgement of general suffering in war.

Anzac (Australia and New Zealand armed corps) forces landed with other Allied troops at Gallipoli on 25 April 1915 as part of a First World War campaign to defeat the Ottoman Empire.[37] After months of bloody and inconclusive fighting, the last Anzac forces left on the night of 19 December 1915.

While Australia suffered more casualties later in the war in France, Anzac Day is particularly remembered as the Anzacs' first military action in the war. But there have been marked variations in how the campaign is remembered. At the 2005 Anzac Day dawn service at Gallipoli, Australian Prime Minister John Howard paid tribute to the Anzacs, saying the Anzac spirit has 'sharpened our democratic temper and questioning eye'. It lived on in the valour and sacrifice of young Australians serving in the Solomons, Iraq and Afghanistan.[38] At the same service, New Zealand Air Vice Marshall Bruce Ferguson struck a somewhat different note. He:

> praised the Anzacs as 'the bravest of the brave' but said there had been no glory 90 years ago, only a tragic slaughter of young men on all sides. The Gallipoli campaign was warfare at its worst, at least on the British side. 'There was inspired leadership at the lower levels, and gross incompetence at the senior levels.' At Gallipoli 'We learnt to shake off the shackles of colonial dependency – we learnt that we must stand for what we believe in'.[39]

Differences in responses to Anzac Day have a long history. The differing tones between heroism and imperial slaughter were already present in 1916 and 1917, not least in two bitter referenda on whether Australia should have conscription for overseas service.[40]

Some proponents have had clear agendas in presenting events in a particular way. Prime Minister Howard's speech was in part trying to build a bridge between respect for previous soldiers and his Government's unpopular involvement in the current war in Iraq. But he was hardly the first politician to use such 'spin'. From the start, the Anzac legend (and Simpson's image) were co-opted into First World War recruitment campaigns. As an ex-Labor man leading a conservative government from 1916 to

1922, Prime Minister Billy Hughes' political position was often precarious. He was skilled at building support by popularist appeals, and by using his reputation as 'the little digger'. Hughes' courting of ex-servicemen was an important factor in the remarkable political strength of returned service groups in the 1920s.[41]

The agenda of the Returned Soldiers and Sailors' Imperial League of Australia (RSSILA) had strong influence in the 1920s and 1930s. As its title suggests, the League was strongly imperial – indeed, this was one reason it had difficulty maintaining numbers among ex-servicemen. Fewer than half the 270,000 returning servicemen ever joined the League, and its membership numbered only 41,000 in 1929, less than 20% of surviving servicemen.[42]

Nonetheless, the RSSILA had remarkable political power in the 1920s, and put its stamp on the commemoration of Anzac, with strongly military and imperial organization.[43] Despite opposition from business groups against another holiday for their workers, the RSSILA succeeded in making Anzac Day a full public holiday across Australia by 1930.[44]

After the Second World War, with large additional numbers of returned servicemen, the League changed its image, dropping the 'Imperial' and becoming the Returned Servicemen's League (RSL). A less reverential aspect infiltrated the annual Anzac Day commemoration, which Russell Ward described in 1958 as schizoid:

> Solemn religious services are conducted and patriotic orations are delivered by prominent citizens, but the rank and file carry out also, different, unofficial ceremonies. During and after the official performances knots of old soldiers gather in the public streets and squares, there to assert their birthright by playing, in the face of the law and the constables, ritualistic games of 'two up'. For most of the players, too, it seems both natural and fitting to end the day with a serious attempt to make it the greatest alcoholic debauch of the year.[45]

By the mid 1960s, the *Sydney Morning Herald* called together a panel to debate the subject 'can Anzac Day survive?'[46] Servicemen returning from Vietnam subsequently boosted numbers – but the passions over that conflict brought further agendas into play. Those in the annual march in the late 1970s faced protestors demonstrating against 'the futility of war'.

More recently, the numbers attending Anzac Day marches each year have grown remarkably. But the tone has changed, with less emphasis on the battles, and more on human values and shared suffering in war. This has meant a broader scope for involvement in the ceremonies.[47]

A symbol of this is changed attitudes towards Turks taking part in the annual Melbourne Anzac Day march. In the early 1980s, a Turkish request to participate was rejected by the Returned Services League (RSL): 'Anyone who was shooting us doesn't get in.' By the mid 1990s, the Victorian RSL branch invited two representatives of the local Turkish returned soldiers association to join the Melbourne march.[48]

At the same time, the RSL made other efforts to encourage observance, arranging with the AFL and the ARL to hold high profile football matches on Anzac Day. While both started recently, the Anzac Day Essendon-Collingwood game in Melbourne (first played in 1995) and the Australia-New Zealand test in Sydney (1997) are now referred to as part of the Anzac tradition, and draw huge crowds.[49] The military presence is strong: the 2006 match in Melbourne saw air force fly-overs, and veterans whisked around the ground in a lap of honour. The scope of the national imagery is growing stronger – many more games now play the national anthem. And 'a Hawthorn-Carlton match, four days before Anzac Day 2006, began with the two teams lined up before an enormous Australian flag, with the crowd being asked to stand while two buglers played the Last Post'.[50]

There are however limits to how far the blurring of sporting and military images goes. The word 'digger' has had widespread usage for Australian (and sometimes New Zealand as well) soldiers. On 2 August 2001, Athletics Australia announced that it would use the title for the Australian athletics team. While the proposal had been discussed beforehand with the RSL, neither party seemed prepared for the storm of protest that was unleashed. Critics felt that the word for soldiers who had fought, with some dying, for their country should simply not be used for a team of professional athletes. The furore was such that within two days Athletics Australia backed down, scrapping the proposal.[51]

So while entreaties to the 'Anzac spirit' are powerful, there are some important differences in the ways that Anzac is remembered – and in the agendas that lie behind the calls. With Anzac, there has been a gradual shift from more militaristic imagery to images of Simpson and his donkey. But, as evident in the different tones struck at the 2005 Anzac Day dawn service, different agendas still emphasise different elements in the story, constructing particular views and uses of this national symbol.

Constructing national identity

This collection centres on the role of sports in the Australian national identity. Developing themes introduced in the previous paper, this paper has discussed three key national symbols. It has emphasized that the development and presentation of these symbols has varied considerably over time, and between different observers (and social groups) at any one time.

Social class strongly flavoured attitudes in most of the above discussions. For example, upper-class Anglophiles in the mid-twentieth century were much keener on keeping God Save the Queen as the national anthem, while working-class and Irish descendants were much more likely to support an Australian anthem. The two same social groups varied in their attitudes towards either celebrating the imperial links of Anzac or complaining about incompetent Pommie generals butchering valiant Australians.

In the changes over time, economic developments played an important role. Cheaper airfares have given backpackers the ability to attend the dawn service at Anzac Cove in large numbers. As discussed in Paper 12, declining support for God Save the Queen and other imperial ties in the 1960s accompanied economic changes, with Australia increasing trade ties to Asia rather than the traditional British market.

But social class and economic developments were not the only driving forces. The demise of the cooee as an Australian identifier took place alongside strong political efforts to reinforce imperial links. The political strength of the RSSILA, and Billy Hughes' wooing of ex-servicemen, influenced the celebration of Anzac Day. Political agendas had strong impacts on the choice of the national anthem.

For all the dynamics outlined in this discussion, there are many views in Australia that sports madness transcends such parochialism – whatever differences on other issues, Australians all 'love their sport'. There are two responses to this. The first is that this, like other images of national identity, also needs to be considered in terms not only of the reality behind it, but also in terms of the agendas encouraging the image. Secondly, differences and changes in various aspects of the national identity have had demonstrable impacts on sport. This has occurred both in the way that particular sports have developed, and in the presentation of Australia's image as a sporting nation.

Later papers investigate how and why Australia's image as a sporting nation has developed. A key theme, drawing from the above discussion, is how diverse views and visions have interacted. Emphasizing the importance of such diversity, the next two papers discuss patterns of sports attendance and sports participation in Australia.

Notes

1. Cashman, '*Ave a Go, Yer Mug*, 98. Other citations give the famous 'Yabba' credit for this barrack: see, for example, Kleinman and Shtargot, 'What a day at the 'G'. *The Age* December 30, 2005, 3.
2. Smart, ed. *The Penguin Book of Australian Sporting Anecdotes*, 144–5.
3. Gallup polls in June and August 1963 found less than 15% support for the 'royal', with majority and growing support for the 'dollar' – see Gallup poll summary, Sept.–Oct. 1963.
4. Extending a point made by Davison, 'Welcoming the World', 76, it is possible to cite a considerable number of dates when various people claimed Australia had 'come of age'. These include Federation in 1901, the Anzac (and western front) battles of the First World War, victory in the Second World War, the Melbourne Olympics of 1956, the cultural resurgence in the mid-1970s, and the Sydney Olympics of 2000. As Davison notes, what is interesting here is not so much the individual events as the perpetual adolescence that the commentators seem to reckon Australians need to grow out of. This attitude is strongly related to the 'cultural cringe' discussed below in Paper 10.
5. Stephens, 'The View Beyond the Battlefield', *Sydney Morning Herald*, August 26, 2005; and Flanagan, 'What would Simmo have thought of Howard?' *The Age*, November 5, 2005.
6. This and the following discussion draws heavily on Cochrane, *Simpson and the Donkey*.
7. Cochrane, *Simpson and the Donkey*, 214–35. The 1956 book was Alan Moorehead's *Gallipoli*. Reflecting the wider commemoration of Simpson by 1989, publisher Macmillan produced an illustrated version of Moorehead's book, with Simpson now appearing in one (disputed) photo, in a page of text on the Anzac medallion, and in an excerpt from a letter from his mother to her son at the front.
8. Cochrane, *Simpson and the Donkey*, 224.
9. Flanagan, 'What would Simmo have thought of Howard?'
10. Inglis, 'Imperial Cricket', 168.
11. On-line text of Sir Arthur Conan Doyle, *Boscombe Valley Mystery*. http://camdenhouse. ignisart.com/canon/bosc.html.
12. This and subsequent paragraphs draw from White, 'Cooees across the Strand', 109–27, and Blainey, *Black Kettle and Full Moon*, 120–8.
13. Blainey, *Black Kettle and Full Moon*, 128.
14. Meaney, 'Britishness and Australian Identity', 79.
15. Firth and Hoorn, 'Empire Day to Cracker Night', 31.
16. Ross Warneke, *The Age*, October 5, 2000, Green Guide, 10.
17. Cashman, *Sport in the National Imagination*, 94–5.
18. Meaney, 'Britishness and Australian Identity', 80.
19. Gallup poll summaries, respectively December 1943–January 1944, July 1946.
20. Inglis, *This is the ABC*, 150–1.
21. Ibid., 259.
22. Gallup poll summary, January 1953.
23. Cashman, *Sport in the National Imagination*, 95. See the more detailed discussion of the battle over imperial images at the Melbourne Olympics in Paper 11 below.
24. Gallup poll summaries, published in April–June 1964, Feb.–March 1965. The statistics for dual national feelings were calculated by assuming that anyone in the smaller group on each Australian/English question would also make the respective choice in the other question. Forty per cent wanted an Australian song on both occasions, while one in five wanted God Save the Queen for both.
25. Gallup poll summaries in respectively Jan.–March 1957, April–June 1964, Feb–March 1965, Feb.–June 1967, June–July 1969, and Nov. 1972.

26. Gallup poll summaries, July 1946, Nov. 1968, Feb, 1969. Comparing the results of the 1968 nationality question with the 1969 anthem question, it appears that a quarter of those considering themselves Australian were still happy with 'God Save the Queen' as the anthem.
27. Australian Bureau of Statistics (www.abs.gov.au), *Year Book Australia 2007* (1301.0), Table 7.39.
28. Gallup poll summary, Feb.–March 1965.
29. National Library on-line archive on Waltzing Matilda (www.nla.gov.au/epubs/waltzing-matilda/4-Anthem-Choosing.html).
30. This turned out to be a Pyrrhic selection, as Australia won no gold medals in Montreal.
31. Melbourne *Herald-Sun*, April 19, 1984, cited www.hamilton.net.au/advance.html.
32. Australia's national song has a remarkable number of words undecipherable to most English speakers. The four lines of the first stanza alone have six such words:

Once a jolly *swagman* camped by a *billabong*
Under the shade of a *coolibah* tree
And he sang as he watched and waited 'til his *billy* boiled
You'll come *a-waltzing matilda* with me

A swagman is an itinerant bush worker, carrying his possessions in a swag or pack. A billabong is a cut-off arm of a river (known as an ox-bow in the US). The coolibah is a native tree. The billy can was used by swagmen to boil water for their tea. A-waltzing matilda is slang for going on the road, carrying 'matilda', another term for the swag.

33. Davidson, 'A Nation of Barrackers'. *The Age*, January 27, 2007.
34. Barry, *Rise and Fall of Alan Bond*, 135.
35. Wright, *Turn Right at Istanbul*, 223, cited by Damousi, 'The Emotions of History', 28–39.
36. Fewster, Basarin and Basarin, *Gallipoli*, 21.
37. Despite the commemoration of Gallipoli in Australia and New Zealand, the Anzac troops were a small minority of the allied forces, suffering 36,000 casualties, compared with 120,000 British (including Indian) casualties, and 47,000 French. The Ottoman defenders suffered some 250,000 casualties – in each case about one third were fatalities. See Fewster, Basarin and Basarin, *Gallipoli*, especially 6, 7.
38. Reported in *The Age*, April 26, 2005, 6.
39. Ibid., 1.
40. White, *Inventing Australia*, 130, and see the detailed discussion in Paper 11 below.
41. Horne, *In Search of Billy Hughes*.
42. Seal, *Inventing Anzac*, 109, 206.
43. Damousi, 'The Emotions of History', 32.
44. Seal, *Inventing Anzac*.
45. Ward, *The Australian Legend*, 233.
46. Cochrane, *Simpson and the Donkey*, 232.
47. Fewster, Basarin and Basarin, *Gallipoli*, 11, and Damousi, 'The Emotions of History', 32–7 who refers to 'an inspiring story of the power of courage, endurance, mateship and heroism'.
48. Fewster, Basarin and Basarin, *Gallipoli*, 18–19.
49. Adair, 'Diggers are not Athletes', 72.
50. Jim Davidson, 'A Nation of Barrackers at the Expense of all else'. *The Age*, Opinion, January 27, 2007.
51. Adair, 'Diggers are not Athletes', especially 64–5 and 77.

References

Adair, Daryl. 'Diggers are not Athletes'. In *Beyond the Torch: Olympics and Australian Culture,* ed. Daryl Adair, Bruce Coe, and Nick Guoth. 61–82. Melbourne: Australian Society for Sports History Studies No. 17, 2005.
Barry, Paul. *The Rise and Fall of Alan Bond.* Sydney: Transworld Publishers/ABC, 1990.
Blainey, Geoffrey. *Black Kettle and Full Moon.* Camberwell, Victoria: Penguin, 2003.
Cashman, Richard. *'Ave a Go, Yer Mug': Australian Cricket Crowds from Larrikin to Ocker.* Sydney: Collins, 1984.

Cashman, Richard. *Sport in the National Imagination.* Sydney: Walla Walla Press, in conjunction with the Centre for Olympic Studies, University of New South Wales, 2002.

Cochrane, Peter. *Simpson and the Donkey: the Making of a Legend.* Melbourne: Melbourne University Press, 1992.

Damousi, Joy. 'The Emotions of History'. In *The Historian's Conscience: Australian Historians on the Ethics of History,* ed. Stuart Macintyre, 28–39. Carlton, Vic: Melbourne University Press, 2004.

Davison, Graeme. 'Welcoming the World: the 1956 Olympics and the Re-presentation of Melbourne'. *Australian Historical Studies* 109 (1997): 64–76.

Fewster, Kevin, V. Basarin, and H.H. Basarin. *Gallipoli: The Turkish Story.* New South Wales: Allen and Unwin, 2003.

Firth, Stewart, and Jeanette Hoorn. 'From Empire Day to Cracker Night'. In *Australian Popular Culture,* ed. Peter Spearitt and David Walker, 17–38. Sydney: Allen & Unwin, 1979.

Gallup Poll Summaries, every 2–3 months, 1941–1973, mimeo sheets held by State Library of Victoria SLTF 301. 154 AU7GAL.

Horne, Donald. *In Search of Billy Hughes.* Melbourne: Macmillan, 1979.

Inglis, K.S. 'Imperial Cricket and Test Matches between Australia and England 1877–1900'. In *Sport in History: The Making of Modern Sporting History,* ed. Richard Cashman and Michael McKernan, 148–79. Queensland: University of Queensland Press, 1979.

Inglis, K.S. *This is the ABC.* 2nd ed. Melbourne: Black, 2006.

Meaney, Neville. 'Britishness and Australian Identity: The Problem of Nationalism in Australian History and Historiography'. *Australian Historical Studies* 116 (2001): 76–90.

Moorehead, Alan. *Gallipoli.* New York: Harper, 1956.

Seal, Graham. *Inventing Anzac: The Digger and National Mythology.* St Lucia, Queensland: University of Queensland Press, 2004.

Smart, Richard, ed. *The Penguin Book of Australian Sporting Anecdotes.* Ringwood, Vic: Penguin Books, 1996.

Ward, Russell. *The Australian Legend.* Melbourne: Oxford University Press, 1958.

White, Richard. *Inventing Australia.* Sydney: George Allen and Unwin, 1981.

White, Richard. 'Cooees across the Strand: Australians in London and the Performance of National Identity'. *Australian Historical Studies* 116 (2001): 109–27.

Wright, Tony. Turn Right at Istanbul: A Walk on the Gallipoli Peninsula. Crows Nest, NSW: Allen and Unwin, 2003.

The roar of the crowd

Early in the twentieth century, a visiting English fast bowler criticized Australian crowds and 'the bitterness of the disappointed mob of cricket fans':

> Australia was being beaten so the crowd, not knowing what sportsmanship means, shouted abuse at the men who were winning. Can you imagine my feelings when 50,000 people booed my every step as I ran at the wicket? ... The Australian people seem to be out to throw us off our game. When they failed they shouted insults, and hoped to win in that way.[1]

A rather different take came in another comment from an English bowler, who achieved his best Test batting performance at the Sydney Cricket Ground (SCG). When he was finally out, just short of a century,

> Every man on the Sydney Cricket Ground stood and cheered me. The applause and the cheers from the mob on the Hill were thunderous. I never realised the approach of the Australian crowds until that moment. It proved to me Australians like a trier, they go for the underdog, and they appreciate good cricket no matter who provides it. They are tough: they barrack to unsettle a player, but they like anyone who attacks. I never expected the Hill mob to get up and cheer me after the abuse they had hurled.[2]

These situations differed – with the crowd responding first to a bowler dishing it out, and then to a batsman showing he could take it. But there is a world of difference between the first crowd image 'not knowing what sportsmanship means' and the second, of a tough but knowledgeable crowd that 'appreciates good sport no matter who provides it'. Across the years, many commentators have used one or the other of these images. Whichever is being used at the time often comes with the implication that something about the real Australian national identity is being revealed.

So will the 'real' Australian crowd please stand up? Or at least start a Mexican wave? Our search for a national crowd identity is complicated by the fact that the above two accounts actually came, at different times, from the same person – Harold Larwood, the English strike bowler in the controversial bodyline series in 1932–33. The first was written for English readers in the *Sunday Express* on 7 May 1933, shortly after the series finished. The second came in Larwood's career recollections, published 30 years later in both England and Australia – 15 years after he migrated to Australia, where he lived within earshot of the SCG.

The effects of time and context on one person's perceptions of Australian crowds reiterate the emphasis of the last paper on differing perceptions of national images, and their relation to proponents' agendas.

   This paper concentrates on the images and the underlying reality of sports atten-dances, particularly looking at motivations behind attendances. As we will see, these attendances are much more complex than generally realized – and are also affected by how sports organizers present their game, and how potential fans respond to the opportunities and offerings.

Those surprising fans

Maybe it's the media's interest in controversy, but it seems that the critical comments of unsporting partisans outnumber the numbers of images appreciating knowledgeable and sporting crowds. There is a long history of this. In his speech at the jubilee of Australian football in 1908, Prime Minister Alfred Deakin saved any qualms about this 'sporting people' for 'those who are putting their energy into their voices instead of their muscle'. The sense of fair play, which is always present in the breast of the players, is not always first in the minds of those who applaud merely something which makes for the success of their own side.[3]

   A common recent image in such criticisms is the archetypal 'ocker' sports fan. Typically male, the diehard sports fan, decked out in his team colours, is loud, hard-drinking, and shows little interest in things beyond his immediate ken,[4] and writes his football club in the space for religion on the Census form.

   But if we start thinking of different sports, we immediately come across different images. Taking the four most popular sporting events in Melbourne each year, the male fan at the Australian Rules Finals is perhaps the closest to the 'ocker' image. But this image is some distance away from the well-dressed young party girl at the Spring Racing Carnival, the older well-heeled matron at the Australian Open tennis, or the 'petrol head' male at the Australian Grand Prix.

   In 1995–96, these four major sporting events each attracted some 300,000 people.[5] The gender balance in these crowds followed the images to some extent: women were about half of those who attended the tennis and the Spring Racing Carnival, while men dominated with two-thirds or more of the crowds for the AFL Finals and the Grand Prix.[6] And some of those attending would certainly have confirmed the above images.

   But there was considerably more diversity, and overlap, amongst the fans than the images would suggest – and some other surprises as well. Of the people attending the Grand Prix, one quarter also attended the tennis. Compared with the 8% of the overall population that went to the tennis, this means Grand Prix patrons had a tennis atten-dance rate three times that of the general population. This was the general pattern across all four big events. Those attending each event were generally three times as likely as the general population to also attend the other major sporting events.

   There are also problems with another frequent image in Australia, which contrasts the philistine ocker with a more refined attendee at cultural events. Given the common image of the tennis fan, it is perhaps not surprising that those who attended the tennis were four times as likely as the general population to attend the predominantly high-brow International Festival of the Arts. However, attendees at the Grand Prix often swapped their petrol head T-shirts and caps for Arts Festival glad rags: their Arts Festival attendances were three times those of the general population. And attendees at any of the big four sports events were twice as likely as the general population to also go to the Comedy Festival in April.

   These patterns go beyond major sports events. In 2003, the Australian Bureau of Statistics compared children's involvement in sports with cultural pursuits such as playing a musical instrument, singing, dance or drama. One fifth of boys in sports teams also took part in at least one of the cultural pursuits – close to double the 11% cultural score for boys not taking part in organized sport. Similarly, girls playing organized sport were 33% more likely than non-playing girls to also follow cultural pursuits.[7]

Among adults, one factor in enjoying both sport and cultural events was probably a greater ability to pay for tickets to any sort of event. Family income was certainly a big influence for the children: involvement in both sports and cultural activities was much higher for children in dual income families than for children with non-working parents.[8]

A second big factor was attitudinal. An 'event-going' attitude meant people attending the big sports events were again twice as likely as the general population to attend local (and free) street festivals. And, overall, they were 60% more likely to visit an art gallery during the year (tennis patrons slightly higher, AFL people slightly lower).[9] The family environment affected children's involvement, with much higher rates of sport participation if fathers or siblings were also actively involved.[10]

This attitudinal pattern applied to more generic activities as well. People attending the big events were consistently 20% more likely to exercise than the general population, and even more likely to attend the casino.[11] There is a small influence here from the age patterns of the groups – people in their 20s and 30s more likely to go to events, to exercise, and to go to the casino. However, by far the more important factor is that across all age groups, people attending these events also choose to be more physically active, and to attend cultural events.

This discussion has challenged several of the key elements in the common image of the sports fan. The comparison with different images at different events introduced some complexity, with things rapidly getting more complicated with the findings of the overlaps between fans at different sports – and at other social and cultural activities. The idea of a single sports fan image is looking increasingly unsustainable – a point reinforced if we look at differing motivations among sports fans.

Fans and motivation

As discussed in Paper 2, Australia is well ahead of the United States in the extent of sports attendance – almost half of Australians attend at least one sports event each year, compared with just over one third of Americans. But the difference between the two countries is not due to the diehard fans. Frequent fans (those going at least once a month) form about one in eight of each population.[12] The difference in the overall statistics is due to those who attend infrequently – with the numbers in this group in Australia (36% of the population) well ahead of those in the United States (23%). Such a disparity makes a huge difference in social dynamics: for example, it makes it much more likely that a new acquaintance in Australia will be interested in sports, and hence makes sports a useful topic of casual conversation.

There is an irony here. Taking attendance at sports events as a symptom, Australia's international sports image is due not to those in the population who have the full sports mad influenza, but to those afflicted with sniffles. We need something more than the image of a diehard fan to explain the greater level of sports interest in Australia.

In 2004, writer Gideon Haigh had no doubt that sports fans had responded to a more attractive style of cricket under Australian captain Steve Waugh: 'on only five occasions in Waugh's fifty-three tests have his teams been stalemated. Guaranteed an

Table 1.   AFL Grand Finals: TV viewer numbers 2000–07.

	2000	2001	2002	2003	2004	2005	2006	2007
	Essendon	Brisbane	Brisbane	Brisbane	Pt Adel	Sydney	W Coast	Geelong
GF teams	Melbourne	Essendon	C'wood	C'wood	Brisbane	W Coast	Sydney	Pt Adel
Melbourne	1,190	1,216	1,244	1,325	1,215	1,200	1,180	1,210
Sydney	290	323	315	352	314	991	762	320
Brisbane	172	461	375	575	490	341	328	270
Adelaide	314	340	390	330	431	314	325	377
Perth	234	260	302	384	349	511	549	385
National	2,200	2,604	2,626	2,966	2,800	3,400	3,150	2,560
Melb share	54%	47%	47%	45%	43%	35%	37%	47%

Note: C'wood is Collingwood, Pt Adel is Port Adelaide and W Coast is West Coast.
Source: Newspaper reports of viewer numbers in week following each Grand Final.

outcome, Australian test audiences have risen from 411,335 in 1999–2000 to 568,324 in 2002–03; everywhere they go now, Australians are feted for their enterprise.[13]

The level of excitement was also a factor in recent trends in the TV ratings for the AFL Grand Final – especially the excitement of seeing a home-town team. From 2000 to 2005, the numbers of people watching the Grand Final on TV in the five major Australian cities soared from 2.2 million to 3.4 million – although it fell again in the two following years, to 2.6 million in 2007. This growth was uneven across the country, with little change in Melbourne or Adelaide (where about a third of the population was already watching in 2000), while numbers were much more variable in the other cities.[14] The full data, with figures in thousands for average numbers watching across the entire match, is:

At first sight, this might indicate the success of the AFL administration's efforts to promote Australian rules across Australia, and especially into the Sydney and Brisbane markets (traditionally Rugby League towns). Certainly there was some effect from this – but there were at least two other potent influences.

The first, which suggests that at least some of the audience are far from died-in-the-wool footy fans, is the weather. For example, in 2002 when the weather in Adelaide was an inhospitable 15 degrees with showers, 390,000 watched the Grand Final on television. The previous year, when fine weather and 31 degrees made alternative outdoor pursuits more attractive, the Adelaide TV audience was 340,000.

But the influence of the weather was little compared to that of a home-town team being in the Grand Final. Teams from each city outside Melbourne played in at least one Grand Final in these years. In each case, the number of viewers in that city at least doubled compared with the previous year, without a local team. The most spectacular increase in TV audience was in Sydney in 2005, when almost a million watched Sydney beat West Coast – the previous year, one-third of that number had watched.

Viewer numbers declined, often dramatically, if a local team was not in the Grand Final the following year. Even in Melbourne, with strong viewer numbers across these years, numbers dropped by 8% in 2004 when no Melbourne team made the Grand Final. However, when Sydney was not in the Grand Final in 2007, viewer numbers there slumped by more than half.

Following the local team is also a big drawcard in regional areas of Australia, where attendance rates are generally higher than in major cities. Two major factors seem to drive this result. The first is the greater range and availability of alternative leisure pursuits in urban areas. The second is the broader social role of sport and sporting clubs in country areas, as indicated in the comments on country football above.

That broader social role was a central concern of a 2004 Parliamentary Committee inquiry into the state of Australian Rules in country Victoria. The Wimmera Football League told the Committee

football and netball are where everybody in this area meets, where they get to intermingle with others from nearby towns, and what they do for enjoyment and relaxation. In this area football and netball are not just games; they are part of life.[15]

Former AFL Coach Tom Hafey remembered

doing a night at Beulah up in the Mallee, with a 300 population. An old fellow came rushing over. He said, 'I used to collect your garbage down in St Kilda'. I said, 'What are you doing in Beulah?' He said, 'I retired, bought a house — $30,000. I've never been a football person, but I am now. I've got 50 new mates.'[16]

And another witness mentioned other social connections:

With parents working and kids at school, Saturday is the main day when a family is in its unit. They all leave together and they all go home together. On the flip side of the family day out is that I personally do not have a family and I find that Saturday is an opportunity to see who else is out there that has no family.[17]

So we have a variety of reasons for watching sports. Some are diehard fans. Others are encouraged by the excitement. A significant proportion only watch if they can cheer on their local team. Still others see the occasion as a crucial part of local social networks. Some take the opportunity to establish new relationships. And these motivations can overlap and reinforce each other – there are plenty of diehard fans quite happy to take advantage of pick up opportunities if they present themselves.

Starting from such differing motivations, Melbourne academic Bob Stewart has described a number of different 'types' in those attending sporting events. He outlines five types, varying on how often they attend matches, and whether their key motivation is the excitement of the game or loyalty to a particular team.

Those attracted to the excitement of the game Stewart terms the 'Aficionado' (frequent attendee) and 'Theatregoer' (less frequent). Those motivated by loyalty to a team are termed the 'Passionate Partisan' (died-in-the-wool supporter, attending most matches); the 'Champ follower' (less frequent attendances, with team support more conditional on success); and the 'Reluctant partisan' who is loyal to one team, but doesn't attend much.[18]

The factors influencing interest in AFL TV ratings and country football, as well as Stewart's types, emphasize the number of different motivations behind attendances at sports. While the diehard fan is an important part of the story, that image needs to be supplemented by those attracted by the excitement of particular events. Both Stewart's more detailed list and the overlaps between sports discussed earlier indicate shades of grey between these two types – a diehard fan for one sport could well be an occasional event goer for other sports. The next section discusses the patterns of attendances at different sports.

Table 2. Attendance patterns, major Australian sports, 2006.

	Million people attending at least one match/event in the previous year	Frequent fans as % of those attending	Female % of those attending	Ratio of professionals attending to non-professionals
Australian Rules	2.5	34%	40%	1.3
Horse racing	2.0	11%	46%	1.2
Rugby league	1.5	27%	37%	0.9
Motor sports	1.5	12%	31%	0.6
Cricket (outdoor)	0.7	16%	25%	1.9
Rugby union	0.7	18%	34%	1.8
Soccer (outdoor)	0.6	34%	38%	1.6
Harness racing	0.4	10%	43%	0.9
Tennis	0.3	15%	61%	2.2
Basketball	0.2	34%	44%	1.3

Patterns of attendances

In 2006, 2.5 million Australians attended at least one Australian rules game, while horse racing also attracted over 2 million people.[19] Motor sports and rugby league each attracted 1.5 million people, while cricket, rugby union and soccer were attended by 600-700,000. The ten most popular sports were:

These figures indicate considerable diversity in sports attendance, and also challenge some common images. Cricket, long considered a major part of Australian sporting obsessions, only just outranked soccer, often considered a poorly followed sport here. And tennis, which was a major focus of Australian sporting attention in the 1950s and 1960s, attracted 300,000 people, ranking it ninth of the top ten sports, behind harness racing (400,000), which receives very little media coverage.

In later papers, this collection demonstrates that social cachet can be important in establishing the power of images. Certainly it helps explain the relative strength of the cricket and tennis images versus soccer and harness racing. Both cricket and especially tennis attract higher income and status crowds. The higher-paid occupational groups of managers, administrators and professionals make up 30% of the workforce, but contribute significantly more than 30% of the audience for cricket and tennis (and also rugby union). In contrast, harness racing, rugby league and motor sports are more blue collar sports (as soccer has been until recently), with much less than 30% of the audience from the professional occupations.[20]

Consistent with the patterns outlined for the four major sporting events in Melbourne, Australian sports crowds also vary on gender lines. The most male dominated sport is cricket, with women making up only a quarter of those attending; rugby union and motor sports audiences are also heavily male-dominated. In contrast, women make up just over half those attending tennis, and just under half the attendees at basketball.[21]

It is significant that the two most popular sports, Australian rules and horse racing, are also the two sports with the broadest social appeal. Both have a fairly even spread across all occupational groups, and both also attract large numbers of women (40% of those attending rules and 46% at the races). The success of sports that aim at an inclusive social spread is also a theme that later papers will develop further.

The patterns differ across states as well, especially between the Australian Rules states along the southern coast and the rugby states of the east coast. In addition, horse racing and tennis attract especially large groups in Victoria, while motor sports are most popular in Western Australia.[22]

There are also differences between sports in the proportion of fans who come regularly. AFL, soccer, basketball and rugby league all had the largest proportions of fans attending once a month or more. In contrast, sports such as horse racing, motor sports and tennis had very small proportions of frequent fans, and high numbers attending just once or twice. These sports often base their marketing on one or two particular events in a year. The Australian Open Tennis is a leading example, and many of those attracted to the excitement of the Melbourne Cup Carnival attend no other race meetings during the year.

The interaction between different motivations, and the ways sports try to attract crowds, can differ over time. This is evident if we look at the rates of sporting attendance over the years.

Since 1995, several sports have tried new marketing campaigns, with some showing significant benefits. In response, the numbers of people attending rugby union doubled in the next ten years, while Australian rules enjoyed an increase of one-third. Horse racing had a modest increase, with a big factor being the attendances at Flemington events in Melbourne Cup week discussed in Paper 14. However, other sports saw declines: tennis and cricket losing one third of their patrons, while basketball crowds fell by more than half.[23]

Similar changes occur in the broader measure of sports interest published in the biannual Sweeney Sports Report. The Report calculates overall 'interest' by combining data about participation, attendance, television viewing, radio listening, print media readership and internet use.[24] Over the past 20 years or so, total interest in sports has remained high, with interest shown by a little above half of the population (most frequently through television watching). The figures for individual sports have however varied. The first important element has been the success rate of Australian competitors in international sports, with, for example, golf viewing on TV considerably less now than when champion Greg Norman was playing. The second element has been the organizational changes and better marketing from sports such as Australian Rules, rugby union and soccer.[25]

Going further back in time, getting a good picture of attendance patterns can be complicated by the quality of the statistics. In the early 1980s, Australian cricket captain Greg Chappell was sceptical of official crowd numbers, asking 'you don't believe the figures that they give out, do you?' Further back, in January 1914, a Victoria versus New Zealand cricket match attracted the unlikely official total of $4,739^{1}/_{2}$, although a New South Wales match against England in 1874 avoided other numeration problems by insisting beforehand that no horses would be allowed into the ground.[26]

Thankfully, better quality statistics – albeit still with some idiosyncrasies – are available from the Australian Bureau of Statistics since 1975, and from opinion polls before that. Table 3 gives the broad trends in attendance at sports events since 1950. The figures show the proportion of the adult population who attended at least one sports event in the past year.[27]

The figures show a considerable decline in the proportion attending sports events from 1953 to 2006, although with a slight increase from 1995 to 2002. Over this time

Table 3. Percentages of adults attending major sports events.

	1953	1975	1995	2002	2006
Football (all codes)	39%	34%	25%	32%	29%
Horse and Harness Racing	26%	16%	16%	16%	15%
Cricket	17%	4%	8%	6%	5%
Tennis	14%	n.a.	3%	3%	2%
All sports (excluding motor sports)	75%	53%	42%	45%	40%

period, both cricket and tennis saw remarkable drops in attendances. This was particularly in state-level competitions: cricket Tests and the Australian Tennis Open still draw good crowds, but the Sheffield Shield cricket competition between state sides and the state tennis tournaments attract many fewer fans. It is worth noting that cricket attendances, after a severe drop from 1953 to 1975, then rebounded, with the introduction of one-day cricket a major factor.[28]

One element in motivating fans, especially the occasional attendees, has been the attraction of local champions. In the 1930s, the Australian cricket Board of Control was certainly aware of this, spruiking ads extolling Don Bradman as 'Australia's champion'. In three Ashes series against the English team, in 1932–33, 1936–37 and 1946–47, crowds averaged some 39,000 on days when Bradman was batting, well ahead of the average 27,000 who came along on other days of the same cricket matches.[29]

Bradman's star status thus helped increase crowds by close to half on days when he was batting. However, crowd numbers for cricket Tests against England varied for a number of other reasons as well, as a recent study of these crowds between 1920 and 1966 has shown. Two reasons related to the excitement levels: if either side was well ahead in the match, attendance fell by some 40% – and if the match was a foregone conclusion, average attendances fell 80%.

The other factors fall more into the 'opportunity' category. Rain interrupting play reduced numbers by a quarter, while numbers would climb by some 40% for days of play on the weekend or public holidays. Most important was the size of the ground – average crowds at the Melbourne Cricket Ground were twice those of the Gabba in Brisbane, and those at the Adelaide Oval were 70% up on Brisbane.[30] The typical crowd in Melbourne or Adelaide without Bradman batting was bigger than a Gabba crowd when he was batting.

The availability of facilities was also a significant factor in regular attendances at Australian rules matches in Melbourne. The graph shows the remarkable proportions of Melbourne's population attending VFL Australian rules games each weekend (not including the finals series).[31]

As is discussed in Paper 14, the VFL was worried that the 5% attendance figure in the 1970s demonstrated a decline in the game. In fact, this figure was still remarkable in international competition, being comparable with similar figures for the most sports-mad cities overseas. The closest competition probably came from Glasgow, home to two stadia at that stage capable of holding more than 100,000 patrons.[32] And Melburnians turned out at twice that rate, at close to 10% of the total population, in the interwar years, with attendances still consistently above 8% until 1960.

What generated such remarkable attendance figures? Explanations here can rapidly become circular, and certainly there are a number of reinforcing factors. A

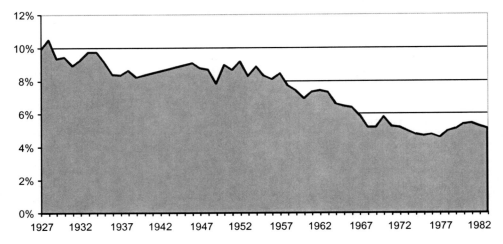

Figure 1.   Average weekly attendances, VFL Home and Away games, as percentage of Melbourne's population.

common explanation is that Melbourne has a 'football culture'. But culture is heavily influenced by what people do, so the large number of attendances is both a cause and an effect of such a culture.

One critical factor was Melbourne's ability to accommodate such large numbers. In addition to the massive Melbourne Cricket Ground, the inner suburbs of the city had 10 venues capable of holding substantial crowds. Circularity is involved here as well – Australian rules attracted large paying crowds from the 1870s, and the grounds were able to expand facilities to accommodate even larger crowds.

Paper 8 discusses this early development of Australian rules. Again, an interaction occurred between the development of the sport and a variety of motivations among fans. Such patterns can be illustrated at the grass roots level, tracing changes in the way country football has presented itself to the community.

Initiatives and community response

Mick Stone, the ARL umpires' boss, was touring small country towns giving lectures on the rules. At one meeting he asked,

> 'Now, what would happen if, at the last kick of the game, the ball burst in mid air, with half the ball going over the bar, and half going under?' The old committee man thought for a moment and said 'Well … the way I see it, the club would be down about \$60.'[33]

The old committee man and his colleagues often play crucial roles in social life in country Australia – indeed, sport is often described as the social cement in small towns. Alarmed by stories of decline in many Australian rules competitions, a Victorian Parliamentary Committee conducted an inquiry into the state of country football in 2004.

A number of witnesses talked of the 'proud tradition and long history' of country football since the Victorian Country Football League (VCFL) formed in 1927. They also documented declines in club numbers, with the number of clubs reducing by 69 between 1990 and 2003, half from clubs disbanding, the other half from mergers into combined clubs. The two most cited reasons were the diminishing populations in some farming areas, especially in the Mallee and Wimmera in the north west of Victoria, and the movement of young men and women into the cities for education and employment.[34]

As with many of the images discussed in this collection, this initially plausible picture provides only part of the overall story. The Committee noted that the VCFL statistics were still impressive: it has 870 affiliated clubs, 29,000 registered players aged 19 years or over, and 40,000 juniors.[35] Each club also had some 20–30 very active volunteers. The reasons given for decline were not the full picture either: while populations in some farming areas had declined, other areas have been attracting more people. And while some young people were leaving for education and employment, football participation was falling even amongst young men staying in rural areas.

A key aspect in the Committee's view was club culture. Increasing numbers of people were turned off by the traditional strongly male-oriented culture in many clubs, with an emphasis on drinking. One witness to the Parliamentary Committee described the 'old' environment at his local club in Swan Hill:

> When I first came to Swan Hill it was very much a men's club, and alcohol was the top end of it; there was football first and then alcohol. Alcohol made all the money. You would go to training on a Thursday night and there would be beer there, on Friday night you would have a beer there, and certainly on Saturdays after the game there would be beer well into the night, and then on Sunday the barrel. It would roll on and on.[36]

The Committee noted two recent studies showing the pattern was continuing. In 13 football clubs in Gippsland, half of those drinking at the club consumed hazardous amounts of alcohol each time they drank at the club. The second study, of metropolitan clubs, found that more than 10% of 18–20-year-olds drank 13 or more standard drinks each time they visited the club – and nearly all of those left the club as the driver of a vehicle.[37]

Most clubs have taken steps in recent years to improve this culture, to make their club more attractive to women and more 'family friendly' – recognizing, as the Committee put it, that 'their viability is dependent on their ability to actively include women as participants, spectators and volunteers'.[38] Most football clubs have integrated with netball clubs over the past 25 years; by 2004, 47 of the 48 senior football leagues had incorporated netball competitions.[39]

While the process of change has sometimes been slow, the Committee found many clubs that had successfully reoriented their culture to restore a central role in their local communities. One outstanding example was the Yinnar Football and Netball Club. Yinnar District is located in the Latrobe Valley, east of Melbourne. The District has a population of 650 – from which the Football and Netball Club has a membership of 500. Operating from the Yinnar Recreation Reserve, the club fields 15 netball teams and seven football teams, as well as running junior Auskick and Nettaball programmes. Yinnar's senior team won the 2004 Mid Gippsland Football League grand final.[40]

But it would be a mistake to take this impressive example as an indicator of unchanging Australian sports culture, or of inherent social 'glue'. While the club has been operating for 115 years, its viability was under threat in the early 1990s – and many clubs in similar circumstances failed to survive. Decisions made by the

Committee, in particular to change the Club's culture and to welcome family and female participation, were critical in seeing off those threats.

The club's problems in the early 1990s came from both external and internal sources. The general decline of interest in football was exacerbated in the Latrobe Valley by the restructuring of the area's biggest industry, electricity generation. The State Electricity Commission (SEC), which had previously provided considerable assistance to local sporting clubs, was dismantled and privatized. But the club also had its own internal problems. These were particularly associated with a long-time culture of heavy drinking. As Club President Russell Cheffers noted, 'When I first got involved about 18 years ago, to put it crudely, the more grog you could serve the more money you made.'[41] In the early 1990s, the club got into strife with the local community over some well-publicized episodes of drinking at juniors events, and these worsened problems it was already having in attracting sponsorship.

The Club took three broad initiatives. The first was to encourage more netball teams:

> We place a lot of emphasis on our netballers, because most footballers have partners, wives or girlfriends. To have them involved is very important. You have got to have the right atmosphere again to encourage the ladies to be involved ... We certainly support the netballers in every shape or form. The netball courts have been resurfaced, we have just put in change rooms for netballers, and we have just put in place things like new balls and bibs and whatnot.

The second was the redevelopment of the club facilities and social rooms.

> We have just put a $100,000 extension into our social rooms, which has been funded from grants but more particularly paid for by volunteer labour, both trade and non-trade labour that has come from within the Yinnar community.

The redevelopment doubled the size of the club rooms, and included better facilities for netballers, for women umpires, and for the disabled. The 'excellent' facilities are now shared with the local cricket and tennis clubs.

The third initiative, related to the first two, was other encouragement of families, women and children. This included a smoke-free environment in the club rooms, and a 'responsible alcohol' policy:

> making sure that we do not serve people who have had too much to drink – there is a fine line near; it is difficult – and certainly not allowing people to go anywhere near a car if they have had anywhere near the level in that context. All those factors have had a positive impact in that we attract families. They buy a different form of drink across the bar but because there are more of them [club memberships have grown by 30% in the past 5–10 years] we have found that our bar sales have increased.

These successes of the Yinnar Football and Netball Club, and country football more generally, show the importance of the interaction between the decisions sports make and how people and communities respond. But, as we will see in later examples through the collection, responses have not always been as positive as in Yinnar. One initiative that misread the market response was recent efforts to introduce gambling products based on the very strong social phenomenon of footy tipping in southern Australia.

Each week in the footy season across southern Australia, a remarkable number of people participate in AFL footy tipping competitions. Participants attempt to better work or club colleagues by picking the winners of the eight matches each winter weekend. Even the most knowledgeable about Australian rules rarely score better than 70% right over a season.[42] The most popular tipping website claims it hosts 20,000 competitions, attracting almost 250,000 tipsters.[43]

And the competition can be intense. In a small town in northern Victoria, the local butcher was the town's dominant tipster, finishing each season streets ahead of his nearest competitor. But one year the butcher faced a tense fight, being pushed to the edge by an 11-year-old girl who picked teams based on their colours.[44]

Writer Sean Dooley reminisces about a road trip he took with his ageing father through Western Victoria, and about the many stops they made for a cleansing ale. If there was a choice of pubs in the town, his Dad chose on one criterion alone – which pub had the biggest footy tipping competition. The reasoning was simple; the locals wouldn't come in every week to submit their tips in a pub that served dud beer. His theory proved unerringly on the money: the longer the list of names on the footy tipping board, the fresher the beer tasted.[45]

The widespread interest in footy tipping tempted various gambling venues, and the Victorian State Government, to see a potential revenue source from commercial tipping contests. But there are limits to how far footy tipping fever goes, and here again fans' reaction was critical – there was very little response. While interest is intense, it is a social interest. Dooley recalled a friend's 101-year-old Great Aunt Mary, a footy-tipping fiend whose mood improves each March as she revs up for another season. Like most tipsters, Mary has no interest in the various betting possibilities. 'What matters to this 101-year-old is that she gets more correct tips each week than that upstart 84-year-old Bombers fan in room 17.'[46]

This paper has stressed the diversity of sports interest in Australia, from the diehard fan to the attendance at country football to check out the talent to Great Aunt Mary. The impressive attendance figures, and other involvement, are influenced by many factors – the sporting culture, certainly, but also an event-going attitude, the facilities and star attractions, be they home town teams or international champions. Another important factor has been the actions that sports clubs and administrators themselves have taken in both retaining old, and attracting new, fans. And, crucially, how people respond to those offerings. The next paper follows similarly diverse factors in discussing patterns of sports participation in Australia.

Notes

1. Larwood with Perkins, *The Larwood Story*, 210–11.
2. Ibid., 197–8.
3. Deakin's speech, 'The Australasian Game' reported in *The Argus*, August 29, 1908, 17.
4. Oxley, 'Ockerism, the Cultural Rabbit', 193–5, and see discussion in Paper 3 above.
5. Arts Victoria, *The Arts Industry in Victoria*, 114. This draws on data from Australian Bureau of Statistics (ABS, www.abs.gov.au), *Leisure Participation Victoria, year ended October 1996* (4176.2).
6. The female percentages amongst those who attended the four events were: tennis 54%, racing 46%, AFL 33%, Grand Prix 30% – see ABS, Table 1.
7. ABS, *Children's Participation April 2003* (4901.0), 6, 21, 17.
8. Ibid., 21.
9. Arts Victoria, *The Arts Industry in Victoria*, 115.
10. Olds, *Children and Sport*, 96–7.
11. ABS, *Leisure Participation Victoria,* Table 5.
12. Frequent fans form one third of the 35% of Americans who attend sports – and about a quarter of the 48% of Australians attending. This means frequent fans are about 12% of the

population in each country. The US Census report (www.census.gov), *Statistical Abstract of the United States 2006*, Table 1237 asked for those who attended particular sports monthly or more frequently. ABS, *Participation in Sport and Physical Activities* (4177.0) asks for those who attended six or more times in one year. As sports are seasonal, these measures give similar results. The Gallup poll in Australia, asking questions about church attendance, classified anyone attending once or more a month as 'regular' – see discussion in Paper 12 below.

13. Haigh, *Game for Anything*, 82.
14. The TV audiences for the AFL Grand Finals 2000–06 were taken from newspaper reports of ratings in the week following each Grand Final (e.g. for the 2007 Grand Final, *The Age*, October 1, 2007, 2).
15. Victorian Parliament, *Inquiry Into Country Football*, 41.
16. Ibid., 33.
17. Ibid., 32.
18. Stewart, 'Channelling Passion', 117. In 2006, Octagon research conducted a similar analysis for the US Tennis Association Office of Diversity, termed 'Passion Drivers for Tennis'. The USTA kindly provided the author with a copy of this presentation.
19. ABS, *Sports Attendance 2006* (4174.0). The following discussion draws especially on Tables 5, 8, 10, 11.
20. Ibid., Table 8.
21. Ibid., Table 7.
22. Ibid., Table 6.
23. Ibid., Table 11. Timing may have affected cricket's declining numbers. The surveys asked people whether they had attended a particular sport in the previous 12 months. In 1995, the previous 12 months included the 1994–95 Ashes test series between Australia and England. The 2002 and 2006 surveys were each 12 months early for subsequent Ashes series.
24. See Sweeney Research website www.sweeneyresearch.com.au. The following discussion draws largely on the Summer 2007 report, released May 10. 2007.
25. In recent years, the AFL overall interest figures have grown from 45 to 55, while soccer (30 to 50) and Rugby Union (20 to 40) have seen even stronger growth. Interest in golf declined from 50 to 30.
26. Cashman, *Australian Cricket Crowds*, respectively 3, 4 and 319. Cashman suggests that the $1/2$ person in 1914 was due to officials counting each child as half an adult.
27. Gallup poll summary 1953, ABS, *Sporting Attendance* (4174.0) publications in 1995, 2002 and 2006, and ABS, *General Social Survey: Leisure Activities away from Home 1975* (4104.0). The author is grateful to Kathryn McGrouther of the ABS General Social Survey section for locating this report for this study. The 1975 ABS survey asked a slightly different question from the other surveys, asking respondents to nominate up to seven activities in which they spent most of their leisure time away from home. The leisure activities were coded into 72 categories: if someone attended only one or two games in a year they probably would *not* include that activity on their top seven list. The 1995 ABS survey gave the percentage of those attending each sport who attended more than five times. The 1975 figures were then adjusted by this percentage, to give an estimate of the total number of people attending, including infrequent attendees. The resulting estimates were checked against a Gallup Poll summary Nov. 1966–Feb. 1967 which gave results for various numbers of attendances at the races across the year.
28. See the more detailed discussion of recent cricket crowds in Paper 13 below.
29. Blackman and Chapman, 'The Value of Don Bradman'. Blackman and Chapman give a lower estimate of the impact of Bradman, due to the more sophisticated way they account for other variables. Bradman's crowd-drawing power was even greater in Shield cricket – in matches at the SCG and MCG, his batting almost doubled the size of the crowd. See Cashman, *Australian Cricket Crowds*, 309.
30. Results from econometric analysis by Blackman and Chapman, 'The Value of Don Bradman'.
31. Vamplew, ed., *Australian Historical Statistics*, 41, 383. The VFL competition included one club, Geelong, from outside Melbourne, so the figure as a percentage of Melbourne's population is distorted slightly upwards for the one weekend in two that Geelong played at home. On the other hand however, Melbourne also hosted two other city-wide Australian rules competitions: the VFA and the amateur VAFA. While crowds were much smaller for these games, they would still have increased overall attendance numbers.

32. Hay, 'Sports Mad Nations'.
33. Walker and Doyle, *Sports Jokes*, 413.
34. Victorian Parliament, *Inquiry Into Country Football*. The proud tradition was cited on 151, the changes in club numbers 76, and the population changes in north west Victoria cited by e.g. Hindmarsh Shire Council, 82.
35. Ibid., 58, 66–7, 44–5.
36. Ibid., 41. For an extended analysis of the male-dominated culture in rural towns in the early 1990s, see Dempsey, *A Man's Town*, 54–5 cited by the Victorian Parliament, 34.
37. Victorian Parliament, *Inquiry Into Country Football*, 41.
38. Ibid., 34, 97.
39. Ibid., 60.
40. Details about the Yinnar Football and Netball Club are drawn from ibid., especially 32, 42 and 191, from the club's submission to the Inquiry, from the transcripts of the Inquiry's interview with Club President Russell Cheffers in its *Public Hearings* in Leongatha, 7 April 2004, and from the Australian Drug Foundation's 'Good Sports' website, at http://www.goodsports.com.au/about/benefits/case_studies/yfnc.html.
41. This and the following quotes from Mr Cheffers are drawn from Mr Cheffers' testimony in the *Victorian Parliament, Inquiry into Country Football, Public Hearings* transcript, 2–5.
42. Leon Gettler, 'Is Footy Tipping Over the Edge?' *The Age*, March 31, 2007, Business, 10.
43. see www.footytipping.com.au.
44. Sean Dooley, 'It's That Time Again ...'. *The Age*, March 29, 2007, 21.
45. Ibid.
46. Ibid.

References

Arts Victoria. *The Arts Industry in Victoria: A Statistical Overview.* Victorian Government. 2000.
Blackman, Julian, and Bruce Chapman. 'The Value of Don Bradman: Additional Revenue in Australian Ashes Tests'. *Economic Papers* 23 (December 2004): 369–85.
Cashman, Richard. *Australian Cricket Crowds: The Attendance Cycle Daily Figures 1877–1984.* Sydney: University of NSW. Bicentennial History Project, Statistical Monograph No. 5, 1984.
Dempsey, K. *A Man's Town: Inequality Between Men and Women in Rural Australia.* Melbourne: Oxford University Press, 1992.
Gallup Poll Summaries, every 2–3 months, 1941–1971, mimeo sheets held by State Library of Victoria SLTF 301. 154 AU7GAL.
Haigh, Gideon. *Game for Anything: Writings on Cricket.* Melbourne: Black, 2004.
Hay, Roy. 'Sports Mad Nations: Some Research Already Done'. *Australian Society for Sports History Bulletin* 33 (February 2001): 18–24.
Larwood, Harold, with K. Perkins. *The Larwood Story.* 2nd ed. Sydney: Bonpara, 1982.
Olds, T.S, Dollman, Ridley, Boshoff, Hartshorn, and Kennaugh. *Children and Sport.* Report for the Australian Sports Commission, University of South Australia, September, 2004. www.ausport.gov.au/research/youthandsport04.asp p109-110.
Oxley, Harry. 'Ockerism, the Cultural Rabbit'. In *Australian Popular Culture,* ed. Peter Spearitt and David Walker, 190–209. Sydney: Allen & Unwin, 1979.
Stewart, Bob. 'Channelling Passion or Manufacturing Identity'. In *Fanfare: Spectator Culture and Australian Rules Football,* ed. Matthew Nicholson, 109–24. Balaclava, Vic: Australian Society for Sports History, 2005.
Vamplew, Wray, ed. *Australian Historical Statistics.* Broadway, NSW: Fairfax, Syme & Weldon Associates, 1987.
Victorian Parliament Rural and Regional Services and Development Committee. *Inquiry Into Country Football Final Report* No. 95. Session 2003–04.
Walker, Max, and Brian Doyle. *Sports Jokes.* Carlton, Vic.: Allen and Unwin, 1997.

Lifeblood of the community

> When the younger of my two brothers was 15 years old, he was (despite his disinterest in the game and his low level of the particular skills needed) pressured into playing football for the local team in the small rural community of which we were a part. The team was short of players and if he didn't participate chances were that the team would fold and the cohesion that existed among the community of scattered farms in the area would disappear. And so he played his part, not just in keeping the football team going but also in sustaining the wellbeing of the community as a whole.[1]

Many explanations for Australian sporting success focus on the opportunities for active involvement in sports in this country. Paper 2, in discussing the reasons for women athletes' success at the Olympics, agreed that wider access to some sports played a big part. But, as the reluctant 15-year-old footy player illustrates, there is considerably more to participation in sports than one image of enthusiastic youngsters all chasing Olympic dreams.

Furthering this collection's discussion of the interplay between underlying realties and the creation of images, this paper assesses the realities of active participation in sports. As with sporting attendances noted in the previous paper, motivations can differ, and be complex. And to an even greater extent than for sports crowds, participation levels have varied considerably over time. Those differences, and the reasons for them, provide important background to the changing images of sports in this country.

The paper starts by looking at current patterns of sports participation, and then at how these changed over the twentieth century, especially since the Second World War. The following section looks at recent changes in children's participation rates.

Active participation

Ten million Australians aged over 18, two thirds of the population, take part in sport and physical activities – informal, organized or both. If the focus is narrowed to just those involved in organized sport, the figure is four million, over one quarter of the population.[2]

In the total numbers, the most popular activity is walking for exercise, undertaken by four million Australians each year. Aerobics attracts two million, swimming and cycling more than one million, while running, golf, and bush walking also have many adherents.[3]

This paper concentrates mainly on participation in organized sports, for three reasons. First, organized (and especially team) sport is more commonly referred to in assessing sports culture than is walking for fitness. Secondly, in tracing patterns over time, we have much better data for organized sport than for informal activities. And thirdly, the ways sport was organized (and the ways people reacted to that organization) are an important part of the story of sports in Australia.

Differences in motivation for active sports participation occurred in the city as well as the country. Nearly all the adolescents surveyed in the Melbourne suburbs of Doncaster and Templestowe in 1967 belonged to at least one sporting or social club. When asked the primary reason they joined that club, almost half gave the particular activity of the club, while a quarter wanted to meet new friends, mix with people, or just get a change from home. Amongst swimmers, the most popular organized sport, a small group were quite happy to give up swimming if facilities were available for other sports they found more attractive – ten pin bowling, squash or ice skating.[4]

A dozen years earlier, 13 to 18 year olds in Sydney reported tennis as their most popular organized sport (as it was for adults as well in the 1950s). The sport was popular across all social groups, not just for the sport itself but also for a socially sanctioned setting 'particularly useful for meeting adolescents of the opposite sex'.[5]

Whatever the motivation – and individuals may well be swayed by more than one – the patterns of involvement across Australia in particular organized sports are impressive.[6]

The most popular organised sport in Australia in 2006 was aerobics (with 5% of those aged over 18 participating), followed by golf (3%) and then netball, tennis and soccer (all 3%). The top four maintained their rankings since earlier counts in 1997 and 2002, although in those years lawn bowls, not soccer, had been the fifth most popular.[7]

Some sports had seen quite marked changes since 1997. Lawn bowls and tennis, while still popular, had lost numbers, while declines were even more marked for organized swimming and ten pin bowling. Yoga and touch football joined soccer in becoming more popular.

The strength of aerobics, and the growth of yoga, indicate a trend noted in the discussion of country football in the previous paper – away from more traditional organized sports and towards more individual sports (albeit still organized through health clubs). However, there is also an impact from how the sports themselves responded to that trend. The three sports of club tennis, swimming and lawn bowls, all of which had been very popular in earlier years, declined markedly in the 1997–2006 period. In contrast, sports like soccer, cricket and Australian rules adopted new

Table 1.   Participation in organised sports, Australian adults, 2006.

Sport	Participants ,000	Per cent
Aerobics / fitness	731	4.6%
Golf	405	2.5%
Netball	348	2.2%
Tennis	316	2.0%
Soccer (outdoor)	287	1.8%
Basketball	237	1.5%
Lawn bowls	235	1.5%
Cricket (outdoor)	219	1.4%
Australian rules football	205	1.3%
Touch football	202	1.3%

strategies to develop their sports, and these efforts clearly bore fruit with increasing participation rates between 1997 and 2006.

There were also differences across age groups in the different sports. Sports requiring more physical exertion, such as Australian rules and basketball, are most popular with people in their 20s, and attract very few participants beyond age 40. Cricket and netball participation rates also decline steadily with age, while aerobics and tennis have a slower rate of decline across age groups, still attracting many people in their 40s and above. The two sports most popular with older people are golf (with increasing rates until the 50s age group) and lawn bowls (which has very few participants younger than 50).

There are some other differences across society. Men, and especially younger men, have a higher involvement in organized sport than do women. Organized sport is also stronger in country areas than in the big cities, but total involvement in physical exercise is actually slightly stronger in the cities. This probably reflects both a wider range of options for physical activity in the cities, and sporting clubs' larger role in social life outside the big cities.

Participation also varies with income and social status. In 1990, usage of local swimming pools was fairly evenly spread across all income groups. In contrast, higher income people were much more likely to make use of tennis courts and golf courses than were people on lower incomes. A couple of factors are probably at work here. The first, especially for golf, is the ability to afford the cost of golf equipment and, for organized sport, club membership. The second, which applies to tennis as well as golf, is the social cachet of the sport.[8]

Overall Australian sports participation rates, as noted in Paper 2, are similar to those in the United States, and somewhat behind those in New Zealand. But the discussion thus far indicates that considerable diversity underlies the overall rates. The patterns are influenced by factors such as people's sports motivation, their dedication to particular sports, their age and income levels, the availability of facilities, and the social environment surrounding particular sports and clubs. And, as the next section documents, there have been marked changes over time.

Changing patterns in participation

The image of the sports-mad Australian suggests a relatively consistent absorption in sports. This was challenged for sports attendances in Paper 5 – and changes over time are even more marked in sports participation. The patterns can be gleaned from Australian Bureau of Statistics data after 1975, public opinion polling data from the end of the Second World War, and a number of other sources in earlier years.

Sports participation rates were not high before the Second World War. Immediately after that war, a Gallup Poll in early 1948 asked, 'How far can you swim?' and about half of the men, but only one in six of the women, could swim more than 50 yards. Half the women had never learnt to swim at all.[9] Another 1948 poll asked people what they did with their weekend leisure time. One third of the population, including nearly all women in lower income groups, responded 'what leisure time?' Conversely, sports participation was strongest among younger men, especially those from better-off backgrounds. 'Sport is played by almost two of every five well-to-do and better-off men, compared with only one out of every five wage-earners'.[10]

Even lower participation occurred in the early days of cricket. In South Australia around 1900, local cricket teams struggled to survive if their town population was less than 1,000. Finding 15 cricket players from the some 385 men aged over 15 suggests a low participation rate of only 4% of adult men and only 8% of the active sporting age group 15–34.[11] And cricket teams were also drawn heavily from the higher income groups, as historian Clive Forster noted:

> Many teams, as today, depended for viability on itinerant professionals – bankers, teachers, lawyers, doctors and clergymen – and reports of speeches at farewell dinners to prominent local sportsmen often reflected fears that the departure of even one active player could cause a club to lose viability.[12]

Class distinctions were still present in cricket in the 1980s. When pace bowler Merv Hughes joined the Victorian team, only two in the squad were from the western (and more working-class) suburbs. Years later, Hughes reminisced on the 'huge rift between east and west': 'basically the western suburbs people are down to earth, honest and hard-working, the eastern suburban people are stuck up snobs who live off their mum and dad's money'. Realizing he was sharing these memories with the still largely upper-crust Melbourne Cricket Club dining room, Hughes added, 'This is probably not the right place to say that stuff.'[13]

As discussed in Paper 11, tennis was also very much an upper-class preserve before the First World War. In contrast, the social background of Australian rules players in the Riverina changed. A majority in the 1890s came from business, farming and white collar backgrounds, but by just before the First World War, players' backgrounds mirrored the social spectrum, with large percentages of farmhands and other manual labourers. And local football legend 'Poddy' Slade attested that 'almost the whole town went to the football'.[14]

Participation rates, if still skewed heavily to the upper social groups, climbed in the interwar years. In 1934, *Australian Women's Weekly* writer Ruth Preddey claimed one million Australian women were members of sporting associations. In a total population of seven million, with some 2.5 million women over 18, this number certainly looks impressive. The source of this statistic is unclear – and in any case it is somewhat misleading, as it adds up membership numbers, not individual people. Other accounts note many better-off women (then the overwhelming readership for the *Weekly*) played several sports in both summer and winter. If a woman was a member of both a tennis club and a swimming club, she would contribute two memberships to Preddey's total. Adjusting for this might make the participation rate say 20%.[15] More anecdotal evidence attests to a growth in participation in the 1930s – above all in tennis. Other sports waited until after the Second World War for their most dramatic growth. This was true of swimming, and also lawn bowls, which is discussed in Paper 12.

But there were still constraints on participation. As late as 1954, a survey in the outer northern (and more working-class) suburbs of Adelaide found that less than 10% of youths in the 15–25 age group attended youth or sports clubs, 'mainly because the range and standard of attracting facilities were not available'. A key reason for this was that many local governments, in South Australia at least, were reluctant prior to 1950 to provide sports facilities. Following pressure from the Fitness Council, the SA Local Government Act was amended to give councils specific powers to provide such facilities.[16]

While earlier sources were partial, more reliable information on sports participation started with public opinion polls after the Second World War – and indicated very

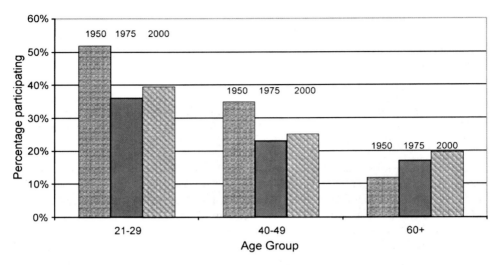

Figure 1.   Percentages by age participating in organised sport 1950-2000.

impressive sports participation rates. Combining such data with later polls and Australian Bureau of Statistics reports, Figure 1 shows total participation in organized sport
since 1950.

Participation in organized sports was strongest in 1950, when about one third of
adults took part. This fell to just over one quarter by 1975, and since then has recovered
slightly, to around 28%. But, as the Figure shows, these combined figures mask some
divergent trends between those aged in their 20s, their 40s, and 60+.[17] In particular,
while younger people are always more active in sports than their elders, 20 somethings
are less likely to be involved in sport now than they were in 1950. In contrast, participation in the 60+ age group has close to doubled.

There have also been differences between male and female involvement. The
decline in participation between 1950 and 1975 occurred amongst both men and
women. In the last 25 years however, male participation has been largely stable –
while women's involvement has grown back to the levels of the 1950s.[18] The detailed
figures are:

The most favoured sports have also changed. Tennis has slumped from remarkable
highs in the 1950s, when 15% played. Swimming and squash grew very rapidly in the
post-war years, encouraged by the growth of facilities such as War Memorial swimming pools and squash centres. However, numbers have fallen considerably since
1980. Golf and lawn bowls also saw strong growth in numbers from 1950 to the
1980s, due not least to popularity amongst older age groups.[19] Most recently, boosting

Table 2.   Participation rates in organised sports 1950–2000, men and women.

	All	Men	Women
1950	32%	38%	26%
1975	26%	31%	19%
2000	28%	30%	26%

the numbers of women participating, the sports of aerobics, netball and yoga have gained ground.[20]

This overall slight improvement in organized sport numbers since 1975 may give too optimistic a picture. Declining numbers of people have registered with affiliated organizations of the Confederation of Australian Sport (CAS). In 1980, the 107-member organizations of CAS represented six million sports people – equivalent to 40% of Australians. By 1999, the 120 organizations affiliated to CAS had 4.5 million members, a quarter of the population.[21]

In contrast, non-organized physical recreation has boomed since 1975. Two surveys in the 1970s found less than 40% of the population interested in exercise to keep fit,[22] and deducting the 26% involved in organized sport leaves just over 10% solely in non-organized exercise. By the end of the 1980s total involvement had grown to half, and by 2006 it has reached two-thirds of the population: 28% in organized sport and over one-third in solely non-organized pursuits.[23]

This picture is some distance away from an unchanging image of a 'sports mad' member of an organized team. Not only have the sports followed changed, but there have been divergent trends between older and younger people and, since 1975, between men and women. In addition, there has been strong growth in interest in physical exercise over the past 30 years, but, especially for men, little of this interest has translated into organized sports numbers.

Why have organized sports become less popular? Surveys in 1975[24] and 1997[25] found that 'no time' or 'too busy' was the most common reason given by people who either felt unable to participate in a sport they liked, or had recently stopped participating. Other, less-often-cited, reasons included the expense of sport, or, especially for women, 'no-one to look after the kids'. However, as indicated by the falling participation rates across age groups shown in the graph, there has always been movement away from sports as people grow older, careers become more demanding, and children need looking after.

The most frequent explanation of the longer term decline in organized sport was expressed in 2004 by Garry Squires, President of the Orbost Snowy Rovers Football Club:

> There are [now] other things for kids to do. Football used to be the only thing you would get in a town. When I and many of the other people were young, if you did not play football you did not do anything in the town. That is certainly not the case any more.[26]

An increasing general pace of life, together with the growth of alternative pursuits, is perhaps the most compelling reason for the longer term decline in organized sports. But while undoubtedly a factor, this explanation faces two major hurdles. Why have participation rates fallen especially for younger men, while growing for older people and, since 1975, for women? And why, in a period since 1975 of rapid growth in interest in physical exercise, have most organized sports not been able to increase their numbers?

Discussing trends in country football in Victoria, the previous paper noted the importance of the culture of football clubs, and the successes that some had in response to changes in that culture. This pattern of reactions to the existing culture seems to be repeated in participation in organized sports. Some of the overall decline in participation was due to an image of sports clubs being regimented and conservative.

The 2004 Victorian Parliamentary inquiry into country football noted clubs had used a range of strategies to maintain numbers. These included providing cars and other inducements to encouraging young people to return 'home' to play football (and netball), increased player payments, and encouraging older players not to retire but to remain active.[27]

As indicated in the declining CAS membership numbers, most sports do not seem to have responded effectively to the social changes, nor to the trends towards more informal sports. Similar patterns appear in the significant shifts in participation amongst school children, discussed in the next section.

Children's participation

The coach called little Jimmy to the sideline.

'Now listen Jimmy, you know the principles of good sportsmanship that Little League promotes. No shouting at the umpires, no abusing opponents, no displays of bad temper. You understand what I'm saying?'

'Yes sir, but it wasn't me sir ...'

'No matter. Would you please explain these to your mother?'[28]

Even with occasional embarrassment from over-enthusiastic parents cheering on the sidelines, sport has always been a popular pastime for Australian children. Since the late 1950s, boys have consistently nominated sport as their most favourite pastime, while girls have frequently seen sport as most favourite, and never less than third on the list. Sport's major challengers for children's attention have changed considerably: from 'going to the pictures' in 1957 and 1961 surveys, to 'watching TV' in 1994 to 'hi-tech entertainment' in 2002.[29]

In 2003, two thirds of boys aged 5–14 and just over half of girls in this age group played organized sport, either at school or in clubs. About one fifth of both boys and girls swim, with similar numbers for boys playing soccer and girls netball.[30]

Some differences in activity levels reflect where children live. Sport participation is strongest in rural areas, reflecting again the 'role organised sports play in the culture of small towns and rural areas, often being the impetus for bringing together families and communities'.[31] Better facilities in larger schools mean school sport is most popular in town, while in rural areas, children more typically use sporting club facilities.[32]

Other factors affecting participation include family income and whether other family members take part in sport.[33] The immediate peer group also has an influence. A recent University of South Australia study used 'cluster' analysis, as applied by marketing firms, to identify broad social types for children aged 10–15. The study found three clusters of boys: 'sporties', 'screenies' and 'autonomes' (the last group spending a lot of time in self-starting pursuits, either by themselves or with peers). Girls split into four clusters: 'sporties', 'screenies', 'players' (active but non-sport socializing) and 'inactive socialisers'.[34]

Such differing motivations suggest limitations to any campaign to encourage more physical activity based on a 'one size fits all' approach. Most comments about changes in activity levels bemoan the increasing time children spent in front of TV and computer screens. Contrary to these images, the study found a group of 'techno active' boys who have high physical activity levels as well as lots of screen time, and a group of 'socializing' girls who have the lowest physical activity ratings but also very low screen time. While a strategy of reducing TV time may help encourage some kids into more exercise, it is unlikely to be effective for either of these two groups.

Trends over the past 20 years suggest similar patterns to those amongst adults. A Sydney University Study found that levels of 'Moderate to Vigorous' physical activity increased somewhat between 1985 and 2004.[35] These increases occurred despite substantial declines in the incidence of walking and cycling to school, and a remarkable fall in unsupervised play in the neighbourhood. A 1999 study in Newcastle found that only 25% of children were 'allowed to play in the neighbourhood unsupervised, compared with 83% of children in the generation preceding them'.[36]

Again similar to adult trends, the overall pattern of physical activity contrasts with a strong drop in organized sport. In the 1980s, more than four out of five kids aged 9–15 participated in at least one organized sport, with 40% playing three or more sports. In 2000, 64% of kids in the same age group played at least one organized sport, with only 10% competing in three or more sports.[37]

Ian Kett, the Executive Director of VicFit, analysed the patterns:

> We know the trends lean very strongly towards unstructured, unorganized flexible time-efficient sorts of activities, too. So there are some issues there. I think it's moved away from where it used to be, where football, cricket, netball and maybe a couple of others such as tennis would have been the main staples of the physical activity diet. Now that is certainly not the case. We see kids moving on to skateboarding – which is very popular with the young kids and growing – soccer, and a whole range of things.[38]

Apart from the taste for unstructured activities, the Australian Sports Commission[39] reckons key factors pushing children away from organized sport include overly authoritarian attitudes from coaches, and too much emphasis on winning (particularly from parents yelling from the sidelines).

This paper has discussed the details of sports participation in Australia. Contrary to any image of an unchanging sports culture, it has emphasized how much things have in fact changed, and the need to consider both how sports are organized and the varied motivations of players. For participation in one sport, lawn bowls, these themes are investigated further in Paper 12.

But if, as both this and the previous paper have shown, there is considerable diversity behind the images, how did those images come about? Using these findings, together with the discussion in Papers 3 and 4 on the creation of national images, the next paper looks at how Australia's sporting image first started.

Notes

1. Townsend, Moore and Mahoney, 'Playing their Part'.
2. Australian Bureau of Statistics (ABS, www.abs.gov.au), *Participation in Sport and Physical Activities* 2006 (4177.0), Table 3. As noted in the discussion in the statistical appendix to the paper, these 2006 figures differ from those in 2002, which were about the same for total physical activity, but somewhat higher for organized sport.
3. Ibid., Table 9.
4. City of Doncaster and Templestowe, *Survey of Recreational Facilities*, esp. 54.
5. Connell *et al.*, *Growing up in an Australian City*, 61.
6. ABS, *Participation in Sport and Physical Activities* 2006 (4177.0), Table 9. The differences between capital cities and other areas were noted in the same publications, ABS 2002, 11; 1997, 6.

7. ABS, *Participation in Sport and Physical Activities* (4177.0), 2002, 20; 1997, 8.
8. Department of the Arts, Sport, the Environment, Tourism and Territories, *Recreation Participation Survey February 1991*, Table 17, 28. These results have also been documented in other studies – see the sources cited by McKay, 'Sport, Leisure and Social Inequality' in the statistical appendix below.
9. Gallup Poll summary, Feb.–March 1948. The various sources of statistical information on sports participation are discussed in the statistical appendix at the end of these notes.
10. Gallup Poll summary, May–June 1948.
11. Forster, 'Sports, Society and Space', with the participation figures compared with the age structure for the period from Vamplew, ed., *Australian Historical Statistics*, 40 .
12. Forster, 'Sports, Society and Space', 42.
13. Merv Hughes, quoted in *The Age*, December 28, 2007, Sporting Life, 2.
14. Gillett, 'Where the Big Men Fly', with 'Poddy' Slade quoted, 171.
15. Preddey articles on women's sport, *Australian Women's Weekly* on February 17, 1934, and April 1934. The articles were cited by Stell, *Half the Race*, 74 (see especially the footnote on p.274), and Stell noted the multiple membership of clubs.
16. Simpson, *National Fitness Council of South Australia*, 10–13 (the survey), and 2–5 (the need for changes to the Local Government Act).
17. The detailed figures are discussed in the Appendix at the end of this paper. As argued there, despite some statistical quirks, the broad picture shown appears to be an accurate one.
18. The figures for 2000 are averaged from the ABS surveys in 1997, 2002 and 2006. See the statistical appendix for more discussion of these figures.
19. In one survey, golf was the most popular sport in Australia in the 1980s, with club and regular social players together totalling 11% of the over 20 age group. See McKay, 'Sport, Leisure and Social Inequality'.
20. Statistics from a range of sources, discussed in the Statistical Appendix.
21. Sport 2000 Task Force, *Shaping Up*, 86.
22. Bloomfield, *Australia's Sporting Success*, 49; Stewart, 'Leisure: The Changing Patterns', 178.
23. Stewart, 'Leisure: The Changing Patterns', 178 (1987 result); ABS, *Participation 2006*, Table 3.
24. ABS, *General Social Survey: Leisure Activites away from Home* 1975 (4104.0), 33, Table 22. The author is grateful to Kathryn McGrouther of the ABS General Social Survey section for locating this report for this study.
25. ABS, *Participation 1997*, 20, Table 10.
26. Victorian Parliament, *Inquiry Into Country Football*, 94.
27. Ibid., 69.
28. Walker and Doyle, *Sports Jokes*, 336.
29. Olds, *Children and Sport*, 46.
30. ABS, *Children's Participation April 2003* (4901.0).
31. Booth et al., *NSW Schools Physical Activity and Nutrition Survey 2004*, 49.
32. Olds, *Children and Sport*, 49.
33. Ibid., 21, 96–7.
34. Ibid., 58–67.
35. Booth, *NSW Schools Physical Activity and Nutrition Survey 2004*, 46.
36. Olds, *Children and Sport*, 32–7.
37. Ibid., 23–4, citing a 1985 Australian Health and Fitness Survey, and a 2000 ABS survey. However the most recent ABS survey, in 2003, showed small increases in organized sport: ABS, *Children's Participation 2003*, 22.
38. Evidence to Victorian Parliament, *Inquiry Into Country Football*, 91. This is supported by evidence cited by Olds, *Children and Sport*, 52 and 96, suggesting a strong interest in individual sports such as surfing.
39. http://ausport.gov.au/junior/parents/factsheets_reasons.asp (no date).

References

Bloomfield, John. *Australia's Sporting Success: The Inside Story.* Sydney: UNSW Press, 2003.

Booth, Michael et al. *NSW Schools Physical Activity and Nutrition Survey (SPANS) 2004: Full Report.* North Sydney: NSW Department of Health, 2006.

City of Doncaster and Templestowe. *Survey of Recreational Facilities, Interests of Youth, and Use of Leisure Time by Youth of this City,* co-authored with Institute of Social Welfare and the Chief Secretary's Department, Melbourne, 1967.

Connell, W.F., E.P. Francis, E.E. Skilbeck, and a group of Sydney University Students. *Growing up in an Australian City: A Study of Adolescents in Sydney.* Melbourne: Australian Council for Educational Research, 1957.

Department of the Arts, Sport, the Environment, Tourism and Territories. *Recreation Participation Survey February 1991.* Canberra, 1992.

Forster, Clive. 'Sports, Society and Space: The Changing Geography of Country Cricket in South Australia'. *Sporting Traditions* 2, no. 2 (May 1986): 23–47.

Gillett, Rodney. 'Where the Big Men Fly: An Early History of Australian Football in the Riverina'. *Sporting Traditions* 4, no. 2 (May 1988): 162–75.

McKay, Jim. 'The Democratization of Australian Sport: Some Preliminary Observations of a National Survey'. *International Review of Sport Sociology* 18, no. 3 (1983): 91–111.

McKay, Jim. 'Sport, Leisure and Social Inequality in Australia'. In *Sport and Leisure: Trends in Australian National Culture,* ed. David Rowe and Geoff Lawrence, 125–60. Sydney: Harcourt Brace Jovanovich, 1990.

Olds, T.S, Dollman, Ridley, Boshoff, Hartshorne, and Kennaugh. *Children and Sport.* Report for the Australian Sports Commission, University of South Australia, September, 2004. www.ausport.gov.au/research/youthandsport04.asp p109-110.

Simpson, A.E. *The National Fitness Council of South Australia: A History 1939–1976.* Adelaide: Department of Recreation and Sport, 1986.

Sports 2000 Task Force. Shaping Up. *A Review of Commonwealth Involvement in Sport and Recreation in Australia.* Report for the Australian Sports Commission, Canberra, November 1999.

Stell, Marion. *Half the Race: a History of Australian Women in Sport.* North Ryde, NSW: Collins/Angus and Robertson, 1990.

Stewart, Bob. 'Leisure: The Changing Patterns of Sport and Exercise'. In *Sports and Leisure: Trends in Australian National Culture,* ed. David Rowe and Geoff Lawrence, 174–88. Sydney: Harcourt Brace Jovanovich, 1990.

Townsend, M., J. Moore, and M. Mahoney. 'Playing their Part: The Role of Physical Activity and Sport in Sustaining the Health and Well Being of Small Rural Communities'. *Rural and Remote Health* 2 (2002). http://rrh.deakin.edu.au.

Vamplew, Wray, ed. *Australian Historical Statistics.* Broadway, NSW: Fairfax, Syme & Weldon Associates, 1987.

Victorian Parliament Rural and Regional Services and Development Committee. *Inquiry Into Country Football Final Report* No. 95. Session 2003–04.

Walker, Max, and Brian Doyle. *Sports Jokes.* Carlton, Vic.: Allen and Unwin, 1997.

Watkins, G.G., P. Prosgrove, and R. Becker. *Recreation in Australia: An Inquiry into Present Patterns of Participation in Recreation, 3.1 Kew.* Report for the Federal Department of Environment, Housing and Community Development, and the Department of Youth, Sport and Recreation of Victoria, 1976.

Appendix: Note on the statistics used in this paper

Despite the differing bases for some statistics, the above broad picture can be treated with a high level of confidence. This Appendix discusses some of the issues involved, and the basis for this confidence. It acknowledges that this paper uses statistics from a variety of sources, compiled on different bases, and that some care is needed in comparing these figures.

A good starting point for the discussion is differences in the Australian Bureau of Statistics' comprehensive surveys of Australians' participation in sports in 1996–97, 2001–02 and 2005–06, published in *Participation in Sport and Physical Activities, Australia* (catalogue number 4177.0).

For example, between the 2002 and 2006 surveys some divergent trends appear. Overall activity is up strongly, especially amongst women, while participation in organized sport is down significantly, especially for men.

Indeed, the 2005–06 publication is cautious about such comparisons. It notes:

Changes in methodology mean that it is not possible to compare the overall participation rates from the 2005–6 Multi-Purpose Household Survey (MPHS) and the 2002 General Social Survey (GSS) as there were changes to the question wording and the actual collection method, both of which may have impacted on the results ...

It is not possible to determine the extent to which the differences between the 2005–06 MPHS and the 2002 GSS methodologies have contributed to any difference in results. (Explanatory Notes, paras 28 and 31)

Similar caution is advisable for earlier data, which is available from a number of sources. The key sources of statistic used above, checked where possible against other material, were:

- Gallup Polls in 1948 (participation in individual sports) and 1951 (overall participation rates).
- Australian Bureau of Statistics (1975) *General Social Survey: Leisure Activities away from Home* catalogue no 4104.0, May (this survey was analysed in detail in 1983 by McKay 'democratization of Australian sport')

In comparing the results for 1951, 1975, and the averages from 1996 to 2006, a couple of difficulties presented themselves:

- The surveys grouped respondents in different age groups. Figure 1 uses standard age groups, with interpolated results (e.g. if a survey used the age groups 35–44 and 45–54, the figures for the 40–49 age group used in the graph were broadly averaged from these two).
- The surveys had differences in the sports, and frequency of activity, they asked people about. The 1975 survey did not include swimming as an organized sport – it was listed under 'water activities' instead. Summarizing the coverage, and differences, between the key surveys gives:

Table 3. Overall sport and recreation activity, percentages of population.

	Male	Female	Overall
2002	65.0	59.9	62.4
2006	66.0	65.7	65.9
Percentages involved in organized sport			
2002	34.3	28.5	31.4
2006	29.0	26.0	27.5

Table 4.   Differing coverage of surveys 1951–2000.

	Date of survey/poll		
	1951	1975	1996–2006
Regular v occasional	Regular	Mainly regular	Both
Organised v organized and recreational	Mainly org	Both	Org
Swimming included?	Yes	No	Yes
Aerobics included?	No	No	Yes

In 1951, the Gallup Poll asked people what sport or sports they 'regularly' participated in. The 1975 ABS survey asked people to nominate up to seven social activities, including sport, in which they spent most of their leisure time away from home in the past year. The leisure activities were coded into 72 categories: irregular participation in a particular sport would probably not make it onto a respondent's top seven list. Indeed, the survey also thought to ask (p.27, Table 16) whether that activity was in the past week (77%), or the past month (15%), leaving only 8% participating less than monthly. Thus, 92% of those reporting participation did so on at least a monthly basis – which seems a reasonable match for 'regular'.

Because the 1975 question included some participating less than monthly, this could have added some 8% to the 'regular' figure needed for a proper comparison with 1951. The reduction in participation activity between the two dates was therefore even greater than shown in Figure 1. However, this would have been counteracted by the exclusion of swimming in 1975. The impact of this is unclear, as while swimming was a popular sport at this time, many if not most of the participants would also have participated in other sports, and hence still would be included in our total data.

While the 1975 General Social Survey and the later ABS surveys all asked about participation in the last year, the 1975 figure covered all sport, while the later surveys made a distinction between 'organized sport' and 'recreation'. In 1975, three quarters of those enjoying participation in sport were doing so as part of a club (p.32, Table 21). On this basis, the 1975 figure covers more activities than that the later 'organized sport' figures. However, changes in what was considered 'sport' (e.g. the exclusion of both aerobics and swimming in 1975) reduced the comparative coverage of the 1975 data. As the first definition gave a greater coverage for the 1975 data, while the second definitions gave a greater coverage for 1995, it is reasonable to treat the overall figures as broadly comparable.

These benchmark data were compared with other survey data available especially for the late 1970s and 1980s, which broadly confirms the patterns shown in the table for 1975 and 1996:

Table 5.   Detailed participation data by age group.

	1951	1975	1996	2002	2006
21–29	52%	36%	38%	44%	37%
30–39	40%	31%	31%	36%	29%
40–49	35%	23%	23%	28%	23%
50–59	20%	21%	21%	24%	21%
60+	12%	17%	17%	22%	19%
All	**32%**	**26%**	**26%**	**31%**	**28%**
Men	38%	31%	29%	33%	29%
Women	26%	19%	23%	28%	26%

- G.G. Watkins *et al.* (1976) *Recreation in Australia: 3.1 Kew*
- McKay, 'Sport, Leisure and Social Inequality' reported data from several other surveys, including:
  - 1984 A survey by pollsters REARK on leisure activities as part of a Recreational Fishing Survey
  - 1985–86 Surveys of Australian leisure activities by Morgan research
  - 1985–86 Recreational Participation Survey by McNair Anderson for the Department of Sport
- Stewart, 'Leisure: The Changing Patterns' refers to Morgan research on participation in specific sports in 1975 and again in 1985.
- Department of the Arts, Sport, the Environment, Tourism and Territories (1992) *Recreation Participation Survey February 1991.*
- Other surveys referenced in the text above.

Other discussions in the text use patterns of activity (e.g male versus female participation, or by income or occupational level) that are found in several or most of the surveys. The popularity of specific sports also draws on information in several surveys, checked against other data where possible.

Start of this 'sporting people'

One hundred years ago, the local hall in an Australian country town was packed for a visiting celebrity. As the introductory applause died down, the visitor heard alarming noises from beneath the stage, 'as though a miniature earthquake was in progress' ,and asked what was going on. The inquiry revealed dozens of people, desperate to hear the proceedings, were lying beneath the stage and repeatedly bumping their heads in the cramped space.

Local halls have long gathered attentive crowds for speeches from sports celebrities, so this story might well meet with a small smile and an accompanying sigh, 'well, Australians are sports-mad – what do you expect?' But this crowd gathered not to celebrate sporting success, but for a performance by an opera singer – Nellie Melba, in her 1909 'Sentimental Tour'.[1]

If such an anecdote were indeed about a sporting celebrity it would confirm the popular 'sports mad' image. But this story jars with the image – despite many stories similar to the above, there are few references to 'opera-mad' Australians.

The year before Nellie Melba gave fans sore heads, at a dinner on 28 August 1908 to celebrate 50 years of Australian football, Prime Minister Alfred Deakin proposed the principal toast, to 'The Australian Game':

> in this country, with its splendid endowment of sunny skies and green fields, its ample leisure, with all assistance to the pursuit of sport which we possess, we are bound to remain, as we always have been, a sporting people.[2]

Deakin's enthusiasm for sport was not always shared. Throughout this period, horse racing was the most popular spectator sport, much to the disdain of one correspondent of the sporting paper *Bells Life*:

> In New South Wales if you see a long and greasy haired ruffian, to whom soap and water are abominations, the filthiness of whose appearance is only equalled by the foulness of his tongue, you may take your oath he is in some way or another connected with a racing stable. They manage these things much better in Melbourne.[3]

So, from the start, enthusiasm for sport varied, and overlapped with other emotions, such as inter-colonial tensions and social distaste for ruffians. Nonetheless, whatever the factors involved, the foundations were laid between 1860 and 1900 for Deakin's 'sporting people' claim.

This account starts the story from 1860. While European settlement in Australia went back 70 years before that, and Aboriginal settlement tens of thousands of years, there are three reasons for choosing this date. The first is the sheer size of the population.

In 1861, despite having doubled with the gold rushes in the previous decade, Australia's non-Aboriginal population was only 1.2 million. This number trebled in the next 40 years, to 3.8 million in 1901, giving a size worthy of considering in discussions of the various components of national identity. Secondly, in Australia as around the world, there was precious little organized sport much before 1860. Games of cricket and horse races occurred in this country soon after 1800, and rough-and-ready games of football, and athletics races, also took place early on. However, most of these events were ad hoc and occasional affairs, often put together by local pubs. While they set some basis for later development they hardly created the regular tourneys or organization necessary for a title of a sporting nation. Thirdly, again as around the world, there was little 'national identity' in Australia in a popular sense prior to 1860. And if a fourth reason is required, the first Melbourne Cup was run in 1861, with Archer winning in front of a crowd of 4,000.

So how did the shambles that passed for sport before 1860 develop to the stage where 50 years later the Prime Minister could claim, 'we always have been a sporting people'? This paper traces this transition, and also looks at why it was sports rather than anything else that came to dominate the national image.

International start of organized sport

Previous papers have emphasized the importance of international comparisons. Around the world, with Australia leading some of the trends, the latter years of the nineteenth century were critical in the development and codification of mass sports. They were also critical in the adoption by various communities of what became their favourite sports. And there were a number of sports vying for favour. A memorable nineteenth-century newspaper editorial argued,

> About twenty-five years ago there was an effort made to introduce cricket, but it failed. We were not, at that time, worthy of the game, and in our ignorance and indolence we said 'Give us something easier.' ... But the time is now ripe for the revival of cricket ... Cricket will probably become as popular here as it is in England, and we shall be contented to play a game worth playing, even if it is English in its origins, without trying to establish a national game of our own.[4]

Such pomposity was not unusual in early editorials of the *Sydney Morning Herald* or the Melbourne *Argus,* but it might be tolerated in this case with a grudging acknowledgement given Australia's subsequent success in cricket. Might be, that is, if these words had appeared in an Australian newspaper. However, the editorial appeared on 30 August 1881 in the *New York Times,* and the 'national game' the writer was so unimpressed with was baseball.

So as late as 1881 even the American passion for baseball was not fully cemented. In addition, the codes and rules inside particular sports were also fluid. In 1874, a team from Montreal's McGill University visited Harvard, and played two games of football, the first resembling soccer, the second rugby. It was only after that date that Harvard started to develop the game that became gridiron.[5]

In the 1850s variations in rules meant that the game of rugby (from the English private school of that name) differed from the football games of Eton, Harrow and Winchester. By the 1890s these games had coalesced into two: rugby and soccer, with rugby then splitting on different fault lines to become rugby union and rugby league. Similarly, there were no standard rules for soccer in England in 1850, but by 1900 both standard rules and the national competitions such as the Football League and the FA Cup existed.[6]

The period from 1860 to 1900 thus saw the birth of organized sport. By 1900, rules had become codified, regular competitions had been established – even some international competitions – and major new facilities constructed to accommodate fans.

As sports developed, so communities and countries adopted particular talisman games. The iconic games became settled by 1900, with little change since. Soccer, for example, dominant in much of Europe and Latin America, would always struggle to make headway in countries and regions already committed to rugby, gridiron or Australian rules.[7]

But the associations that now seem obvious did not seem so while the traditions were becoming established. New Zealand, long seen as devoted to rugby union, had a flourishing Australian rules competition from the 1870s. In 1893 there were 44 clubs in the country, centred in the main cities. The game began to wane in the first decade of the twentieth century, due to successful rugby union tours of Britain. Nonetheless, New Zealand sent a competitive team to the 1908 Australian Football Carnival in Melbourne.[8]

Early diversity and competition between codes was not merely limited to football. In its pro-cricket editorial in 1881, the *New York Times* cast a jaundiced eye over the development of baseball, with particular disdain that professional players 'made the national game a national instrument of gambling, and gradually succeeded in placing it on a level with the game of three card monte'. However, events proved the *Times* was well off the mark with its conclusion, 'the time is now ripe for the revival of cricket'.[9]

But the eventual success of baseball does not support those seeing the game standing 'as a symbol for larger truths and trends of human existence' – or even as a working out of particular US symbols. Its organization proved even more hit and miss than the game itself. In the US between 1869 and 1900 more than 850 professional teams started up – of these 650 failed within two years, with only 50 lasting more than five years. A key factor for successful teams was support from urban crowds – the more rural southern states saw 12 failed attempts to establish a Southern League in the 1880s and 1890s.[10] And the rules of the game also changed. While there were regional variations, most early professional pitchers followed New York rules in throwing underarm, and it was only in the 1880s that the game adopted the Boston practice of pitching overhand.[11] Rather than the working out of some manifest destiny, as Yankees fan Steven Jay Gould argued, 'baseball became America's defining sport for the far more ordinary and concrete reasons of simple persistence and pervasiveness'.[12]

On the other side of the Atlantic, English cricket too went through changes in its rules and organization. Similarly to pitching in baseball, early bowling was underarm – prior to 1864, the rules required the umpire to call 'no ball' 'if any part of the hand be above the shoulder at time of delivery'. Over-arm bowling gained popularity after the rule change.[13]

And while county cricket has long had the image of the foundation of a genteel, upper-class game,[14] this game too could easily have developed in a different direction. The first regular matches of cricket to attract sizeable crowds were from travelling groups of professionals. The county championship did not start until 1873, and was not fully organized until the 1890s. Its several day matches between predominantly amateur teams (although most bowlers were professionals) faced considerable competition for audiences in the North of England and the Midlands from League Cricket, where professional players competed in Saturday afternoon forerunners of one-day cricket.[15] Many of the early county sides were financially precarious, and only survived in the 1880s and 1890s because of the spectator drawcard of occasional tours by Australian teams.[16]

But if such pressures affected the precise way that individual sports developed, the dominant trend between 1860 and 1900 was the mainstream sports becoming more codified and better organized. This occurred especially in the United Kingdom and the United States, and also, as we will see later, Australia. Why did this pattern happen when it did, rather than before 1860 or after 1900?

The key driving force was that these sports became mass spectator sports. Prior to 1860, crowds were minimal – indeed even in the early 1880s, the final of the FA Cup in England attracted only 6,000 people. In marked contrast, after 1900 in the UK, major bank holiday race meetings were attracting up to 80,000, and Scotland versus England football internationals never had a crowd of less than 100,000 fans from 1906 to 1914.[17] Similar trends in crowd sizes happened for baseball and football in the USA – it took baseball until the 1880s to beat a record crowd size of 40,000 for a game in 1862, between two teams representing different regiments in the Union Army.[18]

The massive growth in crowd sizes stemmed from four aspects of the buoyant economic and social growth of the period. The most important was the ability of people to attend sports events, most especially on Saturday afternoons. Both economic growth and trade union pressure led to reductions in working time for white collar and skilled blue collar workers, with Saturday afternoons increasingly leisure time. Secondly, average incomes rose strongly, giving people (and especially young single men) more money to spend on entertainment and leisure. Thirdly, increasing urbanization, together with improved transportation such as railways and trams, ensured much larger pools of people had easy access to events. And fourthly, both economic growth and the spread of mass literacy (compulsory schooling started in the 1870s) encouraged rapid development and readership of newspapers, in which sports reports and betting information loomed large from the 1880s on.

These trends produced larger and larger potential audiences for sports. Sports organizers themselves responded in a number of ways to turn those potential audiences into actual 'bums on seats'. In a mutually reinforcing process, as crowds grew organizers built more seats in better grandstands and other facilities, enhancing sports' ability to accommodate and attract still further bums to those seats. Organizers also codified sports more clearly, assisting fans to better understand and follow the games.

As internationally, changes in individual Australian sports came both from the general trends and from the way organizers and audiences responded. But overall, Australia was well up with the international trends – and in some respects led the way. One talisman of this leadership is the fact that of the seven football clubs now extant worldwide that can document their foundation to before 1860, three are Victorian football clubs: Melbourne (May 1858), Castlemaine (June 1859) and Geelong (July 1859).[19]

The next sections discuss why Australia was in the vanguard of this sports development.

Australian crowds

The second half of the nineteenth century saw massive development in Australia – in social, economic and political dimensions. As noted above, the non-Aboriginal population of Australia trebled between 1861 and 1901, reaching 3.8 million when Federation occurred in 1901. By then, the population of Melbourne and Sydney were each approaching 500,000, significant cities by world standards.[20]

The average Australian standard of living was probably the highest in the world in these years, driven by the gold rushes, rapid expansion of farming and urban development. Up to 1890 Australian average incomes were 40–50% higher than those in the United States, and 20–30% higher than in the United Kingdom. The averages seem to have been even higher in the big cities, above all in Melbourne. And while drought and depression reduced incomes in the 1890s, now averaging close to the UK and USA levels, the earlier years of high incomes had created a strong legacy.[21]

The overall wealth of the population meant a strong market for entertainment of various kinds. For sport, this was reinforced by the age and sex structure of the times. The vast majority of people attracted to the gold rushes of the 1850s and 1860s were single men aged between 15 and 44. In 1861, a quarter of the Australian population were single men in this age group – and this demographic not only provided participants for any sport, but also most of the audience for the sports, the drinks and the bets. By 1901, when a more settled population pattern had emerged, single men in this age group comprised some 12% of the population.[22]

As elsewhere in the world, there were some marked disparities in wealth and income. Dispossessed Aborigines, selectors struggling to eke an existence on hard farmland, and the urban unemployed all faced difficulties. But for many Australians this country was something of a social laboratory, leading the way for the rest of the world to follow. And however disparate the benefits of the economic growth, the early high standard of living had big implications for sport. The size of early Australian sporting crowds attracted many comments. American author Mark Twain visited Melbourne in 1895, and termed it, 'the mitred Metropolitan of the Horse-Racing Cult':

> every man or woman, of high degree or low, who can afford the expense, put away their other duties and come … They come a hundred thousand strong … and they pack the spacious grounds and grandstands and make a spectacle such as is never to be seen in Australasia elsewhere. It is the 'Melbourne Cup' that brings this multitude together.[23]

The crowds at the Melbourne Cup were indeed remarkable by world standards. The Cup attracted its first 100,000 crowd in 1880 – equivalent to 40% of Melbourne's then population of 250,000.[24] But in totals across the year, even such numbers were put in the shade by regular attendances. In the 1910s, crowds of 10,000 regularly turned out for Saturday evening boxing at the Sydney Stadium – not bad in comparison to the 10,150 who attended the world heavy weight boxing championship at Madison Square Gardens, New York in March 1916.[25]

And in Melbourne, by the 1870s Saturday afternoon football was described as 'a weekly carnival':

> Immediately after they finished work at one pm, a few employers, but hundreds of thousands of young 'clerks, shopmen, bagmen, mechanics, larrikins, betting men, publicans, barmaids, working girls and the half-world' swarmed to the sports arenas by foot and by train. Here they cheered on their suburbs team 'loudly applauding' the players' systematic 'cruelty and brutality'.[26]

As noted above, internationally leisure time on Saturday afternoons was critical in creating potential audiences for sports. Australia, and particularly Melbourne, led the way in having Saturday afternoon free for leisure. On 21 April 1856, following negotiations between building tradesmen and contractors, and with the approval of the colonial government, an eight-hour day was introduced into the building trades in Melbourne. Stonemasons leading the movement argued that eight hours a day was appropriate in the Australian heat – and would also give them time to improve their 'social and moral condition'. Two substantial employers resisted the new working hours agreement, but in the face of union strike action they gave way within a fortnight.[27] This success in 1856 was a world leader. It came 30 years before the strikes and demonstrations in Chicago in May 1886 in favour of the eight-hour day became commemorated in international workers' day on May Day.

Attendances at sports events were also assisted in Australia by extensive areas of land available for sports. The cheaper cost of land compared with England, and the more recent development of towns, meant most towns and cities started with considerable space, and could set aside areas (often called the 'domain') for public use, including sports, and for race courses. And the big cities soon had good transport networks to move the growing crowds to and from the events. These factors helped generate the internationally impressive crowds at sporting events in the 1870s and 1880s. Huge crowds also attended other events related to sport, with two notable examples being the numbers at the funerals of sporting champions.

Sculler Henry Searle, one of Australia's early world champions, successfully defended his world championship in England in 1889, but contracted typhoid on the way home and died shortly after he reached Melbourne. When the cortège placed Searle's body onto the train to Sydney, a crowd of 40,000 attended – a similar number to that which turned out to welcome the Earl of Hopetoun, the new Victorian State Governor, some weeks earlier. The radical *Bulletin* commented acerbically that 'the people thought as much of a dead sculler as they did of a live earl'. When the casket reached Sydney, some 170,000 people attended Searle's funeral.[28]

Thirty years later, Australian boxer Les Darcy died in Memphis from septicaemia after a dental operation. His embalmed body was shipped back to Sydney, where some 100,000 people filed pass his coffin on 26 and 27 June. A 'huge congregation' attended the Requiem Mass the next day at St Joseph's in Woollahra, and a crowd estimated at 250,000 (30% of Sydney's population) watched the funeral procession take the coffin to the train station.[29] But, as historian Wray Vamplew has cautioned,

> too much should not be read into these instances of mass public mourning. The funerals of the explorers Burke and Wills, politician WC Wentworth, and militarist General Monash also drew large crowds and surely no-one would claim that Australians were particularly obsessed by their activities![30]

Burke and Wills were two ill-fated explorers who set out in August 1860 aiming to be the first whites to travel to the north through inland Australia. They died on their return journey, in June 1861. On 21 January 1863 their remains received Australia's first state funeral, with a procession stretching for four city blocks and drew the largest crowd ever seen in Melbourne. Prior to the funeral, the remains of Burke and Wills lay in state in the hall of the Royal Society for two weeks, where they were viewed by more than 100,000 people, out of a total city population of 120,000.[31]

Nor was the attraction of big events limited to funerals. In 1885, the New South Wales Government offered troops to serve with the British forces in the Sudan. Two hundred thousand people, two-thirds of Sydney's then population, turned out to see the troops leave.[32] In 1888, Melbourne held an International Exhibition as part of the celebration of the centennial of white settlement. Total attendance (including repeat visits) was two million people – equivalent to 175% of Victoria's population. This was more than double the comparable numbers attracted to the USA centennial exhibition in 1876. Philadelphia's attendances were equivalent to 80% of the population living within 200 miles, a similar catchment area.[33]

Thus, big attendances at sport went alongside large attendances at other events. And, despite a long-standing image that Australians' obsession in sport precludes any interest in the allegedly finer things in life, crowds were also impressive for cultural activities.

Sport and culture

Launching the Bell Shakespeare Melbourne season of plays in February 2005, former AFL player Paul Salmon reminisced that one of his coaches often motivated his team by citing famous warriors. Before one match, the coach reminded the players of Alexander the Great's exploits at the Battle of Hastings. Salmon reckoned, 'it didn't matter that Big Alex wasn't there, but I knew where coach was coming from'.[34]

As we saw in Paper 3, part of the common image of the Australian 'ocker' sports lover is 'a self-satisfied vulgarian' with a 'narrow outlook never rising to anything above mindless hedonism'. Not much room there for knowing – or caring – whether Big Alex was around in 1066 or not. Such criticisms of prevailing philistine mores in Australia have been frequent since the 1880s. Historian John Hirst summed up the concerns in the last decades of the nineteenth century:

> The characteristics of the native-born that made their future doubtful were widely agreed on: a love of sport, a disinclination to mental effort, lack of respect for author-ity, and persistent swearing. Books, learned articles, editorials and speeches elaborated on their failings, added speculation on the effects of climate and the environment, physical and social, and produced forecasts, more or less insulting, of the future Australian character.[35]

There are two key points to be made about such criticisms. The first is to see them in comparison with comments made on other new and wealthy societies – and indeed about working-class youth in the UK at that time. The second, to use the terms of 'a self-satisfied vulgarian', is that they were largely bullshit.

Historian Richard White compared such comments with contemporary comments in other countries, and expressed surprise at how often such attributes 'were seen as being peculiarly Australian when they can more properly be ascribed to the age-old dismay with which one generation greets the ascendancy of the next'. When many 'condemned larrikinism they did so in the same terms in which their counterparts in Britain and America condemned the appearance of relatively affluent working-class youth'.[36]

But such comments, and especially the contention that love of sport was matched with 'disinclination to mental effort' were remarkably wide of the mark. Certainly early entertainment entrepreneurs did not see such a conflict. The first English cricket tour of Australia, in 1861–62, was organized by two Melbourne publicans, Felix Spiers and Christopher Pond. Following the success of the tour, which made a substantial profit of £11,000, their next venture was to bring actor Charles Kean to Australia two years later.[37]

As mentioned above, one of the justifications that stonemasons in Melbourne gave for seeking the eight-hour day was to further workers' 'social and moral condition'. The colonies had remarkable numbers of mechanics' institutes, and showed strong interest in public lectures on a wide range of subjects. In 1875, a Rev. Charles Clark filled the Melbourne Town Hall to capacity four times with a lecture on the Tower of London, and made an impressive £1,000 from these appearances.[38]

Reading was also very popular, with the country a leader in newspapers. The most remarkable circulation numbers were those of *The Age* in Melbourne. With the advent of mass literacy,[39] the paper's circulation grew to 120,000 in 1899. This was equivalent to more than 40% of all Victorian households,[40] and in proportion to population was by far the largest circulation of any daily newspaper in the British Empire. And Melbourne had three other daily papers (*The Herald* in 1892 having the boast below its masthead, 'the largest circulation of any newspaper in Victoria, with the exception of 'The Age'[41]), and the major Victorian regional centres also had dailies. For one international comparison, *The Times* in London had daily circulation of 38,000 in 1900.[42]

In the 1880s, Australia reportedly absorbed one-third of Britain's total output of books – which, as the UK population was eight times that of the colonies, means the Australian per capita absorption of British books was four times that in the UK.[43] David MacKenzie, writing a guide for English migrants in 1885, noted 'everyone reads' – though he was a little concerned how many read Dickens rather than more serious works. A similar modern commentator would be exultant over people reading Dickens![44] And 1911 Census returns show the proportion of people employed as 'authors, editors and journalists' as 40% higher in Australia than the United Kingdom.[45]

But for popular enthusiasm for cultural events in early Australia, little compares with the rapturous response Australian soprano Nellie Melba received on her tours in 1902 and 1909. Melba, born in Melbourne in 1861, left for England in 1886 and soon established herself as one of Europe's leading singers, with successful tours to the United States as well.[46]

In 1902, Melba made a triumphant return to Australia, netting a massive £21,000 from nine concerts in Sydney and Melbourne alone. She set a long-standing world record for the highest fee ever paid a singer for a single performance, with that £2,350 in Sydney dwarfing her usual fees, such as $3,000 (then worth £625) for each performance in a New York season of 15 performances in 1907.[47] If Sydneysiders and Melburnians were prepared to pay world record prices to see Melba, their enthusiasm was also shared in country areas. In 1909 Melba conducted what she termed her 'sentimental tour', travelling 10,000 miles (mostly by train) to give extraordinarily popular concerts in some 50 towns throughout eastern Australia, Tasmania and New Zealand. She stayed one or two nights in each town, with saturation coverage of her visits in local papers.

The tour produced many memorable moments as well as the anecdote which opened this paper. On another occasion, a group of leading citizens, 'of a ca'canny sort' decided they would be able to enjoy the Melba concert without the inconvenience of paying their ten-and-sixpences. Dressed in their Sunday best, they walked with the rest of the town to the hall, and then slipped around the back to climb a ladder to the roof of the hall, and sat themselves around the open skylight. By the end of the concert however, the group found that the gardener had unwittingly removed the ladder. The night became chilly, and it was not until five in the morning that they managed to attract the attention of a policeman, who found the ladder and fetched them down.[48] When Nellie Melba died on 23 February 1931, the *Argus* obituary reckoned she had strong claims to the title of 'the greatest Australian'. Such lauding of an opera singer seems at variance with most images of the Australian sporting nation.

The discussion in Paper 5 noted that people attending major sports events are more likely than the general population to also attend cultural events. And children in organized sports teams are also more likely than other children to learn piano, drama or dance. A similar conclusion can be drawn for the interaction between sports and other, including cultural, events in the pre-1900 period. The wealth of the new country, the success of many workers in winning greater leisure time, and the high degree of urbanization, created audiences for a wide range of activities, not just for sport.

Which raises a central question – why, out of all these possibilities, was sport singled out as the key marker of Australian national identity? As we have seen, there was rich material in sports showing Australia was indeed leading the world in various respects. But there was also similar rich material in other fields of endeavour, which has been largely overlooked in the weaving of the image.

To answer the question, we need to look at the dynamics of the creation of that image.

The sporting image

A special role for sport in establishing the Australian image was apparent in the reaction of the *Sydney Morning Herald* to events on 8 February 1879. That Saturday, a Sydney crowd of 10,000 watched a cricket match between England and New South Wales. When local batsman Murdoch was adjudged 'run out', the umpire's decision was 'dissented from by the betting ring, and thereupon the larrikin horde rushed onto the field to … stop the play'. The day's play ended in chaos, with the match resuming the following Monday.[49]

The *Herald* editorial on Monday drew many lessons from the riot at the cricket:

> Everyone with the slightest spark of national pride, or who is at all conscious of the feeling of national humiliation, or who values the physical and moral training which may be got from well-contested public games, must greatly regret the rude interruption of the cricket match on Saturday … a sense of disorder, which at one time threatened to turn into a general row, disgraced the colony.

Such a fear of 'disgracing the colony', while influential, was only one of the strands which together contributed to the national sporting image. This collection has discussed the diversity and complexity of elements contributing to national identity – and the differing motivations that people bring to their involvement in sport.

In a similar way, a number of motivations and elements contributed to early descriptions of the Australian sporting image. Five strands appeared, sometimes conflicting, sometimes overlapping. These related to markedly different visions of sport in Australia, as discussed in Paper 9.

The first was a disdainful, condescending comment on the new colonials; often expressed by self-importantly superior English, but also echoed by some Australians. To some extent, the disdain for large Australian sporting crowds was also a complaint that the 'proper' social order as existed in England was not being replicated – that especially the skilled working class were getting beyond their proper stations in life. More generally, the supposed obsession with sport (the cultural aspects were little mentioned) was confirming evidence that the colonists would never amount to much.

Some of these critics also claimed that the Australian climate would 'slowly debilitate and enfeeble' the English stock.[50] In 1893 British critic John W. Fortescue wrote an influential article on 'The Influence of Climate on Race': 'in summer even Sydney people showed the 'limp parboiled appearance' sometimes visible in 'degenerate whites' in the West Indies'.[51]

Against such disdain, the *Herald* and the second group looked to sport as a way of demonstrating (to Australians themselves and also hopefully to the English) that the British stock was indeed flourishing in Australia. The *Daily Telegraph* suggested that Beach's 1884 sculling win over Canadian Hanlan was 'a crushing answer to those who have so often and so confidently predicted the physical deterioration of the British race in this climate'.[52] These people looking over their shoulders were forerunners of the 'imaginary grandstand' group we will discuss later.

The third group, along the lines of Alfred Deakin's 'The Australian Game' speech in 1908, saw sport as one element in a social laboratory where progress was being made on a number of fronts to improve the human condition. This view, while still very 'British', was much less subservient to, or nervous about, views from England. Deakin himself was heavily critical of what he saw as the snobbishness and self-obsession of London's high society. In 1887, and on subsequent occasions, Deakin refused offers of knighthoods, and he even refused an honorary degree from Oxford University – who told him nobody had ever refused before.[53]

There was also a very pragmatic and commercial orientation. As we will see in the next paper, promoters of events such as sculling championships advertised strongly on the theme of the 'Australian world champion' (even before Australia formally existed as a Federation). Apparently nationalism sold well even from an early date.

Last, a role developed for at least some sports as nationally inclusive. Appeals could be made to interest in sport that transcended other divisive elements in society, of class or religion. Indeed, this may have been an especially important part of the presentation of the national image in Australia. As noted in Paper 3, nationalism in Europe was based on a number of elements, including cultural/ethnic homogeneity, and while sports images developed as national unifying symbols from the 1920s on, they were always part of that broader suite of imagery.

Australian nationalism was different, for two reasons. First, as Australia was ahead of the pack in a number of developments, so sport as a nationalist symbol developed here earlier too. Secondly, as noted in Paper 4, the cultural/ethnic ethos here was strongly British. But always there were some who did not subscribe to 'Britishness', mostly because either they were of Irish background, or they wanted to see Australia develop in different, less imperial, directions. The 'sporting people' image was particularly useful in reaching across all groups. However, as we will see, there were limitations to how effective this was. When the most dramatic appeals were made to mobilize sporting interest for nationalistic purposes, other factors impinged strongly – this story will be returned to in Paper 11.

Sporting interests are marked by diversity in a number of ways, and similar diversity applied in attitudes to the strands of the national sporting image discussed here. Rodney Marsh, Australian wicketkeeper in the 1970s, was a long way from the colonial cringe:

Marsh, on his first visit to Lord's, asked the MCC type (handlebar moustache, egg yolk and ketchup tie, pinstripe suit) 'Um, where's the dressing room at?'

And the MCC type said 'You colonials, don't you know you can't end a sentence with a preposition?'

And former school teacher Marsh said 'You're quite right. Where's the dressing room at, wanker?'[54]

From Marsh's front foot approach to those cowering before English bumpers, the diversity of views linked to very different visions of Australian sport. They also left strong marks on the early development of key sports in Australia. To illustrate this, the next paper looks at football, racing, cricket and sculling.

Notes

1. Melba, *Melodies and Memories*, 180.
2. Deakin's speech, 'The Australasian Game' at the 1908 Football Jubilee was reported in *The Argus*, August 29, 1908, 17, and is also reproduced from VFL records by Hess in Cashman, O'Hara, and Honey, eds, *Sport, Federation, Nation*.
3. *Bell's Life*, April 17, 1869, cited by Lemon and Freedman, *History of Australian Thoroughbred Racing*, 280.
4. *New York Times*, August 30, 1881, 4 (the initial reference to this remarkable editorial came from Vincent, *Rise and Fall of American Sport*, 121).
5. Mandelbaum, *The Meaning of Sports*, 145–6.
6. Blainey, *A Game of Our Own*.
7. Markovits and Hellerman, *Offside*.
8. Cashman, Headon, and Kinross-Smith, eds, *Oxford Book of Australian Sporting Anecdotes*, 47.
9. *New York Times*, August 30, 1881, editorial, 4.
10. Vincent, *Rise and Fall of American Sport*, 97.
11. Gould, *Triumph and Tragedy in Mudville*, 201–3.
12. Ibid., 210.
13. Harte, *History of Australian Cricket*, 75.
14. Vamplew, *Pay up and Play the Game*, 99.
15. Ibid., especially 58–9 and 122.
16. Dr Vamplew, personal communication to the author.
17. Blainey, *A Game of Our Own*, 64; Vamplew, *Pay up and Play the Game*, 4.
18. Vincent, *Rise and Fall of American Sport*, 93.
19. The listing of the oldest surviving football clubs is from http://en.wikipedia.org/wiki/Oldest_football_club. Also see *The Age*, May 17, 2006, Sport, 2. The other early starters of football clubs are Guy's Hospital (1843) and Blackheath Rugby (1858), both in London, and Liverpool St Helens (1858), and the other the Sheffield Football club (October 1857), from Yorkshire. The earliest US football club, the Oneida club, was formed in Boston in 1861, but like many others did not survive.
20. Vamplew, ed., *Australian Historical Statistics*; Ruzicka and Caldwell, *Demographic Transition in Australia*, especially 72; Sinclair, *Process of Economic Development in Australia*, 108.
21. McLean, 'Australian Economic Growth', 332, gave the following measures of National Income per Head, relative to USA (USA = 100 in each year):

Table 1.   National Income per Head, relative to USA (USA = 100 in each year).

Year	Australia	New Zealand	UK	Canada
1870	155	127	133	66
1890	141	111	121	66
1900	105	105	113	67

See also Sinclair, *Process of Economic Development in Australia*.

22. Calculated from data in Vamplew, *Australian Historical Statistics*.
23. Cited in Cashman *et al.*, eds. *Oxford Book of Australian Sporting Anecdotes*, 50–1. Comparative sizes of football crowds were given in Blainey, *A Game of Our Own*; for sculling Adair, 'Two dots in the distance', 60.
24. Melbourne Cup attendances from the Victorian Racing Club website, http://www.vrc.net.au.
25. Swanwick, *Les Darcy*, 68.
26. Cannon, *Life in the Cities*, 254 – citing 'Manly Sports' in *The Vagabond Papers*, (1932).
27. The start of the eight-hour day in Melbourne is outlined on www.8hourday.org.au.
28. Adair, 'Two Dots in the Distance', 66, and citing *The Bulletin* quote on Searle's death, 81, n.72
29. Swanwick, *Les Darcy*, 100f.
30. Vamplew, 'Australians and Sport', 13. Vamplew could also have added the massive attendances at singer Nellie Melba's funeral in 1931 to this list.
31. See http://victoria.slv.vic.gov.au/burkeandwills/.
32. Hirst, *Sentimental Nation*, 74.
33. Spillman, *Nation and Commemoration*, 51. Spillman cites the Victorian figure at 154% of population: Victoria's population was 1.14 million in 1891, so attendances of two million represent 175% of this number.
34. *The Age*, February 22, 2005, Metro, 8.
35. Hirst, *Sentimental Nation*, 34. Hirst drew heavily on White, *Inventing Australia*.
36. White, *Inventing Australia*, 47–8 and 77.
37. Cashman, *Paradise of Sport*, 188; and Harte, *History of Australian Cricket*, 71. Harte gives a higher figure for Spiers and Pond's profits, at £14,000, but this may have been before they paid bonus payments to the players.
38. Cannon, *Life in the Cities*, 96.
39. Most Australian children received some schooling by the mid-1850s, with legislation requiring school attendance in all colonies by 1880. However, it was not until 1901 that at least 60% of enrolled children would reliably turn up on any particular day. See Ruzicka and Caldwell, *End of Demographic Transition in Australia*, 19–22.
40. *The Age*'s remarkable circulation numbers are given in *Australian Dictionary of Biography*: on-line edition (www.adbonline.anu.edu.au/adbonline), entry for David Syme. The Australian Bureau of Statistics (www.abs.gov.au), *Australian Yearbook 2001* noted the average number of people per dwelling as 4.5 in 1911, so with a population of 1.2 million in 1901, Victoria had some 270,000 households.
41. *The Herald*, January 1, 1892, 1. By 1894 the paper had changed the boast to 'the largest circulation of any evening paper in Australia' – *The Herald*, January 2, 1894, 1.
42. 'London Times's Big Jump', Special Cable to the *New York Times*, May 9, 1914, 9. Accessed from *New York Times* on-line archives, http://spiderbites.nytimes.com/free_1914/articles_1914_05_00002.html.
43. White, *Inventing Australia*, 62, with references to Cannon, *Life in the Cities*, 258, and also Serle, *From Deserts the Prophets Come*, 25.
44. White, *Inventing Australia*, 118–19 and 62.
45. Ibid., 88–9. White gives respective ratios of 1 in 3,200 of Britain's population, and 1 in 2,100 in Australia, but his raw data compared with total population numbers in 1911 gives 2,550 for the UK and 1,835 for New South Wales and Victoria.
46. Davidson, 'Melba', 475–9; Hetherington, *Melba: A Biography*; and McFadzean, 'Dame Nellie Melba: An Australian Icon', 9–10.
47. Davidson, 'Melba', 478; Hetherington, *Melba: A Biography*, 119 and 150–1.
48. Melba, *Melodies and Memories*, 181–2.
49. *Sydney Morning Herald*, February 10, 1879, 4.
50. Blainey, *Black Kettle and Full Moon*, 20–31; and White, *Inventing Australia*, 70–1.
51. Blainey, *Black Kettle and Full Moon*, 26.
52. *Daily Telegraph*, August 18, 1884, 4, cited by Ripley, 'Golden Age of Australian Professional Sculling', 872. For similar comments on cricket, see Harte, *History of Australian Cricket*, 94. Other contemporary comments on this theme were cited by Mandle, 'Cricket and Australian Nationalism', 225–46.
53. Hirst, *Sentimental Nation*, 40–2.
54. Walker and Doyle, *Sports Jokes*, 52.

References

Adair, Daryl. 'Two Dots in the Distance: Professional Sculling as a Mass Spectacle in New South Wales 1876–1907'. *Sporting Traditions* 9, no. 1 (November 1992): 52–83.

Blainey, Geoffrey. *A Game of Our Own.* Melbourne: Information Australia, 1990.

Blainey, Geoffrey. *Black Kettle and Full Moon.* Camberwell Victoria: Penguin, 2003.

Cannon, Michael. *Life in the Cities.* West Melbourne Vic: Thomas Nelson Australia, 1978.

Cashman, Richard, David Headon, and Graeme Kinross-Smith, eds. *The Oxford Book of Australian Sporting Anecdotes.* Oxford: Oxford University Press, 1993.

Cashman, Richard. *Paradise of Sport: The Rise of Organised Sport in Australia.* Melbourne: Oxford University Press, 1995.

Cashman, Richard, John O'Hara, and Andrew Honey, eds. *Sport, Federation, Nation.* Sydney: Walla Walla Press in conjunction with the Centre for Olympic Studies, University of New South Wales, 2001.

Davidson Jim. 'Melba, Dame Nellie (1861–1931)'. In *Australian Dictionary of Biography,* 10. Canberra: Australian Dictionary of Biography, 1986, 475–9.

Gould, Steven Jay. *Triumph and Tragedy in Mudville.* New York: W.W. Norton, 2003.

Harte, Chris. *A History of Australian Cricket.* London: Andre Deutsch, 1993.

Hetherington, John. *Melba: A Biography.* Melbourne: Cheshire, 1967.

Hirst. John. *The Sentimental Nation: the Making of the Australian Commonwealth.* Melbourne: Oxford University Press, 2000.

Lemon, Andrew, and Harold Freedman. *History of Australian Thoroughbred Racing Volume 2: The Golden Years 1862 to 1939.* Melbourne: Southbank Communications, 1990.

McFadzean, Moya. 'Dame Nellie Melba: An Australian Icon'. 2001. http://www.museum.vic.gov.au/lectures/read/010513/melba_lecture.pdf

McLean, Ian. 'Australian Economic Growth in Historical Perspective'. *Economic Record* 80 (September2004): 330–45.

Mandelbaum, Michael. *The Meaning of Sports: Why Americans Watch Baseball, Football and Basketball and What They See When They Do.* New York: Public Affairs, 2004.

Mandle, W.F. 'Cricket and Australian Nationalism in the Nineteenth Century'. *Journal of the Royal Australian Historical Society* 59, no. 4 (December 1973): 225–46.

Markovits, Andrei, and Steven Hellerman. *Offside: Soccer and American Exceptionalism.* Princeton NJ: Princeton University Press, 2001.

Melba, Dame Nellie. *Melodies and Memories.* West Melbourne Vic: Nelson, 1980.

Ripley, Stewart. 'The Golden Age of Australian Professional Sculling or Skullduggery?' *International Journal of the History of Sport* 22, no. 5 (September 2005): 867–82.

Ruzicka, L.T., and J.C. Caldwell. *The End of Demographic Transition in Australia.* Canberra: Department of Demography, Australian National University, 1977.

Serle, Geoffrey. *From Deserts the Prophets Come: The Creative Spirit in Australia 1788–1972.* Melbourne: Heinemann, 1973.

Sinclair, W.A. *The Process of Economic Development in Australia.* Melbourne: Cheshire, 1976.

Spillman, Lyn. *Nation and Commemoration: Creating National Identities in the United States and Australia.* Cambridge: Cambridge University Press, 1997.

Swanwick. Raymond. *Les Darcy.* Sydney: R. Swanwick, 1994.

Vamplew, Wray, ed. *Australian Historical Statistics.* Broadway, NSW: Fairfax, Syme & Weldon Associates, 1987.

Vamplew, Wray. *Pay Up and Play the Game.* Cambridge and Sydney: Cambridge University Press, 1988.

Vamplew, Wray. 'Australians and Sport'. In *Sport in Australia: A Social History,* ed. Wray Vamplew and Brian Stoddart, 1–18. Melbourne: Cambridge University Press, 1994.

Vincent, Ted. *The Rise and Fall of American Sport: Mudville's Revenge.* 2nd ed. Lincoln NE: University of Nebraska Press, 1994.

Walker, Max, and Brian Doyle. *Sports Jokes.* Carlton, Vic.: Allen and Unwin, 1997.

White, Richard. *Inventing Australia.* Sydney: George Allen and Unwin, 1981.

Early sports 1860–1900

The Argus celebrated the opening of the 1892 football season:

> The game is manly and vigorous in the highest degree, and can only be played under conditions which imply the highest state of physical health ... The character of a nation is reflected in its sports; and a race which finds such passionate delight in the conflicts of the football field must have a very robust strain of manliness running through it.[1]

Four years later, another writer in *The Argus* took a much dimmer view of football crowds:

> The women 'barracker', indeed, has become one of the most objectionable of football surroundings. On some grounds they actually spit in the faces of players as they come to the dressing-rooms, or wreak their spite much more maliciously by long hat pins ... One of these gentle maidens at the close of the struggle remarked regretfully that it was a pity they 'let off' the umpire in the Geelong match, as they should have killed him. Yet these women consider themselves respectable and they 'support football' which is consequently in a serious decline.[2]

Along with their reporting of events, these observers gave healthy doses of their visions of sport – what they thought sport should be, and should do socially. There were many such differing visions of sport in the 1860–1900 period, as organized sport became established in Australia. This paper traces developments in the four most popular sports: football, racing, cricket and the now-forgotten sport of professional sculling, in which Australia produced its first world champions.

Each discussion looks at the key drivers pushing the sport forward, the way organization developed, and the differing visions involved. The detail gives good background for the following paper which discusses the differing visions various social groups brought to sport around 1900.

Why does Melbourne play rules and Sydney rugby?

In 2002, one third of adults in Victoria attended at least one game of Australian rules, but only 3% attended a rugby match. The picture was reversed in New South Wales, with one quarter attending rugby matches (two thirds League to one third Union), and only 4% turning up at rules games.[3]

Differences in dominant football codes across the world are generally long standing – the major code had achieved its dominance in most countries by 1900. Once it had become dominant, it seems to have been easy for a code to stay that way.[4] The large crowds for that code would enable better facilities to be provided, hence attracting even bigger crowds. And most young budding athletes and players would naturally want to excel at the sport popular amongst their families and friends. Certainly in Melbourne, and to a slightly lesser extent in Sydney, rules and rugby were already respectively the dominant football codes in the 1880s. Even at that stage, the choice of code tells us something about the differing visions of sport in the two cities.

So if we are to find reasons for the difference between rules and rugby in Australia, we need to look at the circumstances when the sports started, in the 1860–80 period. Some have looked to the larger public spaces in Melbourne, or the lower rainfall than Sydney, as encouraging a faster, more open game.[5] However, the key reasons were social, and revolve around Melbourne being bigger, wealthier, and having stronger trade unions than Sydney.

At first sight, those may not seem likely candidates for explaining a choice of football code. The critical issue was timing. Melbourne started playing rules in a big way in the 1860s, while Sydney did not achieve big attendances at rugby matches until around 1880. Paper 7 argued that the critical factor in the development of mass sport in the late nineteenth century was the start of regular free time on Saturday afternoons for increasing numbers of people. And Melbourne – probably the wealthiest large city in the world in 1860 – was a fertile environment for the stonemasons and other unions to win the eight-hour day. That, together with the city's 120,000 population and access to plentiful parkland, was central to a demand for sport.

Both free Saturday afternoons and the demand for sport in Melbourne came well before codification of the main sports internationally. In his history of the game's origins, Geoffrey Blainey argued that the lack of clearly codified football games in 1858, when the first game was played, was a big factor in early footballers developing different 'rules'.[6]

It took a while for the rules to settle down, with at least five differing drafts between 1859 and 1877, and further changes through to 1900. A driving force behind the revisions to the rules was to create a popular spectacle:

> [Huge] crowds and their preferences helped to shape the game. They longed for the spectacular: they wanted to see the long run with the ball, the high mark, the clever dodging and the sudden physical clash. They shunned the slow moving play and especially the scrimmage.[7]

In contrast, no regular games of football of any sort were played in Sydney until a decade later, and then the number was small. Only a couple of senior matches were played in 1868 and 1869, with the small number of games that latter year attributed to the lack of grounds on which to play, uncertainty about the rules, as well as inclement weather.[8]

The slower introduction of any sort of football in Sydney reflected a number of factors. Sydney's population was smaller than Melbourne's, and the northern city had benefited less from the gold rushes. As a result, incomes were lower, there were fewer single males in the important 15–30 age bracket, and fewer people were free on Saturday afternoons. This contrast gave the crucial difference. The wide social demand for the game meant football in Melbourne quickly developed a democratic reach. In contrast, very small crowds attended rugby games in Sydney in the 1870s, with columnist 'Leatherstocking' in the *Sydney Mail* noting on 30 June 1874, 'the support given to football in Sydney is far short of ... the very liberal support given to football in Victoria'. Rugby stayed a very socially exclusive affair, with teams from the military, the University of Sydney, and gentlemen's clubs – and the one more open club, Waratah, was still markedly upper crust.[9]

Such was the social milieu which formed the Southern Rugby Football Union in Sydney in 1873, with the 'Southern' in its name indicating the self-conscious links to the English game. Rules were still somewhat fluid – the SRFU did not at first adopt the English rules for touchdowns, nor off-side play.[10] Early matches were dominated by the scrimmage, and were consequently low-scoring.

By the late 1870s, dissension emerged in the SRFU. However, while the critics agreed on what they disliked – the dull, unattractive game and the low crowds – they could not agree on which direction to move. Sydney University supported a faster game of rugby. Waratah was happy to move towards the Victorian game. Others suggested soccer. In the end, it was a very small group of Sydney's elite that defensively decided to stick with rugby – albeit with some rule revisions.[11] This was the environment when, early in 1877, the Victorian Football Association wrote to Sydney suggesting an intercolonial match of football. On 7 May representatives of the Sydney rugby clubs declined the proposal:

> the intricacies of the 'Off and On Side' rules of the Rugby game were far too difficult to be readily understood in such a brief space of time to ensure perfect harmony, and prevent any possible unfriendliness from arising through imperfect knowledge generally of the game's fundamental principles, and that the contest had better bide the time when the rules in the respectively colonies had become more assimilated.[12]

Instead of the proposed inter-colonial game, matches did occur between the club sides of Waratah and Carlton, playing rugby on Saturday 23 June 1877, and rules the following Monday. The games attracted by far the largest football crowds seen in Sydney. With an entry fee of one shilling each, 3,000 turned up for the rugby game – and 1,500 for the rules game on the Monday.[13] These paying crowds were certainly large for Sydney at the time. When Sydney University played rugby against the Wallaroo club in July 1880 a non-paying crowd of only 4,000 turned out. The same match the following year attracted only 500 paying fans at the Sydney Cricket Ground.[14]

While the numbers for the Carlton-Waratah games would have been boosted by the sense of the occasion, they certainly suggest that the Victorian game could well have established a base in Sydney. The key reason it did not was the hostility of the exclusive and conservative members of the SRFU.[15] Even dissenters, such as Waratah, were reluctant to fully support rules. One element here may have well been Sydney-Melbourne rivalry. A football reporter in 1881 commented:

> The great objection to the rules in New South Wales was that they were styled 'the Victorian Rules of Football'. Had they been dubbed the Scandinavian rules, well and good; but Victorian – perish the thought![16]

The potential threat from rules seems to have been one factor encouraging the SRFU to make several changes to the game. The SRFU limited scrimmages from 1879, and in the 1880s it agreed to a broader social involvement in the game through the development of the Metropolitan Rugby Union and a number of suburb-based clubs. With those changes, and with the accelerating trend towards free Saturday afternoons, crowds started to improve for rugby – and it established itself as the dominant code in Sydney.

Rugby in Sydney was to see another major change, with the split between Rugby Union and Rugby League in 1907. That schism reflected tensions in many sports at that stage between amateur and professional sport. It is discussed in Paper 9 – along with the way the similar tensions in Melbourne changed Australian rules.

The interaction between social patterns, visions of sport and the development of sports also occurred in other sports. The next section traces these influences in racing.

Racing

In an 1899 'Open Letter to the Australian Jockey Club', remarkable even by his own standards of vitriol, *Truth* publisher John Norton attacked the Club on many fronts:

> Your mismanagement of the high and responsible trust, as guardians of the British national sport of horseracing in this colony ... [has] degraded the AJC to the level of a club clique, actuated by selfish, if not sinister interest, prompted and maintained by class caddishness and society snobbery ... Your whole regime, from first to last, is marked by presumption, prejudice and unfairness ... Unless the wings of your soaring ambition are clipped by the shears of legislation, they will overshadow the law of the land and the right of honest men to gain an honest livelihood in the sphere of sport.[17]

Despite such conflict over the organization of the sport, horse racing was by far the most popular sport in Australia, measured by attendances or broader public participation, in the late nineteenth century. In 1884–85, five major metropolitan racecourses in Melbourne offered 42 meetings between them. There were also a dozen or so smaller race tracks in or near Melbourne, and some 80 country towns and cities conducted at least one proper race meeting. A decade later, with considerable growth in privately-run courses, the 1895–96 season saw 63 thoroughbred meetings in Sydney, and as many as five pony, Galloway or occasional trotting meetings each week.[18] One estimate of newspaper sports coverage in 1900 gave 47% of all sports news to horse racing, compared with 11% for cricket.[19]

In both Melbourne and Sydney, racing had seen massive changes over the previous three decades. In 1860, while most towns of any size had racecourses, often with rudimentary facilities, racing was generally a matter of local events, run by volunteer-based clubs, and dependent largely on the enthusiasm of particular individuals to keep things going. As in England, racing – the 'sport of kings' – was generally organized by the local elite, the gentry or business groups, with attendances predominantly from working-class males. Giving evidence to a 1912 New South Wales Royal Commission, Sir George Clifford, the head of the New Zealand Racing Conference described racing as,

> a sport which is maintained by the wealthy ... for the recreation of the people. It is desirable that the minds of the working classes should be occupied during the time they are not engaged in their work with some form of recreation.[20]

The social elite also presented a military argument for racing. It may seem quaint from a motorized 2009 perspective, but horses loomed large in military thinking prior to the First World War. Accompanying the 330,000 soldiers it sent to the War, Australia sent some 136,000 horses (which would have required a similar amount of shipping space).[21] Even as late as 1928, General Sir Harry Chauvel argued, 'the breeding of remounts and artillery horses ... should be one of the main objectives of studmasters and the industry of horse breeding'.[22]

Such considerations were probably not high on the agenda of most of the audience base, which supported both the 'establishment' events and a second string of race meetings. The latter were organized by hotels, with free entry to the generally much smaller tracks, and profits made from the drinks sales. Even the more formal race meetings borrowed carnival atmosphere from such gatherings.[23]

The way racing grew from occasional meetings in the 1860s to an extensive industry by the 1880s and 1890s reflected the interaction between the audience and those trying to organize the sport. There was a massive growth in the number of patrons, from both Australia's economic growth and the growth of the large cities. The forms racing took reflected the differing agendas of different groups. The Racing Clubs tried to establish themselves as overseers of the industry. Numerous private interests also set up racing facilities, some not interested in registering with the Racing Clubs. Bookmakers flourished, especially in the large cities, as in some states did a new betting technology – the totalizator. And the whole sea of activity attracted disdain from those, like the *Sydney Morning Herald* in 1879, ready to condemn the 'roguery and vile of the deepest and darkest dye'. The strength of the factors and the actors differed between the colonies – and so the outcomes in the structure of racing also differed. Those differences also had some strong influences on subsequent developments in each state.

A good starting point for the growth of racing in this period is the numbers attending the premier race meeting, the Melbourne Cup. The Cup was first run in 1861. By the mid 1870s, it was attracting attendances over 60,000, equal to 30% of Melbourne's population. Both were remarkable figures by world standards, topped in 1881 when attendance reached 100,000, 40% of population.[24] They were encouraged by better facilities at Flemington (a new grandstand was opened in 1873), and in the declaration of Cup Day as a holiday from 1875 on.[25]

Predominant in the audiences for racing were single males aged 15–45. The significance of this group can be seen from racing in Queensland in 1897. While the northern gold mining town of Charters Towers had only a quarter the population of Brisbane, it was dominated by young males. The gold town's two day race meeting in June 1897 to celebrate Queen Victoria's Diamond Jubilee had better stake money and higher turnover than Brisbane had for its Cup meeting. Three races equalled or bettered the £300 stake money for the Brisbane Cup.[26]

The role of single males is also apparent in the Melbourne crowds: as the population became more stable, and the proportion of young single males diminished, so the percentage of the total population attending the Melbourne Cup fell. It was consistently 30% in the 1870s, peaking at 40% in 1880, but by the early 1900s only 15% of the population were attending Flemington on that day.

Also affecting the money in punters' pockets was the health of the local economy. In Melbourne, the boom times in the 1880s encouraged crowds, while attendances slumped with the onset of a severe depression in the 1890s. Economic recovery after 1900 saw consistent Cup crowds of 85,000 or more for the first decade of the twentieth century.

Such was the growing market, the audience, for racing. The market encouraged the racing industry, with growing numbers of owners, trainers and bookmakers. It also led to two types of battles over the organization of the sport. The first was efforts to limit the extent of gambling. The second was struggles between private business ownership of proprietary racing and the establishment racing clubs, such as the Victorian Racing Club (VRC) and the Australian Jockey Club (AJC) in Sydney, to assert pre-eminence over the sport.

The pattern of these battles differed with specific circumstances in each colony. For example, the anti-gambling lobby was more powerful in South Australia than elsewhere. Tough anti-gambling legislation heavily restricted racing in the state between 1884 and 1888, with the somewhat bizarre outcome that the May 1885 Adelaide Cup was held at Flemington, in Melbourne. When a compromise was reached, it involved tight controls on the numbers of race meetings, on bookies, and gave the SA Jockey Club firm control of racing.[27]

However, the biggest difference was between New South Wales and Victoria on one hand and the other colonies on the other. With many fewer people, the other colonies had much smaller racing markets. This limited the amount of interest in propriety racing, and the numbers of bookies – but also meant the leading racing clubs were often financially precarious. This situation created a favourable environment for the introduction of the totalizator in the 1870s. Rather than using starting prices, as the bookies did, the tote's odds would vary depending on the weight of bets for each horse – and the final payouts would only be known after the race. Racing clubs owned and operated the tote – and welcomed the 5–7.5% of turnover they took. The smaller number of bookies in these colonies proved ineffective lobbying against the tote, or against the local racing clubs cementing their position running racing in each colony.

As in the other colonies, both the AJC in Sydney and the VRC in Melbourne also tried to strengthen their control on racing in the 1880s and 1890s. They were hampered by the strength of the racing market in the two colonies, particularly in two aspects – the clout of the bookies, and the growth of unregistered, especially pony, racing.

In Melbourne, the VRC considered the possibility of a tote on several occasions. The financial imperative was less than for the struggling clubs in other colonies, as the VRC was already receiving good income both from generally larger attendances and from its licensing of on-course bookies. In addition, the bookies themselves mobilized against the threat of the tote, and formed an unlikely alliance with some members of the VRC and the churches to oppose it. This alliance defeated seven separate bills to legalize the tote during the 1890s.[28]

The VRC was more united in concern over unregistered racing, with a social gulf between it and the overwhelmingly working-class, unregistered pony racing tracks.[29]

During the 1890s, the VRC made many attempts to restrict unregistered racing. A particular target was the leading owner of pony tracks, and host of the illegal Collingwood tote, John Wren.[30]

In Sydney, the AJC strengthened its powers from 1883 with its own Act of Parliament and new set of rules – registering bookies in the main enclosure, registering clubs and race meetings, and threats of bans on horses and connections racing at unregistered meetings.[31] But the AJC's upper crust membership, and some dubious enforcement of rule breaches by well-connected owners, made it an easy target for criticisms such as John Norton's of 'snobbery, pomposity and ultra conservatism'. By 1900, if the racing clubs were well entrenched in the smaller states there was no resolution in the two biggest cities between the differing visions held for racing.

Cricket

Cricket matches between Australia and England formed the first regular international sporting contests between national teams. From 1877, Australian teams played England every second year or so, generally alternating locations between the countries

– and the Australians were frequently victors, despite the disparity in 1901 between the Australian population of just under four million and the English population of 30 million.

For many, the rivalry went well beyond a sporting contest, with some of the first efforts to ascribe national characteristics to sporting performance. In the searing heat of summer in 1898, and suffering in smoke from nearby bushfires, an English batsman at the MCG lamented, 'it was an odd country that would set itself alight to win a cricket match'.[32]

Twenty years earlier, *The Australasian* greeted the first Australian cricket victory over England as testifying to the vigour of the new country: 'in bone as muscle, activity, athletic vigour, and success in field sports, the Englishmen born in Australia do not fall short of the Englishmen born in Surrey or Yorkshire'.[33] Alongside such identification with national images, the development of cricket between 1860 and 1910 also saw both various changes to the sport and considerable conflict between different visions of how the game should be organized. The lure of money as spectator numbers grew was again a key factor, both in the organizational battles and the way the game developed some distinctive 'Australian' characteristics.

Part of the changes to the game, akin to developments in rules and rugby, was consolidation and refinement of the rules. When Victoria and New South Wales played one of the first inter-colonial matches in January 1857, they had to agree prior to the game on some basic rules. There would be four balls to an over (then common but not inscribed practice), and bowling could be either under-arm or round-arm.[34] In subsequent changes, six-ball overs became standard for inter-colonial matches from 1887, and for test matches from 1892. New South Wales clubs introduced eight-ball overs from 1910, and this became the Australian standard in 1919 – despite heated disagreement from the English, who maintained six-ball overs. Australia stuck with eight-ball overs until 1979, when World Series Cricket, influenced by the possibility of more frequent advertising breaks, moved back to six-ball overs, which is now the worldwide standard.[35]

The number of balls per over was not the only way Australian cricket differed from the English game. Perhaps the most dramatic was the much wider social spread of the sport in the Antipodes, compared with the restricted, mainly upper-class reach in England. Richard Twopeny, author of *Town Life in Australia* in 1883, estimated the number of boys and young men playing cricket in the two countries was roughly equal, despite the 1:8 difference in total population.[36] However, it would be a mistake to overstate the extent of participation in cricket. Twopeny reckoned that perhaps 20,000 'men and boys' played cricket in the early 1880s – but that number represents only 4% of the some 500,000 Australian males aged 15–34 in 1881.[37] As discussed in Paper 6, it appears a slightly higher 8% of this age group played cricket in rural South Australia around 1900.[38]

Interest in cricket went much wider than just those who played. The first match between Victoria and New South Wales in Sydney in January 1857 attracted daily crowds of 10–15,000 (and some £4,000–5,000 in total bets). Forty years later, world record attendances were set by the 100,000 attending the five day fifth test in Melbourne in 1895, and the 36,000 attending one day of the fifth test in 1898 at the SCG.[39] These were big crowds in absolute numbers – the biggest London grounds were Lord's 30,000, and the Oval 25,000.

As discussed in Paper 5, people attend sporting matches for a number of reasons. Two major drawcards in the 1880s and 1890s were the opportunity to see Australia defeat England, and to see icons of the game. Huge crowds turned out to see W.G. Grace on his two tours. Australian Charles Bannerman was a big attraction in 1877, and crowds also followed other Australian heroes, such as bowler 'Demon' Spofforth, all-rounder Monty Noble and batsmen Billy Murdoch and Victor Trumper.

The numbers confirm a much wider social interest in the game than existed in England, and this was encouraged by different attitudes amongst the organizers. In England, when the two-day Eton v Harrow match attracted 40,000 in 1873, organizers increased the entry price from 1/- to 2/6 to reduce the size of the crowd (and presumably also to maintain the social cachet). In Australia, in contrast, organizers were keen to encourage the crowds.[40]

There were several reasons for this wider social spread. First, there was a generally more democratic ethos in Australia. The English maintained a class distinction between gentlemen (amateurs) and players (professionals), even having separate dressing rooms and separate entry gates onto some English grounds. Such distinctions had no place in the Australian team – and as umpire Jim Phillips saw it in 1899, the more democratic air encouraged discussion of tactics, and contributed to the Australian successes.[41]

The second factor was the greater wealth of the population, meaning ticket prices higher than those in England still attracted a broader audience.[42] Such audiences were especially welcome given the much smaller size of the Australian population. A solely upper-class sport would have little chance of viability, especially outside the main centres of Melbourne, Sydney and possibly Adelaide.

The third factor, also financial, lay with the commercial interests of the main cricket clubs. Both the MCG and SCG were used for football as well as cricket – and by the 1890s the football crowds were bigger and more frequent than the cricket crowds. Major stands were built and extended, primarily for the football crowds – but it would have taken a remarkably insular cricket club to refuse paying patrons access to empty seats for reasons of social exclusivity. Indeed, the grounds provided much better facilities for the general public than were available in England. In the mid-1890s both the MCG and SCG installed major scoreboards – which gave players' names rather than the English practice of just using numbers (and requiring patrons to pay extra for a programme).[43]

The wider social spread for cricket gave much of the more democratic and more 'Australian' feel to cricket – along with greater scope for the barrackers.[44] Historian Richard Cashman noted:

> Englishmen, particularly some upper class amateurs, could not fathom Australian humour with the earthy, droll and self-deprecating character – it was totally alien to them, which is not surprising given the class, educational and cultural gulf between the worlds of the English amateur and the Australian Outer patron.[45]

However, it is going too far to conclude with Twopeny that 'all ages and classes are interested in it, and not to be interested in it amounts almost to a social crime'.[46] Throughout this period, cricket ticket prices were at least twice those for football, so the cricket crowds were more frequently upper and middle rather than working class. This is supported by contemporary commentary, and subsequent analysis of head gear worn at the SCG in 1911. The members wore top hats and bowlers, with the Ladies' stand described as the 'millinery department next door'. Other stands saw mainly middle-class bowlers and white-collar clerk boaters. It was only in the outer ground, including the Hill, where working-class cloth caps appeared, alongside bowlers and boaters.[47]

The better-off also dominated the massive crowd of 29,123 noted by *The Argus* at one day of a Melbourne Test in the middle of the hard-hit 1890s: 'There appears to be an idea somewhere that there is a Depression here. To the spectator on Saturday at the MCG that word had no meaning.'[48]

Alongside the development of a more democratic, if still restricted, feel to the game in Australia, struggles occurred over the organization of the game – with results which were far from democratic. A stinging 1912 letter from Australian cricket all-rounder and former Test captain Monty Noble to the *Sydney Morning Herald* illustrated the strength of feelings:

> I say that the Board of Control has acted unjustly and dishonestly ... I believe in the principle of Board control, but I am strongly against its present personnel. They have had six years now to bring everybody into line, and to legislate for Australian cricket, and they have absolutely failed. In these six years they have not been credited with one single act of conciliation or forbearance. They have held the pistol of coercion at the heads of the players the whole time, and gradually taken from them all their privileges. Where a happy issue and solution of the present crisis might easily have resulted, we now have the spectacle of a non-representative team going to England.[49]

Struggles were especially evident in the organization of tours between Australia and England. Early tours had been organized by private entrepreneurs or the players themselves. Two hotel owners, Felix Spiers and Christopher Pond, made considerable profits from organizing the first English team to tour Australia in 1861–62, attracting big numbers such as 15,000 for a game in Melbourne.[50]

Private financiers also backed the first Australian tour of England in 1868, by an Aboriginal team from western Victoria. The emphasis on the six-month tour was on entertaining crowds: in breaks in play, players demonstrated skills in running backwards, and throwing spears and boomerangs. But the team won 14 of their 47 matches, and ran the elite Marylebone club close in a two-day match at Lord's. Historian Chris Harte notes that, despite the team's popularity in England, some in Australia 'seemed stung by the fact that a little-known group of Aborigines was holding its own in a game which was imagined to belong with the privileged white population'. Even in an entertainment context there were already preferred visions for sporting Australians.[51] And the players themselves financed the first white Australian team to tour England, in 1878. Players contributed £50 each to the cost, and eventually made a return of £750. This was a fortune for players like Fred 'Demon' Spofforth, who worked at the Bank of New South Wales for £175 per annum.[52]

Such financial success encouraged a plethora of tours in the 1880s, some organized privately, some by local cricket clubs, especially the Melbourne Cricket Club. Faced with this glut of tours, both the Marylebone Cricket Club in England and the new colonial Cricket Associations attempted to impose their authority on the tours. But such efforts cut across the abilities of the players to organize (and benefit from) their games. Successful Australian captain Billy Murdoch brawled with the Victorian Cricket Association over amateur status, and did not join the 1886 team to England. He was not the last player to stop playing because of disagreements over organization and money.

While a short-lived Australasian Cricket Council (ACC) lasted only from 1892 to 1900, a new Australian Board of Control was set up in 1905, initially just by Victoria and New South Wales. The English, who had become increasingly critical of the organizational arrangements in Australia, refused to tour in the 1906–07 season 'until the new Board of Control was truly representative of Australian cricket'.

The ructions with the English were minor compared with the battles with the players after 1905. The new Board insisted on its authority to appoint team managers, and on new financial arrangements, with its expenses and margin paid before any players' shares of profits.[53] Disgruntlement from Monty Noble and others contributed to poor on-field performance. A visiting English team trounced Australia in 1911–12, with captain Pelham Warner saying, 'At the present time Australian cricket is honey-combed with an amount of personal feeling and bitterness that is incredible and this must, to some extent, have militated against our opponents showing their true form.'[54]

Performances got even worse on the 1912 tour of England, with Noble, Trumper and several other leading players refusing to be selected. The weak team set records for poor performance on the field, and alcohol consumption and disorderly conduct off the field. Long before the tour's end the team had been socially ostracized by their hosts, and the tour made an overall loss of £1,286.[55]

Despite such outcomes, the Board maintained its stubborn ways, and its record of poor management. The malaise extended to lower levels of cricket, with financial losses for the NSW CA in 1913 and 1914. Despite confidence that 'cricket in itself is so deeply rooted in the life of the Britisher' that it would survive, *The Sportsman* in September 1915 warned that cricket 'already in a comatose condition, could be killed off by its friends'.[56]

After surviving these pre-war battles over organization, cricket in the 1920s reasserted its role in the national images, setting new records for crowds (and for beating England). Such happy outcomes did not occur for the fourth of the leading sports in the 1880s, professional sculling.

Sculling

Sydney sculler Elias Laycock challenged the visiting world champion, Canadian Edward Hanlan, to a race on 22 May 1884. The day before, Mr Suttor MLA moved in the New South Wales Parliament that the house should adjourn until 7 p.m. on race day, arguing that getting a quorum during the Hanlan-Laycock race would be impossible. Mr Stuart MLA was shocked:

> I trust the House will not accede to the suggestion? With the enormous amount of highly important work which we have before us it would not be creditable to us as a legislative body to adjourn for the purpose of attending a boat-race. I feel sure there would be no lack of members to form a quorum.

Mr Stuart was wrong. He was beaten 21 votes to 16 and Parliament adjourned for the race period.[57] Indeed, the Government had already declared a public holiday for the people of Parramatta, Windsor, Camden and Penrith to celebrate what was billed as the 'championship of the world'.

Hanlan's extended tour of Australia in 1884 emphasized the immense popularity of professional sculling at the time. On 7 June, 20,000 people attended an aquatic carnival at Albert Park, Melbourne, with 10,000 paying to witness a 'Hanlan regatta'. On 16 August, an estimated 100,000 (equal to one-third of Sydney's then population) assembled on the Parramatta River to see 5 to 1 local underdog Bill Beach beat the visiting champion.[58]

There was also big money involved. Later in the 1880s, when Australian champion Henry Searle raced Canadian William O'Connor, Searle won a race prize of £500. While the money compared well with then average annual wages of £100–£150, the prize was totally dwarfed by the estimated £30,000 won on wagers on the event.[59]

Across the world, professional sports and associated betting was gaining, or being given, an unsavoury reputation by the 1890s. Evangelical and middle-class sporting groups, keen to 'clean up' sport, highlighted examples of sharp practice, and extolled the moral virtues of amateur sports.[60] The debates and efforts, as is particularly discussed in the next paper, were present in Australia as well. Despite such efforts, professional sports thrived for longer here – and had a much wider social acceptance – than in the United States or England. This was evident in pedestrianism (professional running, which the next paper discusses in the story of the Stawell Gift), and in the success of sculling until 1910. As late as 1904, the *Sydney Morning Herald* saw benefits from, 'The speculative sportsman, the man who has ... a fairly good idea of merit, but an overwhelming desire to make money. They are necessary for the sport, for they feed it, and work on the policy of live and let live.'[61]

There were three broad reasons why sculling continued to flourish in Australia. The first, in common with other sports, was the audience, with its wealth and time available to follow the sport. The second was the international success of Australian scullers, and the way that was marketed by the syndicates backing the sport. And third was the way amateur sporting officials, responding to the above factors, worked with the professionals to develop the sport.

Australia's first world champion in any sport was sculler Ned Trickett, who won the world title in England on the River Thames on 27 June 1876. From then until 1907, Australia dominated the international scene, providing seven of the nine world champions. Because the championship was organized on a challenge basis, the defending champion had the right to choose the location, and Australia hosted 23 world title races in these years, generally on the Parramatta.[62] From the first, this success met public acclaim. Some 25,000 people met Trickett at Circular Quay on his 1876 return with the world champion's title. As noted in the previous paper, this reaction was overshadowed by the response when Henry Searle died at the end of 1889.

The two key groups who backed sculling carefully nurtured this public image of sporting success. Backers were a central part of the sport: stake money for races was significant, especially compared with typical wages, and the costs of training and travel were also daunting. Without financial support, such costs were well beyond the resources of watermen (Searle), blacksmiths (Beach) or quarryman Trickett.[63]

Between 1876 and 1893, two Australian entrepreneurial groups effectively controlled the sport: one associated with publican John Deeble, and the other pharmacist brothers Thomas and John Spencer.[64] These backers recognized the commercial value of heavy promotion of 'national' Australian champions. They sought favourable media coverage by initiatives such as making space for the press amongst the officials and dignitaries in the umpire's steamer following the sculls.

The backers took other steps to build popular support and broad social respectability. They asked civic and commercial leaders to take on official roles, and gained government assistance to keep the course clear, supervise crowd behaviour and offer cheap rail and tram packages. The backers also welcomed amateur rowing groups into the organization of races. For their part, the amateur groups received income from providing boating and training facilities, and joined in the general celebration of the success of professional sculling champions.

Despite its popularity, sculling faced organizational problems. One was the challenge structure of the sport, highlighted when Henry Searle died in 1889 and it was unclear who was now world champion. More serious problems came with the depression of the 1890s, and the decisions in 1893 of both the Deeble and Spencer cartels to quit sculling and concentrate on proprietary horseracing and trotting. There were no challenge races for four years until 1896, when Australian James Stanbury lost to the Canadian Jacob Gaudaur, on the Thames in England.

Australia once again held the world title from 1901 to 1907, and during this time proposed new governance arrangements for the sport. Interestingly, in view of the disdain which amateur rowing had for sculling in England, two men prominent in amateur sports, John Blackman and Richard Coombes, led the Australian charge advocating a formal structure. As well as the interaction between many amateur rowing clubs and sculling, the two saw benefits for the profile of the sport generally from international success in the professional arena.[65]

The suggestions included a code of conduct for the championship, regular competition, a stop to champions stalling or obstructing challenges, and limits on the power of backers. Despite little support from the English, who considered it absurd that a group of colonials were trying to set the rules for professional sculling, the world championship in March 1907 followed the Australian-devised rules and regulations. Champions and challengers, from the southern and northern hemispheres, adhered to these codes until 1912.

However, the English world champion, Ernest Barry, who reigned from 1912 until 1919, saw financial advantage in reverting to the old challenge rules. He screened his opponents and refused to race off the Thames. The *Sydney Sportsman* complained that Barry expected the colonials to be 'amenable to the "superiority" of the Englishman and subservient to his arrogance'.[66]

From the international successes prior to 1890, and the stirring newspaper editorials and great speeches that accompanied them, an observer at the time might well have wagered that sculling would be one of Australia's pre-eminent sports through the twentieth century. Yet after 1912 sculling went into terminal decline. Australia no longer had a champion to adulate, and as regular organized spectator sports (especially rugby league in NSW) became more popular, audience loyalties shifted.

Sports and the national vision

Towards the end of 1876, the *Sydney Morning Herald* saw Ned Trickett's sculling victory in broad terms:

> Those who wish New South Wales to be well known throughout the United Kingdom …
> will rejoice because this contest will be a better advertisement for the colony than the
> entire edition of any possible Government handbook.[67]

Similarly broad claims have been made about racing and cricket, most notably in establishing a sense of Australian identity. One MP went so far as to comment in 1886 that the Melbourne Cup was 'achieving Federation in one respect'.[68] And when Australia won the 1897–98 Ashes series, *The Bulletin* argued that the victory did 'more to enhance the cause of Australian nationality than could be achieved by miles of erudite essays and impassioned appeal'.[69]

Certainly a powerful image was being created. Cricket victories over England encouraged both massive crowds to games and a wider take up of the sport by participants. The backers of scullers stressed their 'Australian' heroes in marketing forthcoming contests. But earlier papers have demonstrated that people have a range of reasons for coming along to sports events – and that nationalism itself is multi-hued. The accounts of these early sports have noted the differing agendas involved in developing and organizing the sports – and some of the constraints on people wishing to adopt particular agendas.

The next paper provides more detail on the different visions of sport in Australia around 1900, when the new country was already gaining accolades (and also criticisms) for being this 'sporting people'.

Notes

1. Cited in Smart, ed., *Penguin Book of Australian Sporting Anecdotes*, 389–90.
2. *The Argus*, July 27, 1896, cited in Cashman, Headon, and Kinross-Smith, eds., *Oxford Australian Sporting Anecdotes*, 63.
3. Australian Bureau of Statistics (ABS, www.abs.gov.au), *Sports Attendance 2002*, catalogue 4174.0.
4. Markovits and Hellerman, *Offside*.
5. Blainey, *A Game of Our Own*, 85.
6. Ibid., 23.
7. Ibid., 94–5. In an appendix (103–7) Blainey included various sets of rules – from 1859, 1860, 1866, 1874, 1877, and South Australian and Gaelic rules from 1877 and 1889 respectively.
8. Hickie, *They Ran With the Ball*, 70.
9. Ibid., 120ff.
10. Ibid., 120.
11. Ibid., 120ff.
12. Blainey, *A Game of Our Own*, 85.
13. In repeat matches the following year, 6,000 turned out on the Saturday and 5,000 on the Monday.
14. Hickie. *They Ran With the Ball,* 157.
15. Ibid., 157.
16. Blainey, *A Game of Our Own*, 87.
17. Norton, 'Open letter to the AJC'. *Truth*, August 20, 1899.
18. Lemon and Freedman, *History of Australian Thoroughbred Racing*, 312 (Melbourne race numbers), and 402 (Sydney).
19. Harte, *History of Australian Cricket*, 204.
20. Cited by Lemon and Freedman, *History of Australian Thoroughbred Racing*, 413.
21. Ibid., 414.
22. Ibid., 417.
23. Charlton, *Two Flies up a Wall*, 50–1.
24. Victoria Racing Club website (www.vrc.net.au, attendance statistics); ABS Australian Historical Population Statistics (3105.0.65.001) (Melbourne population numbers).
25. Lemon and Freedman, *History of Australian Thoroughbred Racing*, 301–4.
26. Ibid., 348.
27. Ibid., 325–31.
28. Ibid., 313.
29. Ibid., 309.
30. Ibid., 389.
31. Ibid., 290, 403.
32. Hirst, *Sentimental Nation*, 229.
33. Cited by Harte, *History of Australian Cricket*, 94.
34. Ibid., 35.
35. Ibid., 54, 170, 247, 268 and 296. The switch back to six balls in 1979 is noted in Stoddart, *Saturday Afternoon Fever*, 127.
36. Inglis, 'Imperial Cricket', 166.

37. Ibid., 167.
38. Forster, 'Sports, Society and Space'.
39. Cashman, *'Ave a Go, Yer Mug*, 44.
40. Ibid., 12.
41. Cited by Harte, *History of Australian Cricket*, 200.
42. Inglis, 'Imperial Cricket', 166.
43. Cashman, *'Ave a Go, Yer Mug*, 42–3.
44. Ibid., 42.
45. Ibid., 54. Cashman's original refers to 'middle-class' amateurs – English amateurs generally had independent incomes, so 'upper-class' is a better description than 'middle-class' which usually refers to white-collar workers.
46. Twopeny cited by Inglis, 'Imperial Cricket', 163.
47. Sharp, 'A Degenerate Race', 134–7. While Sharp argues for a broad social spread of attendance, his outline of the hats worn indicates the crowd was thoroughly middle or upper class.
48. Cited by Harte, *History of Australian Cricket*, 85.
49. *Sydney Morning Herald*, February 29, 1912, cited by ibid., 254.
50. Harte, *History of Australian Cricket*, 70–1.
51. Ibid., 78–9.
52. This and subsequent discussion of early tours, and the attempts to set up controlling bodies, draws from Harte, *History of Australian Cricket*, 140, 136, 154, 169, 175, 202, 179, 196, 189, 202 and 225.
53. Ibid., 227.
54. Ibid., 252.
55. Ibid., 254, 255 and 264.
56. Cited by McKernan, 'Sport War and Society', 8.
57. Cited in Cashman, Headon, and Kinross-Smith, eds. *The Oxford Book of Australian Sporting Anecdotes*, 36.
58. Adair, 'Two Dots in the Distance', 60.
59. Ibid., 79, n.15.
60. For a good discussion of these developments in the USA, see Vincent, *Rise and Fall of American Sport*.
61. *Sydney Morning Herald*, July 30, 1904, cited by Adair, 'Two Dots in the Distance', 73.
62. Cashman, *Paradise of Sport*, 46.
63. Scullers' occupations from the Rowing Australia website: www.rowingaustralia.com.au/athletes_history2.html.
64. This and subsequent discussion draws mainly on Ripley, 'Golden Age of Australian Professional Sculling'.
65. As well as Ripley, 'Golden Age of Australian Professional Sculling', see Lane and Jobling, 'For Honour and Trophies'.
66. *Sydney Sportsman*, June 9, 1920, 1, quote cited by Ripley, 'Golden Age of Australian Professional Sculling', 880.
67. *Sydney Morning Herald*, November 10, 1876, cited by Adair, 'Two Dots in the Distance', 57.
68. Lemon and Freedman, *History of Australian Thoroughbred Racing*, 327.
69. *The Bulletin*, March 19, 1898, cited by (amongst others) Mandle, 'Cricket and Australian Nationalism', 241.

References

Adair, Daryl. 'Two Dots in the Distance: Professional Sculling as a Mass Spectacle in New South Wales 1876–1907'. *Sporting Traditions* 9, no. 1 (November 1992): 52–83.
Blainey, Geoffrey. *A Game of Our Own*. Melbourne: Information Australia, 1990.
Cashman, Richard. *'Ave a Go, Yer Mug': Australian Cricket Crowds from Larrikin to Ocker*. Sydney: Collins, 1984.
Cashman, Richard, David Headon, and Graeme Kinross-Smith, eds. *The Oxford Book of Australian Sporting Anecdotes*. Oxford: Oxford University Press, 1993.
Cashman, Richard. *Paradise of Sport: The Rise of Organised Sport in Australia*. Melbourne: Oxford University Press, 1995.

Charlton, Peter. *Two Flies up a Wall: The Australian Passion for Gambling.* North Ryde NSW: Methuen Haynes, 1987.

Forster, Clive. 'Sports, Society and Space: The Changing Geography of Country Cricket in South Australia'. *Sporting Traditions* 2, no. 2 (May 1986): 23–47.

Harte, Chris. *A History of Australian Cricket.* London: Andre Deutsch, 1993.

Hickie, Thomas. *They Ran With the Ball: How Rugby Football began in Australia.* Melbourne: Longman Cheshire, 1993.

Hirst. John. *The Sentimental Nation: the Making of the Australian Commonwealth.* Melbourne: Oxford University Press, 2000.

Inglis, K.S. 'Imperial Cricket and Test Matches between Australia and England 1877–1900'. In *Sport in History: The Making of Modern Sporting History,* ed. Richard Cashman and Michael McKernan, 148–79. Queensland: University of Queensland Press, 1979.

Lane, David, and Ian Jobling. 'For Honour and Trophies: Amateur Rowing in Australia, 1888–1912'. *Sporting Traditions* 4, no. 1 (November 1987): 2–26.

Lemon, Andrew, and Harold Freedman. *History of Australian Thoroughbred Racing Volume 2: The Golden Years 1862 to 1939.* Melbourne: Southbank Communications, 1990.

McKernan, Michael. 'Sport War and Society in Australia 1914–18'. In *Sport in History: The Making of Modern Sporting History,* ed. Richard Cashman and Michael McKernan, 1–20. Queensland: University of Queensland Press, 1979.

Mandle, W.F. 'Cricket and Australian Nationalism in the Nineteenth Century'. *Journal of the Royal Australian Historical Society* 59, no. 4 (December 1973): 225–46.

Markovits, Andrei, and Steven Hellerman. *Offside: Soccer and American Exceptionalism.* Princeton NJ: Princeton University Press, 2001.

Ripley, Stewart. 'The Golden Age of Australian Professional Sculling or Skullduggery?' *International Journal of the History of Sport* 22, no. 5 (September 2005): 867–82.

Sharp, Martin. 'A Degenerate Race: Cricket and Rugby Crowds in Sydney 1890–1912' *Sporting Traditions* 4, no. 2 (May 1988): 134–49.

Smart, Richard, ed. *The Penguin Book of Australian Sporting Anecdotes.* Ringwood Vic: Penguin Books, 1996.

Stoddart, Brian. *Saturday Afternoon Fever.* North Ryde NSW: Angus and Robertson, 1986.

Vincent, Ted. *The Rise and Fall of American Sport: Mudville's Revenge.* 2nd ed. Lincoln NE: University of Nebraska Press, 1994.

Visions of Australian sport in 1900

Peering through her drawing room window shortly before lunch, the benevolent old suburban lady saw a shivering man in a ruined overcoat ... Taking a ten-shilling note from a heavy beaded bag, she scribbled on a piece of paper the words *Cheer up*, put both in an envelope and told the maid to give it to the outcast for her.

While the family was at dinner that evening a ring sounded at the front door. Argument followed in the hall between a hoarse male voice and that of the maid.

– 'You can't come in. They're at dinner.'
– 'I'd *rather* come in, miss. Always like for to fix these things up in person.'
– 'You can't come.'

Another moment and the needy wayfarer was in the dining room. He carefully laid five filthy £1 notes on the table before his benefactress. 'There you are, mum', he said with a rough salute. 'Cheer Up won all right. I'm mostly on the corner, race days, as your cook will tell you; an' I'd like to say that if any uv your friends ...'[1]

Many accounts of Australian identity and sports-madness, like those suggested by Greg Ansley and Nick Afka Thomas in Paper 1, have based explanations on particular factors, such as the amount of sunshine or a desire to eradicate the supposed convict stain. But, as the misunderstanding between the unwitting punter and the bookie illustrates, one situation can mean widely different things to different people. Paper 6 documented varying views of key national symbols, and Paper 8 showed how differing visions of what sports should be affected the organization and development of major sports in Australia. This paper builds on these to look at broad visions of Australian sport.

A good place to assess the differing visions of sport is 1901, when the new Commonwealth of Australia started, a federation of the six colonies. Federation itself had a somewhat rocky road. From the first Constitutional Convention, in 1890, there were differing ideas of how the new country should be established. A key disagreement was between Protectionist Victoria and Free Trade New South Wales. There were also differing ideas on the extent of the new Commonwealth: in 1890 many expected New Zealand to join the federation, and few thought that Western Australia would take part.[2]

The development of sport in the early years of the new country also reflected the interaction between different visions. The first part of this paper outlines four broad visions of sport in Australia around 1900, and how they reflected different social backgrounds and orientations. One of the key differences in visions of sport through to

1970 was between amateurism and professionalism, and the paper also looks at the early patterns here. It also discusses how an iconic Australian event – the professional athletics of the Stawell Gift – managed to be a success in this environment. The concluding section then discusses how the very differing perspectives of the 'benevolent old suburban lady' and the 'shivering man in a ruined overcoat' could possibly combine to give an overall image of Australia as a sporting nation.

International comparisons

Previous papers have shown how useful international comparisons can be in giving a background to events in Australia. Two international illustrations help set the scene for the interactions of social visions and sport – one drawn from basketball in the United States, the other from rugby in New Zealand.

In the United States in the 1850s, the Young Men's Christian Association opposed almost all sports, along with dancing, card playing and vaudeville shows. The YMCA considered these activities 'distinctly worldly in their associations and unspiritual in their influence', and therefore 'utterly inconsistent with our professions as disciples of Christ'. A key concern was the widespread gambling associated with sports.[3]

But 40 years later, both the image of sports and the attitude of the YMCA had changed. Many sports still had a heavy association with gambling. However, other sports had become more organized, and amateur sports had grown, with both these projecting a more 'wholesome' image. In addition, the spread of Saturday afternoon spectator sport, and the massive coverage it received in the papers, meant it was a social phenomenon that could not simply be ignored.

The YMCA's agenda had also changed. Along with other churches, it had become interested in spreading a social gospel, especially into inner city neighbourhoods where church attendance was low. As part of these efforts, the YMCA encouraged sport, especially gymnastics, to involve young people. When gymnastics proved little of a draw-card for the YMCA in Springfield, Massachusetts, instructor James Naismith invented the rudiments of basketball on 1 December 1891. Encouraged by the game's immediate popularity, the YMCA quickly spread it through its organization in other cities.

Similarly, the development of rugby union in New Zealand reflected differences in attitudes towards sport. New Zealand historian James Belich traced three strong elements in the development of rugby in New Zealand around 1900. The game started from the upper-class game played at the British public schools. However, as with Sydney in the 1880s, the upper class in New Zealand was neither sufficiently large nor socially dominant to totally run a mass game. A strong second element in New Zealand was the rough and ready sport played in mining areas, railway construction camps, and some farming areas with many young labourers. The sport played in these environments was hard, fast, frequently violent and strongly linked to drinking and gambling. In marked contrast, the third factor was associated with middle-class moral evangelism, which, like the YMCA, increasingly saw sport as a means to a healthy, and preferably drink-free, body.

Rugby itself was fairly chaotic in its early years, and not all clubs affiliated with the NZ Rugby Union until the 1920s. In the gradual development and enforcement of rules and organization, Belich discerned

a three-cornered contest, 1880s–1920s, between genteel, moralist and popularist rugby, with victory going wherever two opposed one. Gentility and moralism allied against rowdiness and full professionalism. Popularism and moralism allied against social exclusiveness and in favour of improving the game as a spectacle. Muscular gentility and populism allied in favour of robustness, including a persistent degree of violence.[4]

Thus, the way these sports developed reflected the agendas of different groups, and how those agendas interacted with changing social conditions.[5] In tracing such developments in Australian sport, the starting point is documenting what the various visions of sport were.

The three elevens

'Reginald' in the *Melbourne Sportsman* penned a wonderful description of the epic finish to the 1903 Melbourne Cup. Wakeful, well ahead in the Flemington straight despite carrying one of the heaviest weights ever in the Cup (10 stone or 63.5 kg), was run down in the last 100 yards by Lord Cardigan (carrying 6 stone 8 pounds, or 41.5 kg). Still catching his breath, 'Reginald' wrote:

> Those who had the great good fortune to be there on Tuesday can never forget it, even if they live to be a hundred. It stirred the very soul, it lifted us for a spell to a height that only the best impulses can rise to. We came down but there was not one of us who did not feel the better of that sight of a lifetime.
>
> It is this sort of thing that at the time puts the genuine sportsman above the ordinary mortal. Such moments are worth living for, and worth remembering after they have passed.[6]

For many, the length of time at the giddy heights was enhanced by victory over the shivering man in the ruined overcoat. But for others, the genuine sportsman stood apart from the ordinary mortal for quite different reasons. One such was Alfred Deakin, in his 1908 speech at the Australian Football Jamboree. Deakin lauded

> not merely the physical training, but the discipline of sport, its effect upon character and courage, its prominence as an educational process were valuable ... and when the tocsin sounds the call to arms not the last, but the first, to acknowledge it will be those who have played and played well, the Australian game of football, before they play the Australian game of nation-making and nation-preserving to stand by the old land.[7]

Such differences in visions of sport, as an experience in itself, or as a pathway to higher things, were related to other social and political attitudes. Indeed, Deakin in another speech reached for sporting metaphor to explain the shifting alliances in the Parliament of the new Commonwealth. The Parliament then comprised members of three groups: Free Traders (particularly strong in middle- and upper-class Sydney); Protectionists (especially associated with middle-class Melbourne) and the Australian Labor Party (based on working-class votes). As each group had similar numbers of MPs, no one had a clear majority, and the interactions in Parliament could be complex. Deakin explained it thus, on 1 February 1904:

> Ask yourselves the question in machinery with which you are acquainted. What a game of cricket you would have if there were three elevens in the field instead of two, and one of those elevens sometimes playing on one side, sometimes on the other, and sometimes for itself.[8]

Deakin's three cricketing elevens broadly mirrored three strains of thought in early Australia described by historian John Hirst as, respectively, imperial federationists, loyal nationalists and independent nationalists.[9] In terms of strong visions for Australia's future, a fourth eleven, watching predominantly from the Ladies' Stand, was the temperance movement. The groups broadly overlapped on a variety of issues, including sport, with Deakin's three elevens.

As Deakin described it for Parliamentary politics, the relationship between the groups was often fluid. Further, the descriptions of key interests are broad summaries, and there was considerable variation. Nonetheless, an appreciation of the differing views gives a more accurate feeling of the dynamics than one national stereotype does.

Many of the differing attitudes of the 'three elevens' on sport have already been illustrated in the accounts of football, racing and sculling in the previous paper. The conservatives were the most concerned about replicating English sporting patterns, including class-oriented amateurism, as we will see below. They were also the most likely to see sport as demonstrating that the British stock was indeed flourishing in Australia.

The Liberals' agenda was much more socially inclusive. In sport this was a more conducive environment for the broad social reach of Australian rules than the socially exclusive structure in Sydney that rugby had prior to 1880, or rugby union had after 1907.

Working-class fans were much more likely to follow sports that, in Belich's words above, were 'hard, fast, frequently violent and strongly linked to drinking and gambling'. They were keen on spectacle, and not at all fussed about professional and semi-professional sports.

The fourth eleven had influence because Australia shared with New Zealand and many recently settled parts of the United States an especially strong temperance movement. In 1885, more than 45,000 Victorian women signed a temperance petition presented to Parliament. The petition, on a roll of paper half a kilometre long, denounced the liquor traffic 'as the most prolific source of broken hearts, ruined homes and blighted lives'.[10] As well as presenting petitions, the temperance organizations fought for female suffrage – which they expected would give them prohibition.[11] In 1902, Australia became the second country to give women the vote, following New Zealand in 1893.[12]

The rise of temperance supporters, and the prospect of women's suffrage, alarmed some conservative stalwarts. Chief Justice of Victoria, Sir John Madden, declared in 1895 that 'women's suffrage would abolish soldiers, war, racing, hunting, football, cricket, and all manly games'.[13] A direct impact on sport had already occurred in the 1880s in South Australia, where temperance supporters joined with other anti-gambling groups to ban racing. As discussed in Paper 8, the outright ban was soon reversed – but racing resumed with much stricter controls over gambling.

The group's attitude to sport was, as with the YMCA discussed above, along the lines of the muscular Christians in England, who

> sought to evangelise through the medium of sport. Sport gave them a point of contact for conversion, but more than that, sport was character-forming as it taught self-disciple and team spirit and it offered a counteraction to gambling, drink and crime.[14]

The social dynamics of these four elevens can be seen in the debates over amateur and professional sport, to which we now turn. One distinguishing difference in Australia compared with the United States and Britain was the longevity of professional running

Table 1.   Key orientations of main social groups, 1900.

Group	Conservatives	Liberals	Temperance	Workers
Attitude to Empire	imperial federationists	loyal nationalists	imperialist	independent nationalist
Vision for Australia	Vibrant and loyal part of Empire	Social laboratory	Tackling scourges of old world – drink and gambling	'Working man's paradise'
Typical location	Especially upper-class Sydney	Especially upper middle-class Melbourne	Middle and lower middle-class, esp. SA and Victoria	Working class generally, esp. Sydney and Melbourne
Sports ethos	English amateurism	Modern amateurism, some payments	Anti-gambling, anti-drinking, amateurism	Professional sport, gambling
Typical sports	Cricket, racing, rugby union	Australian Rules, racing, cricket	Amateur athletics, later tennis	Aust Rules, rugby league, racing, boxing

in this country, and the central focus for this, the Stawell Gift, is discussed in the following section.

Amateur and professional

In 1958, Australian runner Herb Elliott won gold in both the 880 yards and the mile at the 1958 Commonwealth Games in Cardiff, Wales. After he set a new world record of 3 min. 54.5 sec. for the mile on 6 August 1958, Elliott was offered the equivalent of £100,000 to run professionally in the United States. He declined, keeping his amateur status. Later that year, a Gallup poll asked, 'Was he right to do this?' Men were evenly divided on the matter. Women, however, were adamant – 70% of those with an opinion supported Elliott, with comments such as, 'he did an excellent thing for sport in turning down the professional offer'.[15]

In the late 1950s, there was clearly strong popular support among especially middle-class Australians for the ethos of amateur sport. Many would have agreed with the description *Sydney Mail* writer John Blackman penned on 24 July 1897:

> Amateur sport was good, wholesome and worthwhile, it imbued its participants with the traits of fair play, modesty in victory, dignity in defeat and sportsmanship – all essential elements in the development of character. On the other hand, professional sport was primitive, unworthy, and dangerous, as it was associated with gambling, and was open to cheating, bribery and corruption. The professional, motivated by reward alone, could not hope to aspire to the ideals of the amateur.[16]

Yet there was often a gap between the image of the lofty amateur goals and the reality of how amateurism worked[17] – which was typically with a strong air of social exclusivity. In England, the rules of the Amateur Rowing Association (and some other amateur bodies) excluded from amateur status anyone 'who is or has been by trade or employment for wages a mechanic, artisan, or labourer, or engaged in any menial duty'.[18] And in the United States Ivy League colleges included sport as part of their image of 'virile, masculine, red-blooded he-men' favoured in their admission policies from the 1920s. The explicit goal was to maximize enrolments from elite Protestant private schools, and reduce the numbers of especially Jewish students from public high schools in New York City – who were succeeding in the Ivy League entrance exams.[19]

Such exclusivity is further demonstrated by the fact that, whatever the claimed ideals, early amateurism was certainly not about the best athletic achievements. This is clear from comparing the amateur times for the 100 metres at the Olympic Games with equivalent times at the Stawell Gift (discussed in more detail below) and from other professional runners.[20]

Stawell Gift times were frequently better than the Olympic record for 100 metres until the 1930s. The best times set by Australian professional runners such as Charlie Samuels, Jack Donaldson and later John Stoney (and by American professional Richard Williams) were significantly better than anything achieved at the Olympics before the late 1960s.

But such was the strength of the amateur myth that, for many middle-class observers, professional runners may as well not have existed. As noted in paper 2, when the *Sydney Morning Herald* asked why Australian women runners had done so much better than the men at the Melbourne 1956 Olympics, the article did not even mention that the best male runners were professional and hence not competing. In the United

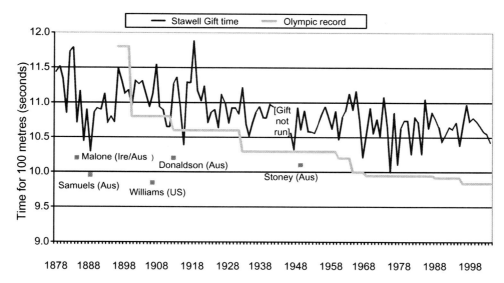

Figure 1.   100 metres Olympic record, and equivalent Stawell Gift and professional time.

States, the remarkable feats of professional runner Richard Williams were airbrushed from history. Before historian Ted Vincent rediscovered them in 1981, their last previous mention had been in 1931.[21]

Any definition of amateur in the first half of the twentieth century had an element of social exclusivity, orienting competition towards those able to afford to compete without payment. But the actual definitions used varied in the strength of their social exclusion, from excluding paid athletes in that sport, to those who had competed against professional athletes, to the manual labourer definition applied by the English Amateur Rowing Association. Definitions differed between sports in Australia, and there was considerable debate in particular sports on the rules.[22]

The two most popular spectator football codes at the turn of the century – rugby and Australian football – both denounced professionalism in 1890. Rugby allowed no compensation for players for time lost from work or injuries, or recompense for equipment or travel. Every expense, at the level of public acknowledgement anyway, came from the pockets of the players. By contrast, Australian football provided players with medical fees, expenses for travelling, training and loss of time from work. An amateur Australian Rules footballer in Melbourne may well have been disqualified from amateur rugby union in Sydney.[23]

Disputes occurred in athletics. Australian Bernard Wise, while at Oxford in 1880, played an important role in the formation of the (British) Amateur Athletic Association. After his return to Sydney, Wise in 1887 turned down an offer to be vice-president of the new NSWAAA because he 'could not agree with the actions of the association in drawing distinctions between labourers and mechanics in the amateur qualification'.[24]

Some of the fiercest battles over amateur definitions in Australia occurred in the 1890s in rowing. The NSW Rowing Association, following the English tradition of gentlemen amateurs, objected to any 'manual labourers', but was quite happy to allow competitors who had won cash prizes in the aristocratic pursuits of sailing and racing. In contrast, the Victorian Rowing Association was happy to include manual labourers, so long as they observed general rules of amateurism, of not competing for money, nor being employed in a rowing-related occupation.[25]

Rowing may have been particularly precious about this. Swimmer Frank Beaurepaire won medals in the 1908 Olympics, and then again in 1920 and 1924. While controversy over his status had disqualified him in 1912, Beaurepaire was considered an amateur in 1920 and 1924 despite having received a £250 publicity grant from the Victorian Government, and a job with that government promoting swimming.[26]

Even stronger hypocrisy existed in cricket with the class distinction between amateur 'gentlemen' and professional 'players'. In 1896, professional cricketers in England had a pay dispute with the county cricket teams. Newspaper the *Guardian* supported the professionals, noting, 'it is an open secret that, if they are not paid openly, allowances are made for "expenses", which leave the humble but necessary "pro" far in the rear'.[27] 'Shamateur' English cricket star W.G. Grace successfully demanded £1,500 as 'expenses' to tour Australia in 1873/74 when the professionals were paid only £170, and 18 years later he obtained £3,000 for another tour.[28]

The class bias of the amateur/professional division was also evident in the split in rugby in Sydney in 1907 into union and league. By 1900, rugby was still run by the upper crust socially conservative groups discussed in the last paper. However, it had become a mass spectator sport, and many fans and players were now working class.[29]

Many players complained of the 'intransigence of rugby officials', especially when, despite healthy coffers, authorities refused to pay medical bills for injured sportsmen. A breakaway group founded the NSWRL in August 1907, and started club league in 1908 with strong working-class, as well as ALP and Catholic, support. The union authorities took a very hard line against professionalism, banning anyone associated with league.[30]

In its early stages, union seemed to weather the professional challenge. Both codes sent teams to England in 1908, but the league Kangaroos tour was a playing and financial disaster, with a largest crowd for any match at 2,000. In contrast, the union Wallabies attracted a peak 22,000 spectators, and won an Olympic gold medal in London.

At the end of the 1909 season, however, disaster struck for union. Hotelier and sporting entrepreneur James Joynton Smith offered members of the 1909 Wallabies team substantial sums to switch codes, and in the 'great defection', most of the Wallabies moved to League. *The Bulletin*, no admirer of rugby league, was critical of Smith's coup, declaring that 'it is reducing football to private enterprise and making it a wild scramble for cash'.[31] The defection reversed the fortunes of both codes. League gate receipts almost doubled from 1909 to 1910, and increased further by 1913. Union receipts, which had been similar to league in 1909, were less than 10% of its competitor's by 1913. Union had to relinquish leases on major sporting grounds (most were taken over by league) and was left with rump pockets of strength, in some schools, and in country NSW.

A decade earlier, south of the border, a less acrimonious split occurred. In 1896, eight of the stronger rules clubs broke away from the Victorian Football Association (VFA) to form the more professional and commercial Victorian Football League (VFL).[32]

Rules had attracted major crowds in Melbourne throughout the prosperous 1880s, with glamour team South Melbourne regularly attracting crowds of up to 25,000. Gambling was also prevalent, and despite the supposedly amateur status of the game, under-the-counter payments to players were common by the end of the decade.[33]

The depression of the 1890s hit hard at revenues from both crowds and wealthy patrons. With some weaker clubs struggling financially, VFA secretary Thomas

Marshall, a strong supporter of amateurism, also saw an opportunity to tighten observance of the amateur rules. In 1896 he proposed central control of club finances, allowing each club only £5 per week for administration, well below the gate receipts of more popular clubs. The bigger clubs, after reaching agreement with Collingwood, which had the biggest supporter base of any club, announced a new Victorian Football League immediately after the 1896 Grand Final.

The VFL was strong from inception, both because it had the stronger teams and it moved to a more attractive, free-flowing game. A new knock-out finals system between the top four teams rapidly won media and crowd interest – after 1902 VFL Grand Finals at the MCG consistently attracted crowds over 30,000. Another feature of VFL crowds was the gender makeup. Around 1900, women were some 40% of the average football crowd, 'proportionately more than of any other football code in the world'.[34]

Measures to attract crowds were also important in the history of the Stawell Gift, Australia's premier professional running event.

Stawell Gift

On 17 April 1981, Good Friday evening, bookies and punters gathered in the Army Drill Hall in Stawell, an old gold mining town in western Victoria. Continuing a 40-year-old tradition, the Call of the Card placed bets on the athletics races held over the Easter weekend – including the Stawell Gift.[35]

A raid by the Melbourne gaming squad disrupted the event. Despite its tradition, the Call of the Card had always been illegal. However, Stawell Athletic Club secretary Hank Neil was not too perturbed by the raid: 'We've been going for more than 100 years … it will take more than what happened last night to wipe us out'.[36]

When some people were subsequently fined for illegal gambling, media statewide complained about the 'oppression of Stawell'. Some 18 months after the raid, legislation was introduced into parliament to legalize the Calling of the Card. All parties supported the legislation, most agreeing with the MP who argued,

> It is appropriate that Parliament should legalize what has been traditional practice prior to the Stawell Gift … It is a bit like two-up – there are certain institutions that are always present in the community and the law sometimes catches up with them and sometimes does not.[37]

The disdain for legal niceties was long part of the celebrated culture of the Gift, a handicap foot race over 120 metres (originally 130 yards). Historian of the Gift John Perry summed up the requirements of a 'legendary win at Stawell': 'cunning tactics and a strategy based on camouflage and dissimulation. But even a straight out victory is not enough – the bookies should be taken for a ride as well.'[38] Such images are a world away from those the amateur sporting groups and the wowsers wanted to see as the image of sporting Australia. But they certainly resonated with a large sector of the population, especially among working-class people in regional Australia.

One such legendary win, with its tales of subterfuge and the larrikin spirit of the Gift, was that of Bill Howard in 1966.[39] Jack King, a trainer in North East Victoria, had spotted Howard, a teenage local footy player, two years earlier. King was well versed in Stawell Gift tricks, having trained winners in 1952 and 1954. Howard started an 18-month training programme on King's farm, on a cinders track that replicated the exact gradient of the rise at Stawell. Secrecy was tight, with Howard running in only five races prior to Stawell, and being hidden away in a horse box on an occasion when a former Gift winner visited the farm. And the team put around rumours that Howard drank heavily and only attended training occasionally – images far from the teetotaller who never missed a training session. When the team went to Stawell, Howard was initially introduced as a visiting nephew of one trainer. All the ruses worked – the stable plunged on the 100-1 odds on Howard, who started on a favourable handicap of 8.75 yards. His first prize was $1,700, and Howard also shared in the stable's punting earnings of $6,000. The following year, further subterfuge was tried in lead-up events to Stawell, with Howard running in old shoes in several, and drinking as much water as possible just before one to slow him down. To little effect however: Howard was still at short odds at the Call of the Card, and his stable won only $400 from the bookies for his second success. The wins changed Howard's life, enabling him to pay off most of a house, and developing confidence he later claimed helped set him up for life. The wins over both handicappers and the bookies added further to the mystique of Stawell.

It is surprising such mystique should find home in a town of 6,100 people. Yet the Stawell Gift, with a first prize of $32,000 in 2005, and a total of $100,000 in prize money, has held this title of Australia's richest foot race for most of its 125 years.[40]

Professional foot races were very popular across Australia in the late nineteenth century, especially in the rough and ready environment of gold mining towns. In country Victoria, many towns maintained 'Gift' handicap races with prize money and even more to be made from betting.[41] Yet Stawell's Gift flourished while many others fell by the wayside. To survive, the Gift had to overcome three major challenges – changes in the mining environment, in the gambling laws and in its own social status and finances.

The Stawell Gift, held each Easter since 1878, was initially a lesser event than the Stawell Miners' Sports, held each year since October 1873. The Sports were successful both in raising money for the Miners' Accident Society, and as venues for politicians addressing the crowds.[42] However, after success for 30 years, attendances at the Miners' Sports started to dwindle after 1900. The event was hit hard both by increasing social division between radical unionism and entrenched conservatism, and by new restrictions from the 1906 Gaming Suppression Bill.[43]

The second major threat to the Gift came from such measures to limit gambling. In 1932 the State Government further tightened the laws, to crack down on regional 'sports meetings' that were little more than crowds betting with bookies on metropolitan races that day. The legislation prohibited betting at any sports meeting held within a municipal district in a city or town.

Both Stawell and neighbouring Ararat up until then were incorporated as 'boroughs'. Ararat, under the stewardship of an anti-betting Mayor, sought 'town' status in the 1930s, and the Ararat Athletic Club decided to close down and abandon its Gift races. Stawell, in contrast, decided to shelve any town aspirations, and remained a borough into the 1950s.[44]

Surviving both these challenges indicated the strength of the third issue – the importance of a strong social status in Stawell. By 1982 most people agreed with the Parliamentary comment: 'undoubtedly the Stawell Gift has meant a great deal to the community and to the people of Stawell'.[45] That 'great deal' did not just happen – and in fact the Gift came close to folding in the 1890s. From the start, the Club tried to keep its image clean, passing a resolution in 1879 that 'the judges and starter shall not have any bets with any person on the result of the races'.[46] Despite this, rumours often spread, and in April 1895 the local newspaper was disparaging, asking, whether Easter cannot be turned to better account in Stawell than it is at present. Professional pedestrianism monopolizes the occasion with us, and of all sports this is the most discredited and discreditable. Professional running has become a by-word for all that is vicious and dishonorable, until it stinks in the nostrils of all honest sportsmen.[47]

Such disdain compounded financial woes from both the 1890s depression, and an expensive legal battle over the awarding of handicaps for the 1893 Gift.[48]

The Club took a number of measures to restore both its financial health and social image. The Committee held a profitable Recovery Meeting in 1896, and Committee members guaranteed the remaining debts themselves. The Club also moved the event to Central Park, in the middle of Stawell in 1898, and tried to attract a broader audience. This move specifically involved moving up market, and appealing more to women. The Gift was re-positioned as a social event, with the local newspaper starting to 'publish detailed lists of how the fair sex had been bonneted, beribboned and begowned'. By 1904 the main newspaper story emphasized that ladies could attend the Gift without having to go close to the bookies' ring.

Once the Club's finances improved, from 1904 it contributed generously towards town charities. Stawell's Mayor welcomed the move: 'no longer could it be said that the club only brought in parasitic loafers, but through its charitable acts it could be shown that it was actively engaged in serving community interest'.[49] Overseeing these changes was a quite remarkable committee. The Club's centenary history noted that the seven members of the Committee organizing the Diamond Jubilee Gift in 1937 had, between them, aggregated 253 years of service to the Club.[50]

As well as its clever moves to broaden the social appeal of the Gift, this Committee established a reputation for tough and honest administration. The Gift attracted visiting sports officials, complimenting leading standards in the athletic world.[51] A 1931 article in *The Referee* described the 'big professional meeting' as having 'the endorsement of the public as the land's most popular athletic carnival'.[52]

With exploits such as Bill Howard's adding zest to proceedings, the Gift continued to flourish in the post-war years. While still other Gifts and meetings eventually closed, the Stawell Gift managed to survive until made secure by the revival of professional athletics and big sponsorship money in the 1970s. General Motors Holden was the first big name sponsor of the meeting in 1975, and Australia Post now sponsors the meet, contributing to the total $100,000 in prize money.[53]

As well as the ruses of runners and trainers, the Gift attracted some great stories among the punters. In 1979 two Scots on their way to Stawell to back runner George McNeill provided 'an eye-opener for most drinkers' in the Southern Cross Hotel in Melbourne when one of the punters withdrew $5,000 in $50 notes out from his underpants,

'For God's sake, man' one of the drinkers exclaimed, 'Why in hell's name do you store your money down there?'

'I've never had anything stolen from there yet' the Scotsman smiled. 'We're off to Stawell tomorrow ... we want to make sure we've got enough money'.[54]

Constructing a national image

The image of pub patrons securing their gambling money in their underpants would have struck horror into temperance hearts, on all sorts of grounds. Yet, as discussed in this paper, a number of different visions of sport have long existed in Australia. Which complicates any effort to move from the above four broad visions of identity and sport towards an overall Australian image.

To some extent, this is a matter of the 'spin'. Each alternate vision could claim to be the 'true' vision for the country, with the others misguided, misleading, or even (especially in the tempests of the First World War) traitorous. And it was quite possible for each different group to claim to its own satisfaction that it had the 'real' vision.

But just noting such competing claims does not help explain the overall national image. Previous papers have emphasized that national identities and images are complex and multi-faceted, so it is possible for differing aspects to co-exist to some extent. But those images have also changed over time, so it is worthwhile asking how much the different aspects affected the whole.

As noted above, New Zealand historian James Belich suggested coalitions between different groups contribute significantly to the development of rugby. In Australia, certain events propelled different coalitions together on some occasions. For example, temperance groups in Victoria had long been pushing for tough anti-gambling legislation, but had found themselves stymied by the tolerance for gambling amongst both the upper crust and the working class. They achieved success in the 1906 Gaming Suppression Bill, in the wake of widespread disgust at the lynching of bookmaker Donald McLeod at Flemington on Grand National Steeplechase day. McLeod had defaulted on his debts and was trampled and kicked to death by an infuriated crowd on the Flemington flat.[55]

Yet even this Bill showed signs of compromise between different interests. It banned betting clubs, restricted betting to racecourses and imposed Government licensing on the racecourses. However, it left the Victorian Racing Club in control of registered racing, and the VRC used its increased market strength to both extend an admission charge to the flat in 1913, and to develop a new 10,000 seat stand at Flemington.

While such events could form critical trigger points, more generally the influence of particular visions on the overall image and vision reflected social, and at times political, strength. Paper 8 noted distinguishing features in Australia in the early development of football, racing, cricket and sculling, compared with the UK. Those often reflected differences between the countries, most notably the less entrenched social strength of the upper class, and the financial strength given to more popular and working-class sports involvement from the higher standard of living in Australia.

Especially from the 1880s, mass spectator sports promised burgeoning finances. While they could pursue their own particular agendas, sports administrators had to keep at least one eye on what their audience and market wanted. In the 1880s the upper crust rugby organizers in Sydney had to accept changes to make the game more attractive to audiences. And when the organizers of the Stawell Gift faced financial troubles in the 1890s, they made a conscious decision to increase the event's appeal to middle-class spectators.

Such strength was also evident in such coverage as *The Referee* gave in a lengthy April 1931 article celebrating the 'historic, thrilling contests of ... champion athletes' at Stawell. Richard Coombes, President of the Amateur Athletic Association of New South Wales from 1894 to 1935, was editor of *The Referee* for several years. Coombes was a staunch imperialist, and vigilant in insisting on amateur rules.[56] In Britain or the United States such a pedigree would have seen the journal giving scant, if any, space to professional athletics. But in Australia, broad social support for professional racing meant that journals such as *The Referee* could not hope to maintain their leading status and circulation if they did not cover the Stawell and other Gifts.

The strength of sports audiences in Australia either limited or forced compromises on some visions of sport that were stronger overseas. But, as discussed in Paper 8, proponents of those visions had their successes as well, notably in the way sports were increasingly organized. Demographic changes also had an impact: as Australia's population grew, and became more settled, the proportion of single young men in the 15–40 age group dwindled. Some of the market for gambling and more violent sport dwindled with them, encouraging those who wished to 'improve' sports through greater organization and control. The strongest efforts to tie sports to such agendas came in the First World War. That story is the subject of our next paper.

Notes

1. Lawrence, *Kangaroo*, 277 – the original story was apparently from *The Bulletin*.
2. Hirst, *Sentimental Nation*.
3. Vincent, *Rise and Fall of American Sport*, especially 227.
4. Belich, *Paradise Reforged*, 382.
5. Other historians have provided similar analyses in other countries – see for example Nielsen, 'Welfare-nationalism?' for some of the dynamics in sport in Scandinavia in the 1920s and 1930s.
6. Cited by Lemon and Freedman. *History of Australian Thoroughbred Racing*, 407.
7. Deakin's Speech 'The Australasian Game' at the 1908 Football Jubilee was reported in *The Argus*, 29 August 1908, 17.
8. Deakin, 'Three Elevens', included in Warhaft, ed., *Well May We Say,* 147.
9. Hirst, *Sentimental Nation*, 67.
10. Blainey, *Black Kettle and Full Moon*, 353.
11. Dunstan, *Wowsers*, 11, and the discussion in Blainey, *Black Kettle and Full Moon.*
12. Some US frontier states led the way with women's votes: the territory of Wyoming, in 1869, and Colorado, in 1893. South Australia was the first colony in Australia, in 1894.
13. Quoted by MacCallum, *Political Anecdotes*, 49–50, citing Clark, *History of Australia.*
14. Vamplew, *Pay Up and Play the Game*, 51.
15. Gallup poll summary Oct.–Nov. 1958.
16. Cited by Cashman, *Paradise of Sport*, 60.
17. For several accounts of the different patterns and complexities of amateurism in the UK, see the special issue of *Sport in History* 26, no.3 (December 2006).
18. Vamplew, *Pay Up and Play the Game*, 8 – the full rules are reprinted in 303, Appendix 2b,.
19. Karabel, *The Chosen,* and see review in *The Economist*, November 26, 2005, 89.
20. Olympic Games times from the International Olympic Committee website, www.olympic.org. Stawell Gift times from the Stawell Gift website, www.stawellgift.com. As discussed late in this paper, the Gift was run over 130 yards (120 metres since the 1970s), with runners receiving different starting handicaps. The Gift website gives winners' times and their handicaps. Times for actual distances run were converted into equivalent times per 100 metres. Other professional times were also adjusted (from either 100 yard times or Stawell Gift-type handicaps) to give comparable distances – see, for example, Vincent, *Rise and Fall of American Sport*, 83 for the times of US runner Richard Williams, who clocked 9 seconds for the 100 yards in 1906.
21. Vincent, *Rise and Fall of American Sport*, 83. As well as the 100 yards, Williams set records which were not bettered by amateurs for more than two decades in the long jump and for almost 50 years in the 440 yards.
22. See the definition from Gordon Inglis in his 1912, *Sport and Pastime in Australia,* cited by Phillips, 'Diminishing Contrasts and Increasing Varieties', 26, and Phillips' discussion of the variations, 24–5.
23. Phillips, 'Diminishing Contrasts and Increasing Varieties', especially 26.
24. Messenger, 'Bernard Wise and Olympic Athletes', 30.

25. Lane and Jobling, 'For Honour and Trophies'.
26. Lomas, *Will to Win*, 41–54.
27. *Guardian*, August 10, 1896, 6.
28. Vamplew, *Pay Up and Play the Game*, 6.
29. Cashman, *Paradise of Sport*, 190–2.
30. Phillips, 'Football, Class and War', and Cashman, *Paradise of Sport*.
31. Phillips, 'Football, Class and War', 162.
32. Cashman, *Paradise of Sport*, 67 and 190.
33. Gow, 'The Victorian Football Association in Control', 45–85.
34. Hess, 'The Victorian Football League Takes over', 86–113.
35. Perry, *The Quick and the Dead*, 255.
36. 'Stawell Gift Bets Swoop', *The Herald* (Melbourne), April 18, 1981, 1.
37. *Victorian Parliament Hansard* Council, 7 December 1982, 1228.
38. Perry, *The Quick and the Dead*, 66.
39. 'Bill Howard's Stawell Gift, 1966'. *The Age*, April 15, 2006, Sport Notes. See also Harms, 'Dasher's Hidden Talent'. *The Age*, April 14, 2006, for the story of the 1946 winner.
40. The following discussion draws heavily from Perry, *The Quick and the Dead*, together with the Stawell Athletic Club, *The First 100 Years* (available on the Stawell Gift website, www.stawellgift.com), and Merrick, 'Stawell Gift – and its Famous Runners'. *The Referee*, April 5, 1931, 13. Mewett, 'Fragments of a Composite Identity', 357–75 discusses some of the symbolic aspects of the Gift.
41. Perry, *The Quick and the Dead*, 2.
42. Ibid., 17–18.
43. Ibid., 57.
44. Ibid., 256–7.
45. *Victorian Parliament Hansard* Assembly, 1 December 1982, 2282.
46. Perry, *The Quick and the Dead*, 30.
47. Ibid., 47.
48. Ibid., 38–47.
49. Ibid., 52–6.
50. Stawell Athletic Club, *The First 100 Years*.
51. Perry, *The Quick and the Dead*, 58.
52. Merrick, 'Stawell Gift'.
53. Stawell Athletic Club, *Centenary History* and the Stawell Gift website.
54. *The Herald*, April 18, 1981, 20.
55. Lemon and Freedman. *History of Australian Thoroughbred Racing*, 391.
56. Gordon, *Australia and the Olympic Games*, Chap. 4.

References

Belich, James. *Paradise Reforged: A History of the New Zealanders 1880s to the year 2000*. Auckland: Allen Lane-Penguin Books, 2001.
Blainey, Geoffrey. *Black Kettle and Full Moon*. Camberwell Victoria: Penguin, 2003.
Cashman, Richard. *Paradise of Sport: The Rise of Organised Sport in Australia*. Melbourne: Oxford University Press, 1995.
Dunstan, Keith. *Wowsers*. Sydney: Angus and Robertson, 1974.
Gordon, Harry. *Australia and the Olympic Games*. Brisbane: University of Queensland Press, 1994.
Gow, Robin. 'The Victorian Football Association in Control, 1877–1896'. In *More than a Game: An Unauthorised History of Australian Rules Football*, ed. Rob Hess and Bob Stewart, 45–85. Carton Vic: Melbourne University Press, 1998.
Hess, Rob. 'The Victorian Football League Takes over 1897–1914'. In *More than a Game: An Unauthorised History of Australian Rules Football*, ed. Rob Hess and Bob Stewart, 86–113. Carton Vic: Melbourne University Press, 1998.
Hirst, John. *The Sentimental Nation: the Making of the Australian Commonwealth*. Melbourne: Oxford University Press, 2000.
Inglis, G. *Sport and Pastime in Australia*. London: Methuen, 1912.
Karabel, Jerome. *The Chosen: the Hidden History of Admission and Exclusion at Harvard, Yale and Princeton*. Boston MA: Houghton Mifflin, 2005.

Lane, David, and Ian Jobling. 'For Honour and Trophies: Amateur Rowing in Australia, 1888–1912'. *Sporting Traditions* 4, no.1 (November 1987): 2–26.

Lawrence, D.H. *Kangaroo.* Harmondsworth: Penguin in association with Heinemann, 1950.

Lemon, Andrew, and Harold Freedman. *History of Australian Thoroughbred Racing Volume 2: The Golden Years 1862 to 1939.* Melbourne: Southbank Communications, 1990.

Lomas, G. *The Will to Win: The Story of Sir Frank Beaurepaire.* London: Heinemann, 1960.

MacCallum, Mungo. *Political Anecdotes.* Sydney: Duffy & Snellgrove, 2003.

Messenger, Robert. 'Bernard Wise and Olympic Athletes'. In *Beyond the Torch: Olympics and Australian Culture,* ed. Daryl Adair, Bruce Coe, and Nick Guoth, 29–44. Australian Society for Sports History Studies No. 17, Melbourne, 2005.

Mewett, Peter. 'Fragments of a Composite Identity: Aspects of Australian Nationalism in a Sports Setting'. *Australian Journal of Anthropology* 10, no. 3 (1999): 357–75.

Nielsen, Niels Kayser. 'Welfare-nationalism? Comparative Aspects of the Relation between Sport and Nationalism in Scandinavia in the Inter-war Years'. *The Sports Historian* 17, no. 2 (November 1997): 63–79.

Perry, John. *The Quick and the Dead: Stawell and its Race through Time.* Sydney: UNSW Press, 2002.

Phillips, Murray. 'Football, Class and War: The Rugby Codes in New South Wales, 1907–1918'. In *Making Men: Rugby and Masculine Identity,* ed. John Nauright and Timothy J.L. Chandler, 158–80. London; Portland OR: Frank Cass, 1996.

Phillips, Murray G. 'Diminishing Contrasts and Increasing Varieties'. *Sporting Traditions* 18, no. 1 (November 2001): 19–32.

Stawell Athletic Club. 'The First 100 Years'. 1977. http://www.stawellgift.com/images/stories/HistoricDocs/First%2520100%2520Years.pdf

Vamplew, Wray. *Pay Up and Play the Game.* Cambridge and Sydney: Cambridge University Press, 1988.

Vincent, Ted. *The Rise and Fall of American Sport: Mudville's Revenge.* 2nd ed. Lincoln NE: University of Nebraska Press, 1994.

Warhaft, Sally, ed. *Well May We Say ... The Speeches that Made Australia.* Melbourne: Black, 2004.

Sports images in a time of turmoil 1910–40

> Sportsmen of Australia, to you is given a great opportunity, upon you rests a heavy responsibility. As you have played the game in the past so we ask you to play the greater game now ... You are wanted today in the trenches far more than you were ever needed in the football or cricket oval ... I ask you to be true to yourselves, and to prove yourselves worthy members of the great brotherhood of sport.[1]

Prime Minister Billy Hughes, a master of political rhetoric, launched a recruiting drive for a Sportsmen's Battalion on 27 July 1917 by drawing on oft-cited links between sport and war. Ten years earlier, his predecessor Alfred Deakin, in his eulogy to Australian rules, had drawn on similar images in assuring his listeners that sportsmen would be the first to respond 'when the tocsin sounds the call to arms'.[2]

Several commentators have cited such views, and Australia's raising of 'sportsmen's battalions' for the First World War as evidence of the strength of sports in Australian society and identity.[3] But Prime Ministerial rhetoric, however eloquent, is not enough to shape national images by itself. We need also to look at how people responded – and as we will see in this paper, Hughes' impassioned appeal was in fact much less successful than he hoped.

From noting differing views of sport in the First World War, this paper also casts a sceptical eye over two other common aspects of the national sporting image in the 1920s and 1930s. There was a renewed criticism of Australians' regard for sport, linked to the 'cultural cringe' and supposed philistine attitudes towards art and culture. The other frequent assertion is that sport – especially in the forms of Phar Lap and Don Bradman – played an important social cohesion role in the 1930s Depression. Asking questions of these aspects of the sporting image, the paper traces how both racing and cricket developed in these years, in their interactions with the social climate and the new technology of radio.

Sport and First World War

Billy Hughes' impassioned 1917 speech, and many others like it, certainly supports the symbolism of sport in Australian nationalism. However, these efforts to raise sportsmen's battalions were largely failures – most spectacularly seen at a special Rugby League match in Sydney in August 1917. Despite the clearly stated objectives of the match, only seven additional recruits came forward. One of the organizers reported back to the recruitment committee that 'the audience was antagonistic to recruiting and expressed itself so by counting out the speakers'.[4]

Rather than demonstrating one all-encompassing sporting image, the experiences in the First World War indicated the strength of the differences in how people saw and responded to sport. The previous paper noted the upper- and upper middle-class views, seeing sport as building character and training for higher things, in contrast to the working-class view of sport as more simply entertainment. The gulf between the two, reinforced by growing class antagonisms, worsened dramatically as the war went on – with echoes reverberating across the interwar years.

The first concerted action for Australian troops in the First World War was at Gallipoli from April to December 1915, with subsequent action primarily in France and also in the Middle East. While Australia had compulsory domestic military service from 1911, troops heading overseas were all volunteers. In the face of massive losses in France, and with recruitment levels falling, a highly divisive conscription referendum was held on 28 October 1916. The Labor Party (which had expelled Hughes and other leaders over the issue) led the 'No' vote. Despite intensive 'Yes' campaigns by the conservative parties (now led by Hughes), the media and Protestant churches, conscription was narrowly defeated, by 42,000 votes.[5] Although Hughes and the conservative parties won a massive victory in the May 1917 election, a second vitriolic conscription referendum later that year was also defeated, by a wider margin of 94,000 votes.[6]

Historian Richard White outlined the images the two sides created in the divisive campaigns:

> Each side strove to portray itself as representing the 'real' Australia, while the other was betraying national ideals. Conservatives, employers, the Protestant churches and the middle class generally saw anti-conscriptionists and strikers as traitors to the war effort, to the heroes at the front, to God, King and Country. The trade unions and the Irish saw the conscriptionists as prepared to throw away Australian lives in a war that was not Australia's own, and to betray Australia to imperialists and war mongers.[7]

The antagonisms in Australia over conscription exacerbated social tensions felt in most combatant countries as the war progressed. Inflation outstripped wages, and there was widespread criticism of the 'war profiteers', the 'sharks', the 'merchants of death'.[8] The climate fostered industrial disputes, the most bitter in Australia being the Great Strike in New South Wales which started in the railways, lasting three months from August to November 1917, with 173,000 men striking.[9] That strike had been running for three weeks when the special recruiting Rugby League match was held, contributing to the tensions amongst the largely working-class crowd.

While tensions took some time to reach the fever of 1917, the situation at the start of the war clearly showed the differing visions of sport – particularly in debates over whether spectator sport should be suspended during the hostilities. In May 1915, Melbourne headmaster L.A. Adamson put the conservative view succinctly. He extolled the virtues of amateur sport: 'from its athletic and its moral side the British love of games [had] proved a magnificent asset to the Empire', and saw sport as useful in building character. In contrast, he saw professional sport as incompatible with true sporting ideals and aims, with money corrupting noble instincts. And, for the duration of the war, spectator sport should be suspended because in Adamson's and many others' view it so clearly interfered with recruiting.[10]

More working-class sports clubs denied that sport interfered with recruiting. Rather, sporting events were, in this view, a good way of maintaining morale – and could be used to raise funds for the war effort. The clubs also pointed out that many in the audience, even in the teams, were ineligible for service either through age or because they were married. Married men, as breadwinners with dependents, had an automatic exemption from enlistment – in consequence over 80% of AIF volunteers were single men.[11] There was in fact a marked difference in eligibility between middle- and working-class men in their 20s. The average male age at marriage was 28, but seems to have been about 25 for working-class males, compared with over 30 for middle-class men.[12] Further, about half of those volunteering for service were rejected, most often on height or fitness grounds, and it seems rejection rates were especially high for inner suburbs working-class men.[13]

Depending largely on social background, sports took different approaches to suspending or continuing operations during the War. Both inter club and Sheffield Shield competitions in the largely upper- and middle-class sport of cricket were suspended from October 1915. In Sydney, the upper middle-class Rugby Union cancelled its 1915 season, while working-class Rugby League kept playing. In Australian rules competitions in the southern states, middle-class clubs generally supported suspension, while working-class clubs argued to continue the competitions. In Melbourne, while the VFA competition ceased, the VFL continued its 1915 season. In 1916, with middle-class clubs dropping out, the VFL ran a truncated competition with only four working-class clubs participating. The VFL gradually recovered numbers to six in 1917, and back to nine by 1919 – with decisions to recommence reflecting both clubs' community's social nature and the financial straights some were in.[14]

In direct recruitment efforts, two campaigns occurred for specific sportsmen's battalions. The first occurred in July–September 1915, alongside a generally heavy recruitment push. It seems there were doubts in Victoria about the whole idea of appealing to sportsmen, and a half-hearted effort attracted only 42 recruits to join in 'the best sport on Almighty God's earth – war'. The NSW effort was more organized, and by the end of September 1,100 had joined up for the Sportsmen's Battalion. This was however a very modest number compared with the Australia-wide recruitment approaching 100,000 in these three months. In addition, the idea of a united sportsmen's battalion was never realized – most volunteers went to different units. Only 300 sportsmen joined a specific unit, forming the 7th reinforcement of the 20th battalion.[15]

Not only were these results unimpressive compared with overall recruiting across Australia, they were less impressive than two efforts in England to raise sports-related units – although those units too had additional agendas. Efforts to raise a Sportsmen's Battalion in 1914 targeted amateur sportsmen, with a goal 'to enable middle class sportsmen from London's commercial classes to serve together in the great crusade without having to rub shoulders with the wrong type of citizen'. In 1915 efforts to build a Footballers' battalion targeted working-class footballers, with one force behind the campaign a public relations effort by the English Football Association to divert the sorts of criticism that League and the VFL received in Australia.[16]

Australia's second, more concerted, effort to raise a Sportsmen's Battalion came in 1917. After the failure of the conscription referendum in late 1916, Government recruitment efforts moved into higher gear. Sports recruitment committees, dominated by amateur sports administrators, were set up at year's end in NSW and Victoria. Proposed leaders for the battalion had both military training and sporting stature and popularity. However, in New South Wales, half the men chosen to command the different units were union footballers, which limited the reach of their popularity across the target market.[17]

Considerable resources were employed. The NSW committee published 5,000 copies each week from July to November of *Sport* magazine, and also paid for extensive advertising. In Victoria, a travelling band recruited through country areas.[18]

Yet despite such resources and efforts, the results were meagre. The NSW committee set a target of 750 new recruits on its first day, but only attracted 241. Over the four months of the campaign, the Sportsmen's Battalion in New South Wales recruited 1,197 men (well below expectations), while the Sportsmen's 1,000 in Victoria raised its limited target of 1,050 men. These were small numbers in terms of the total recruitment at the time. Further, there was always some gimmickry involved – those recruited were used as reinforcements for existing units, and did not form a distinct sportsmen's unit.[19]

Faced with poor responses such as these, recruitment supporters increased their efforts to close sporting events for the duration of the war. In the May 1917 election campaign, the government proposed additional controls on sport.[20] However, no action was actually taken until after the VFL Finals that year – and the action that did come was linked to other agendas. The government restricted the gambling sports of racing (especially weekday meetings) and boxing (only one boxing programme per state per fortnight) while taking no action against VFL or Rugby League.[21] And the implementation of restrictions also reflected status quo prejudices: in Queensland the number of Queensland Turf Club meetings was reduced by a quarter, while private promoter John Wren's Kedron Park course was allowed only 10% of its previous meetings.[22]

While Billy Hughes and the campaign organizers tried to strike a common chord with 'Sportsmen of Australia', their appeals faltered in the gulf between different images of sport, between sport as training for higher things or as entertainment. That gap was aggravated as the war progressed by increasing social tensions, most especially over the conscription referenda. In consequence, the most concerted effort to conscript the Australian sporting image for other purposes was largely a failure.

While not often as vitriolic as during the conscription battles, or the Great Strike, those social tensions remained through the interwar years. As well as on other aspects of life, they had impacts on sport, and on the further development of the sporting image.

The ocker in the sights

The tensions of the war, and the fall out from the conscription referenda, cast a shadow across the interwar years. They were important in the creation of a more negative dimension of the Australian sporting image – that of the sports-loving philistine. Paper 7 noted some earlier critical comments on a supposed Australian obsession with sport and ignorance of the finer things in life. It also noted that there was actually very little basis for these criticisms, and that the creation of the image reflected more the prejudices and agendas of the observer than the reality they were observing.

But those early comments were little compared with the intense criticism of Australian philistinism after the First World War. Cultural critic A.A. Phillips, writing in 1950, described this phenomenon as the 'cultural cringe', with two main aspects. The more important was a strong preference for 'culture' from England – with an accompanying denigration that anything produced in Australia was second-rate. The second element has become known as the 'tall poppy' syndrome, whereby Australians are supposed to take great delight in cutting down to size anyone excelling in any field apart from sport.[23] There is actually scant evidence to support these assertions. Indeed, as Paper 7 discussed for the 1880s, Phillips noted in 1950 that higher levels in Australia of newspaper readership and per capita purchase of books 'would suggest that in fact our cultural attainments are rather above the average Anglo-Saxon level'.[24] Phillips found difficulties measuring the 'tall poppy' aspect – but on at least one test it too had very little credence. He compared British and Australian Prime Ministers in the interwar years, suggesting that the British political parties more frequently chose the safe, mediocre candidate for leader, while the Australians more typically chose the best man for the job.[25]

So if there was actually little basis for the cultural cringe and its associated image of the philistine sports-lover, why did this image become so enduring? And why did it become especially strong in the interwar years?[26]

One explanation, noted by Phillips, was the sheer difference in size between the cultural milieus of Australia and Britain. In 1950, with Australia's eight million population less than 20% of Great Britain's 51 million, whatever the per capita cultural interest, the size of the cultural market in Britain was naturally larger. Phillips saw this as adding to the nervousness of the local intellectual: 'the crust *feels* thinner, because, in a small community, there is not enough of it to provide the intellectual with a protective insulation'.[27]

This provincial/metropolis explanation undoubtedly contributed to the phenomenon – and was quite common internationally, for example in the rest of England versus London, provincial France versus Paris, and the mid West of the United States versus New York or Los Angeles. But it does not explain the particular features of the Australian cultural cringe, nor why it was especially strong in the 1920s and 1930s, alongside the growth of 'white hot indignation' by educated Australians over the broad Australian accent.[28]

Such attitudes overlapped with other social patterns, described by cultural historian Geoffrey Serle:

> down to the 1930s, the products of private secondary schools and the universities – the educated class – were overwhelmingly imperialist and conservative in politics ... The extreme imperialists constantly talked and dreamed of 'home', decried everything Australian, kept alive the tradition of exile ... they debunked all Australian manufactures, they imported English bishops, headmasters and professors and under-rated local candidates. Unlike any other sizeable group in any other Anglo-Saxon community, they were ashamed of the local pronunciation of English. The Adelaide Club – the Adelaide Club – did not serve Australian wines before 1945.[29]

A critical factor here was the social and political push amongst conservatives in the 1920s and 1930s to reassert the British image in Australia. Appeals to 'a British people' were strengthened in the turmoil and aftermath of the First World War. As discussed in Paper 4, between 1914 and 1921 some State Governments introduced oaths of loyalty to the British Empire and the Union Jack in public schools, which lasted until the 1950s.

Australia was far from alone in experiencing social turmoil in the 1920s, stemming from the dislocation of the First World War, the difficult economic times for many, and the spectre (for conservatives) or promise (for those on the left) of the Bolshevik revolution. In November 1933, W.S. Kent Hughes, a young Minister in the Victorian State Government, spoke for many conservatives in seeing attractions in fascism as a 'half way house between the two systems' of laissez faire and socialism. But he argued Australians would maintain democratic institutions, and dislike overt displays such as the black shirts of Italian fascists, or the brown shirts in Germany. Hughes declared, 'I am a Fascist without a shirt', arguing 'an Australian fascist would be more than likely to lose the coloured shirt on a racehorse on the following Saturday!'[30]

And while conservatives in many countries organized against the 'red menace' in the 1920s, the form they took similarly varied depending on particular circumstances. In both the USA and Australia conservatives mobilized some 10–15% of white Protestant men into semi-military organizations.[31] Both the Ku Klux Klan and the Australian paramilitaries were vitriolic anti-red and heavily anti-Catholic. However, while the KKK espoused small town American values, and wrapped itself in Old Glory, the Australian groups saw themselves as upholding British culture, and wrapped themselves in the Union Jack.

This orientation of the paramilitary groups reflected a widespread mood across conservative groups in Australia. The loss of the two conscription referenda had hit hard, as if demonstrating to conservatives that, despite early promise, the new country had betrayed its imperial responsibilities. If this was the way that Australia might lead the world, then it was far better to return to imperial ties.[32]

This helps explain the strength of the cultural cringe and the philistine sports lover image. As we have seen, there was scant evidence in reality to support either. But there was a strong social/political agenda to impose the superiority of British ties and culture over Australian traits, with their dubious imperial loyalty.

On a political level, the crisis for conservatives had dissipated by early 1932. Federal and State ALP Governments, which they had denigrated as 'Communist Langs and Irish Scullins', had been defeated by early 1932, and conservative governments were back in office.[33] But the sectarian antagonism continued for many years, and even greater longevity was shown by the colonial cringe image of the philistine sports lover.

And the tumultuous times of the 1910s and 1920s had also seen considerable social success for the temperance and anti-gambling groups – those derisively termed 'wowsers' by their opponents. Paper 9 noted that the temperance movement had its greatest successes in Australia, New Zealand and newly settled areas of the United States. In these new areas, the social strength of establishment conservative groups was markedly less than in more long-standing societies, and in each area populist and labour movements were gaining ground. This environment created more space for the wowsers to mobilize. It also, as discussed above in the impacts on sport of coalitions between differing visions, meant conservatives accepted more of the wowser agenda in social and political compromises. The temperance movement was at its strongest immediately after the First World War, at a moment when, in the midst of the 'Red Scare' from the Bolshevik revolution, the conservative forces felt especially fragile.

The social strength of the coalition between the conservatives and the temperance movement produced remarkable restrictions on drinking hours and pursuit of leisure on Sundays in the 1920s and 1930s. They also created the image of the kill-joy 'wowser', as historian Geoffrey Blainey noted:

> The wowsers symbolised the deep social divisions raised by alcohol and other leisure pursuits. To many Australians the wowsers were killjoys and spoilsports but in the eyes of others they were evangelical reformers fighting on a wide front.[34]

But overall national culture is not just defined by the visions of the socially powerful, but also by the reactions of others. And such social successes, especially when pushed hard, started creating their own backlash. In the United States, this was seen in the widespread social tolerance for breaking the prohibition laws. In Australia, in the words of historian Manning Clark,

> Wowserism, one of the ugly manifestations of Puritanism in Australia, also contributed to the growth of the larrikin spirit ... This faithless and somewhat mindless wowserism has caused a backlash of protest, which in turn has joined forces with the other well-springs of larrikinism.[35]

The social standing of the larrikin had parallels in the development of Australian sports humour. From 1900, media commentary on cricket at the SCG often saw the Hill as the most colourful, interesting and above all the most Australian element of the crowd.[36] And as noted in Paper 1, 'Yabba' attained cult status for his vociferous and clever barracking of cricket matches in the 1920s and 1930s. The strong elements both of self-deprecation and mocking those in authority in Australian sports humour, were not unique. As with many elements in Australia, early humour drew heavily on British antecedents. Much of early 'piss taking' derived from earthy humour from Cockneys, the north of England and Ireland.[37]

What was different in Australia was the extent of social acceptance, even support, which self-deprecation and mocking authority had here. This was, as Clark suggests, to some extent a reaction to the strait-laced wowser, who was notorious for a complete lack of humour. But it was also indicative of the social and commercial strength of groups ready to mock authority. *The Bulletin* lamented in 1881:

> Our larrikins are as much the outcome of the prosperity of the labouring classes as of anything else ... The peculiar prominence which they attain is clearly attributable to the comparative ease with which they, as compared with the same class in the old world, can acquire the means for indulgence and for idleness.[38]

That prosperity and 'idleness', as discussed in Paper 8, provided the crowds necessary for the early flourishing of spectator sports in this country. It also provided a market for numerous newspapers targeting radical and working-class antipathy to the establishment; a market for John Norton's attacks on the Australian Jockey Club in *Truth*; and a market to support two of the remarkable political cartoonists of the twentieth century.

Both David Low and Pat Oliphant developed their skills in formative years working in Australia. New Zealand-born Low started contributing to the *Bulletin* in 1911, before moving to London in 1919 to work on *The Star*. From the mid-1930s until his death in 1963, he was described as 'the dominant cartoonist of the Western World'. Oliphant was employed as a cadet artist on his native South Australia's main paper *The Advertiser* in 1953, aged 17. In 1964 he became the daily cartoonist in the *Denver Post*. He won the Pulitzer Prize in 1976, the same year he became the daily cartoonist for the *Washington Star*. During this period he was considered the most widely syndicated and highest paid cartoonist in the world.[39]

Low and Oliphant, while outstanding individual exponents, came from a rich tradition of political cartooning in Australia. This was encouraged especially by *The Bulletin* from the 1880s, and *Smith's Weekly* in the 1920s and 1930s, which both provided ample opportunity and employment for cartoonists.

While this social (and commercial) base nurtured the Australian style, appreciation of the sports humour in particular was more widespread than that social base. If cartoonists and other humorists wanted to puncture pomposity, it helped to have pompous targets around. Although it is unlikely that any tests exist for determining if Australia had more pompous targets than elsewhere, certainly the wowser and the Anglophile cultural cringe created a space for robust derision.

As well as having impacts on national symbols generally, these social patterns also affected sports. And the tensions meant that sport was much less of a socially cohesive force in the 1930s than has often been claimed.

Sport and social tensions

While some parts of the common image of the Australian sports fan in the interwar years were not that flattering, a more positive part of the image emphasized that sport gave all Australians a common interest. That the woes of the Depression could be lost for a while in cheering on Phar Lap in the 1930 Melbourne Cup or Don Bradman in the bodyline cricket series. As sports historian Brian Stoddart concluded, specifically talking about cricket followers: 'In a time of Australian stress, there was a degree of social cohesion and identity perhaps unmatched in any other social situation of the time.'[40]

There is no doubting the strength of Don Bradman or Phar Lap in the popular image. Yet here too the statistics cast some queries about the underlying reality. As Paper 5 argued, Bradman's star status helped increase Test crowds by close to half on days when he was batting. However, that discussion demonstrated also that other factors had strong influences on crowds – some having bigger impacts than Bradman.

The three years when Phar Lap ran in the Melbourne Cup (1929–31) were the worst years of the Depression. Those years, average attendances at Flemington on Cup Day were just over 80,000. The previous three years each saw attendances of 109,000, while the 1932 to 1935 crowds averaged 90,000.[41] In 1930, when only 72,000 saw Phar Lap win as short-priced favourite (usually the worst result for bookies), the massive popularity of the horse seems to have had little adverse impact on bookies. In the months after the Cup, only four bookmakers had their licences revoked by the VRC because they could not meet their debts. As this was in the midst of the Depression, and bookmaking is usually a hazardous business, this does not seem many.[42]

Further doubt can be cast on the image of Phar Lap or Don Bradman as a particular source of social cohesion by comparing aggregate attendances at major sports in these years with attendances at the Sydney Show and at cinemas in New South Wales. These are shown in Figure 1.[43]

Figure 1 compares total attendances for the five activities using indexes based on the average attendance from 1928–30 as 1.0. While there is some year to year variation in the figures, the attendance trends for the Ashes Tests, the Melbourne Cup and the Royal Sydney Show are all remarkably similar – and few people have claimed that the Sydney Show was a special source of social cohesion in these years! The two activities that differed from the broad trend were VFL attendances, which suffered less in the Depression, and cinema attendances, which fell further and for longer than the others. Key explanations might be that VFL in Melbourne was relatively cheap, while it is likely the largest group in cinema attendances was young workers – a demographic particularly hard hit in the Depression.

Each of these data series can have their quirks. Both the Sydney Show and the Melbourne Cup can be affected by bad weather. Cricket attendances were affected by the numbers of days of play (there were 33 days played in the 1928–29 series, compared with 25 in 1932–33) and the location of matches (there was one Test in the

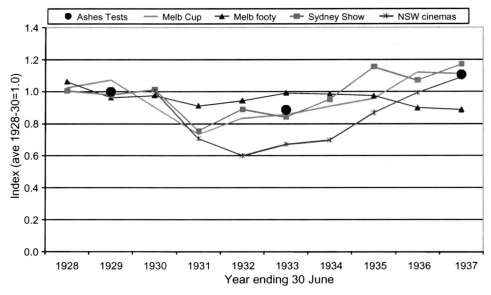

Figure 1.   Attendances 1928-1937 – major sports and other entertainment.

large capacity MCG in 1932–33, but two in 1936–37).[44] Taking these and other factors into account, it seems cricket attendances in 1932–33 were definitely boosted by the presence of Bradman and the controversy of bodyline.[45]

Despite such specific details, and while Phar Lap and Bradman were certainly extraordinary sports figures, this evidence does not suggest that a massive need for social cohesion attracted greater attendances or betting in the depths of the Depression. Once again, we need to look not only at the realities behind images, but also at the agendas of those creating the images. In the social stresses of the Depression, there were certainly those trying to create unifying images.

Whatever their provenance, the strength of the images certainly impressed Hungarian Communist and journalist Egon Kisch, who visited Australia in 1934 to speak to anti-fascism rallies, despite government attempts to prevent him entering the country. Kisch gave considerable space in his memoirs of the trip, *Australian Landfall,* to the phenomenon of sport, and particularly Phar Lap and the bodyline cricket series:

> Bodyline is connected with sport, but it also has a profound political significance. To write about Australia and to omit the bodyline affair would be like describing the Vatican without mentioning the Pope, or – but there is no end to such comparisons if we are to describe the significance of cricket for Australia, or of bodyline for international politics.[46]

'Bodyline' was a bowling tactic used by the English team in the 1932–33 Ashes series in an attempt to frustrate the batting brilliance of Don Bradman. Reviewing Bradman's dominance of the 1930 series in England, English captain Jardine detected one weakness – a dislike of fast short-pitched deliveries on leg stump. Jardine, with bowlers Larwood and Voce, developed what they called 'leg theory'. The Australians termed it 'bodyline', claiming the fast bowlers were aiming at the batsmen, not the leg stump.[47]

After several injuries to Australian batsmen, bodyline was controversial. During the Third Test in Adelaide, Australian captain Bill Woodfull famously told the English manager, Pelham Warner: 'There are two teams out there, and only one of them is playing cricket.' Following that Test, the Australian Board of Control sent its English counterpart (the Marylebone Cricket Club) a telegram complaining the tactic was 'unsportsmanlike'. The MCC, undoubtedly aware of the ACB's reliance on Test revenues, threatened to abandon the tour unless the insult was withdrawn – and maintained its stand despite Government discussions on the matter. The ACB eventually backed down and the tour continued.

All of this was some way from the hopes for social cohesion from one WA politician at the start of the tour 'we look upon these visits as a powerful influence in cementing the bonds of empire.' Or the *Sydney Morning Herald*'s wishes before Adelaide that the game should be 'played in the tradition and the spirit that have made it what it is – the true embodiment of British sport and fair play.'[48]

Years later, spinner 'Tiger' O'Reilly was still incandescent both about bodyline and the Australian cricket establishment's performance:

> the bouncer delivered with malice ... should have been rubbed right off the slate in 1933. England then was offended by the use of one word, and the Australian cricket hierarchy fell to its knees in supplication, fearing that in pursuing their threat to take the bat and ball and go home to Mummy, they would ruin their hopes of record gate takings. The aroma of it still persists.[49]

It was not just the ACB's acquiescence to the imperial power that attracted O'Reilly's wrath. The Protestant/Catholic sectarian feelings of the period loomed in cricket as well. Protestants dominated the ACB in these years, with Masons prominent in the NSWCA hierarchy.[50]

At the end of the third Test in Melbourne in 1937, O'Reilly and three of the four other Catholics in the team were summoned to a meeting of the ACB to discuss suggestions that 'some members of the team were indulging in too much beer, and not showing enough physical fitness and team spirit. Insubordination was also mentioned.'[51] Despite the individual feats of the players concerned in the difficult test series thus far, 'there we were, accused, it seemed, as representatives of an insubordinate and disloyal team of slackers and boozers. It was more than I could take.' O'Reilly interrupted proceedings and asked whether 'we four were being held responsible. The answer was "No". So what then were we there for? The answer was not provided. The meeting broke up in general confusion.' O'Reilly blamed captain Bradman for not supporting him during this confrontation, the incident adding to the sour relationship between the two.[52]

But if cricket, as with other sports, saw reflections of the social tensions of these years, the sports did attract interest across social divides. But the extent of this has been overemphasized. Paper 5 noted that even in 2000 professionals were heavily over represented in cricket audiences, and this was even more true in the first half of the twentieth century. This was partially due to gate fees: in the 1920s typical entry to a cricket match was 2/-, 15% of the daily wage, and four times the 6d entry to the football.[53] Still, it seems the social spread was probably wider in the 1920s than it was in the 1911 SCG crowd discussed in Paper 8 above, which was overwhelmingly upper and middle class. A wider social interest is certainly suggested by the more than doubling of total attendances at Ashes Tests, from the 342,000 in 1911–12 to 858,000 in 1928–29. Indeed, some attracted to Tests in the bodyline series for example seem to have been more from a prize fighting milieu – one report noted boos for the English if they weren't bowling bodyline, as the crowd wanted to see the action. If a bodyline field was then set, the boos were even more vociferous.[54]

Spectacle was also important in racing, still the most popular spectator sport in the country. The Melbourne Cup, as noted in Paper 8, was attracting audiences of 85,000 in the first decade of the twentieth century. In the 1920s, attendances averaged 105,000 each year, and recovered after the depression to a similar average from 1935 to 1939. Numbers were also strong for the two big race meetings either side of the Cup[55] – and the patterns for these give good indication of some of the variations within the racing audience. Derby Day, on the preceding Saturday, attracts punters (tending to be young and often working-class men) to a number of top-line races. Oaks Day on Thursday is traditionally 'Ladies' Day', with higher female, and more well-off, attendances.

Attendance at both events climbed rapidly in the years prior to 1914. While the good economic times of these years were clearly a factor, the organization of the sport also played a part. Punters were encouraged to Flemington both by positive measures, such as a new stand for 10,000 people, and by restrictions on betting off-course in the 1906 Suppression of Gaming Act. The VRC also counted more numbers when it extended admission controls and charges to the Flemington flat in 1913.

Attendances fell during the First World War, with enlistment of many of the key market of young men. They quickly reached record numbers with peace and economic good times in the 1920s. The Depression of the 1930s had a more marked effect on the Derby than Oaks, reflecting the difference in the audiences.

In the later 1930s, Derby Day recovered to a little below its levels of the 1920s. In contrast, Oaks Day was attracting crowds of 25,000 by the end of the 1930s, well above its 20,000 in the late 1920s. At the same time that cricket was widening its social appeal, to bring in more working-class fans, it appears that racing was also broadening, attracting more middle-class fans.

Racing clubs around Australia – particularly in the major cities – shared Flemington's enjoyment of good crowds in the 1920s and later 1930s. While average Australian incomes actually grew little between 1901 and 1941,[56] the market for sports grew considerably, due to both overall population growth (the Australian non-Aboriginal population almost doubled, from 3.8 million people to 7.1 million) and its even greater concentration in urban areas. In 1901, close to half of Australians lived in urban areas; by the 1940s this figure reached two-thirds. The combined population of Sydney and Melbourne grew from just under one million to 2.4 million, from a quarter to one third of the total population. And the earlier prosperity had bequeathed grounds and facilities to accommodate considerable sporting interest. Sports organizers built on these facilities to continue to attract massive crowds by world standards.

As with Flemington, attendances across Australia reflected not just these economic patterns but also how the sport was organized. Conflicting visions of what the sport was and should be were aired in a remarkable series of formal inquiries into racing and betting across these years.

A Tasmanian select committee in 1922 recommended the legalization and regulation of bookmakers. South Australia passed a comprehensive Lotteries and Gaming Act in 1917 to make its existing ban on bookies more effective, and its Parliament considered another 18 bills relating to gambling between the wars. The most far reaching of these followed the 1933 Royal Commission into Betting. Queensland had a Royal Commission into Racing and Racecourses in 1929, and another Royal Commission in

1935 into 'certain matters relating to racing and gaming'. New South Wales had a 1912 Royal Commission into the Totalizator and a 1923 select committee looking into pony racing. The Victorian Legislation Council set up a select committee on racecourses and race meetings in October 1928.[57] The Melbourne Cup field of inquiries testifies to both the importance of racing and to the political passions it engendered.

As many of the activities they were investigating were illegal, the inquiries skated on thin ice. The Tasmanian select committee in 1922 had the following exchange:

Chairman: 'To put it bluntly, Mr X, you are a bookmaker?'
Mr X: 'They call me one.' (He later admitted to turnover of £500 on an average Saturday.)[58]

The extent of illegal bookmaking was certainly impressive. The 1933 South Australian Royal Commission concluded that there were hundreds of starting price bookmakers in the state, and that some 15% of the adult population bet with bookies found in four of every five Adelaide pubs. The Queensland Royal Commission two years later estimated 749 illegal bookies in that state.[59]

The inquiries dealt with three major issues: how to deal with illegal gambling; whether to introduce a totalizator (for those states that did not already have one[60]); and what should be done about unregistered pony racing. Social prejudices flavoured proceedings. The Queensland 1929 Royal Commission approved of registered racing 'conducted by clubs formed by persons imbued with love of the sport', controlled by 'men of standing' and attended by the public of both sexes 'in search of recreation and not primarily with a view to gain'. In contrast, unregistered racing was controlled by personnel 'not of the same standing', with the racing 'of an inferior character' and patronized by a public 'almost exclusively male, who attend the meetings in the hope of gain'.[61]

Variations in such attitudes led to quite different recommendations in response to very similar evidence. Faced with the above figures on illegal bookmaking, the 1933 South Australian report argued such extensive activity could not be eradicated, and recommended legalization and registration of bookmakers. In contrast, the majority Queensland report in 1935 concluded, 'we cannot see any great public demand for off-the-course betting facilities' and recommended tougher measures against off course bookies.[62]

As the implementation of controls differed between the states, so too did the responses from the gambling public. The major contrast here is between the efforts by Victorian and South Australian Governments to register off-course bookies, while the NSW and Queensland Governments banned them. Racing historian Andrew Lemon argues that the bans were counterproductive in the longer term, leading to greater social tolerance of illegal activity, which became a prime source of later corruption.[63]

Differing agendas between sports also influenced how they responded to new opportunities, such as the development of radio.

Responding to new technology

Two punters, strangers to each other, were sitting in a Newsreel cinema. A film of the two horse race between hot favourite Ajax and Spear Chief came on. As the horses turned into the straight, one punter said to the other: 'I'll bet you five quid that Spear Chief wins.'

'That's a bet!' said the other
Of course, Spear Chief did win.
Afterwards, the loser handed over his five pounds.
The winner said: 'I can't take your money, I saw the film yesterday.'
'So did I', was the reply 'but I thought Ajax would be improved by the run.'[64]

While some had difficulty adjusting to new communications technologies, they made quick headway in the 1920s and 1930s. With the combination of wealth and sports interest documented previously, Australians responded readily to the new technologies, with sport often to the forefront. One of the first documentary films anywhere in the world was of the Melbourne Cup, and by the end of the 1920s newsreels showing the Cup were flown that afternoon to country and interstate towns and parachuted to waiting projectionists for screening that evening.[65]

Four years after radio was introduced in 1924, 270,000 people held radio licenses, with half of these in Victoria, representing 'a higher proportion of registered listeners than any other place in the world where such figures were kept'.[66] The fastest three-month growth in radio licences occurred in 1934 when the new Australian Broadcasting Commission (ABC) broadcast 'synthetic' commentaries of the Ashes tour of England. Using techniques pioneered for baseball in the United States, the ABC gave ball-by-ball commentary based on cables sent from England at the end of each over. The commentary was enhanced by recorded sounds in the studio.[67]

But this was not simply a matter of sports organizers and media owners taking advantage of technological developments as they happened. As documented throughout this collection, proponents brought a range of agendas to their response to situations such as new technology. Those agendas shaped how the technology was used, as seen in the development of radio sports broadcasts. Early broadcasts compromised a mix of music and talk, with sporting events the most common 'actuality' or outside broadcasts. Cricket was an early sport, with commentary and scores (though not ball-by-ball description) broadcast during the 1924–25 test matches between England and Australia, and horse race commentary started in 1925. By 1932 the BBC commented that, with some 30 outside sports broadcasts a week, sports broadcasting was 'Australia's most characteristic feature'.[68]

Such sports broadcasts were almost ignored by the 1927 national Royal Commission into Wireless. While it noted one complaint (apparently from a fan of classical music) that radio programmes had 'too much sporting information',[69] the Commission's primary concern, shared with the founders of the BBC, was that broadcasting should be educative and uplifting, with a role of social improvement.[70]

When the Government-owned Australian Broadcasting Commission was set up in 1932, it shared these goals, with a high preponderance of classical music and worthy talks. Such fare attracted a limited audience – in 1936 only 20% of radios were tuned to the ABC, with listeners mainly from higher income and rural groups.[71]

The first ABC annual report talked of the characteristics of Australian society they had to respond to, and mentioned in successive phrases, 'the keen national interest in sport' and 'our position as part of the British Empire and British race'.[72] There was not much doubt which of these two was more popular with the audience. Conscious of its self-proclaimed role as the 'national broadcaster', and a little nervous about the Government's control of its purse strings, the ABC chose coverage of sport – and particularly cricket and racing – as a strategy of building a bigger audience. Such was the audience response that the ABC from 1934 gave test cricket precedence over all other programmes, with continuous coverage, even late into the night for tests in England. The ABC also had extensive coverage of horse racing, but here it faced more competition from the commercial channels. It also ran into a key social agenda of concern over off-course betting. Initially, the ABC agreed not to broadcast starting prices, but as commercial stations were happy to do this, from 1934 the ABC broadcast prices. This lasted until 1939, when the Postmaster General requested the ABC, and required the commercial stations, not to broadcast starting prices.[73]

There were also mixed feelings about the broadcasting of sport amongst sport organizers. Both cricket and racing organizations feared in the late 1920s that live broadcasts would reduce attendances. Cricket administrators blamed radio broadcasts for the numbers attending Sheffield Shield games falling by half between the late 1920s and the early 1930s – although the depression may have been a bigger factor.[74] However, from the time the ABC took up the cause of cricket, cricket authorities seem to have felt the overall popularity of the game benefited strongly.[75]

In racing, by 1934 the ABC had exclusive rights to broadcast most important horse races, with broadcast payments to racing clubs. However, competition continued from commercial stations who broadcast from vantage points just outside the fence.[76] This led to a celebrated legal case in 1937, where Sydney's Victoria Park Racing unsuccessfully sued neighbouring property owner Taylor and others for nuisance and breach of copyright.[77]

By the end of the 1930s, the popularity of sports in Australia had been reinforced by the advent of radio, making keeping up with the action much easier. So much so that in the 1946–47 Ashes cricket series 30% of both men and women reported that they listened to more than four hours of Test radio coverage on one Saturday, and only a quarter of men and 38% of women had not listened at all.[78] The technology thus helped further the image of all Australians being interested in sport. As we will see in the next paper, this became an important part of the post Second World War image of the 'Australian Way of Life'.

Notes

1. Cited by Phillips, 'Sport, War and Gender Images', 78. There are many examples of similar speeches – see, for example, Mrs Valentine Spence's speech later in the campaign: McKernan, 'Sport War and Society', 17–18.
2. Deakin's speech 'The Australasian Game' at the 1908 Football Jubilee was reported in *The Argus*, 29 August 1908, 17. See discussion in previous essay 'Visions of Australian Sport in 1900'.
3. See, for example, Vamplew, 'Australians and Sport', 13.
4. Phillips, 'Football, Class and War', 173.
5. Horne, *In Search of Billy Hughes*, 76–92, and the general Australian histories of Macintyre, *Concise History of Australia* and Molony, *Australia: Our Heritage.*
6. Horne, *In Search of Billy Hughes*, 91–2.
7. White, *Inventing Australia*, 130.
8. Horne, *In Search of Billy Hughes*, 85.
9. Phillips, 'Football, Class and War', 168.
10. Cited by Blair, 'War and Peace', 115 (from a report in *The Argus*, April 22, 1915), and by McKernan, 'Sport War and Society' (from a subsequent article in the *Wesley College Chronicle*, May 1915). McKernan, 4 reported the counter productive advertising.
11. Blair, 'War and Peace', 114–38.
12. Vamplew, ed., *Australian Historical Statistics*, 46 notes that a quarter of men were married by the age of 24, and the vast majority of these early husbands would have been working class.
13. Blair, 'War and Peace', 117.

14. McKernan, 'Sport War and Society', esp. 7; Phillips, 'Football Class and War', 166–8; Blair, 'War and Peace', 125, 128.
15. Phillips, 'Sport, War and Gender Images', 79.
16. Ibid., 80.
17. Phillips 'Football Class and War', 173.
18. Phillips, 'Sport, War and Gender Images', 85–90.
19. Ibid., 81.
20. McKernan, 'Sport War and Society', 14–16.
21. Phillips, 'Football Class and War', 171.
22. McKernan, 'Sport War and Society', 17.
23. Phillips, *Phillips on the Cultural Cringe*.
24. Phillips, *Phillips on the Cultural Cringe*, 3–4, 6. Cultural critic Robert Hughes, *Things I Didn't Know*, 269–70 noted a similar statistic for the early 1960s – although, such was the strength of the cultural cringe image, he expressed surprise and tried to explain this in terms of low levels of TV ownership. Evidence from the Gallup polls suggests that the introduction of TV had little effect on book readership. Polls reported in April–May 1953, Nov.–Dec. 1956, and Feb.–June 1967 (see respective Gallup poll summaries), indicated a very consistent pattern of one third of Australians reading a book at the time, one third occasionally reading, and the final one third non-readers. A poll in March–April 1960 showed an even higher figure of current readers, at 48%.
25. Phillips, *Phillips on the Cultural Cringe*, 6–7.
26. Ivor Indyk noted in *Meanjin* in 2000: 'for Phillips, the cultural cringe was at its strongest in the 1920s and 1930s, which he described as a period of stagnation'. Reprinted in Phillips, *Phillips on the Cultural Cringe*, 73.
27. Phillip, *Phillips on the Cultural Cringe*, 4.
28. Yallop, 'A.G. Mitchell and the Development of Australian Pronunciation', 139.
29. Serle, *Creative Spirit in Australia*, 140.
30. Kent Hughes, 'Fascism without a Shirt', part 1. *Herald*, November 14, 1933; and see Cathcart, *Defending the National Tuckshop*, 31.
31. In the US, estimates of Ku Klux Klan membership range up to five million (Friedman, *Moral Consequences*, 148–50), while in Australia, groups such as the White Army in Victoria and the Old and New Guard in New South Wales had recruited some 130,000 members by 1930 (Cathcart, *Defending the National Tuckshop*, 2).
32. See Rickard, *Australia: A Cultural History*, 119: 'Imperial loyalists were shattered by these twin defeats [in the conscription referenda] and felt humiliated in the eyes of the land they called "home"'.
33. See Cathcart, *Defending the National Tuckshop*, 71, 187, and the notes on the 1931 election from academic Grenville Price, chair of the 'Emergency Committee' of conservative parties in South Australia, cited in Connell and Irving, *Class Structure*, 331.
34. Blainey, *Black Kettle and Full Moon*, 355.
35. Clark, 'Larrikins – The Context', 37–9.
36. Cashman, *'Ave a Go, Yer Mug'*, 60.
37. Ibid., 59–60 reports comments on English crowds around 1900: 'There was always a significant difference between the more working class crowds of the industrial north and the more conservative crowds of the south.'
38. Cited by Gorman, *Larrikin Streak*, viii.
39. See www.cartoonists.org.au.
40. Stoddart, 'Cricket's Imperial Crisis', 136.
41. Figures from Victoria Racing Club website, www.vrc.net.au.
42. Armstrong and Thompson, *Melbourne Cup 1930*, 211.
43. Sources of data: Cashman, *Australian Cricket Crowds*, 297; Racing Victoria website for Melbourne Cup (www.racingvictoria.net.au); AFL website for Melbourne football crowds (www.afl.com.au); Vamplew, *Australian Historical Statistics*, 390 for the Royal Sydney Easter show; and Cashman, *Australian Cricket Crowds*, 313 for cinema attendances in NSW.
44. Cashman, *Australian Cricket Crowds*, 11, and 297, 299. The figures would also have been affected by the fact that 1936–37 was a close-fought series, with Australia winning 3–2: England won each of the two previous series 4–1.
45. Blackman and Chapman, 'Value of Don Bradman', esp. 375.

46. Kisch, *Australian Landfall,* extract reprinted in Zogbaum, *Kisch in Australia*, 186.
47. Stoddart, 'Cricket's Imperial Crisis'; and Larwood with Perkins, *The Larwood Story.*
48. Cited by Stoddart 'Cricket's Imperial Crisis', 128 and 134.
49. O'Reilly, *Tiger*, 97.
50. Harte, *History of Australian Cricket*, 305.
51. O'Reilly, *Tiger*, 159–60.
52. Coulter, 'Great Sporting Feuds', *The Age*, December 4, 2005, Sport, 19; and see Harte, *History of Australian Cricket*, 310.
53. Cashman, *'Ave a Go, Yer Mug'*, 70.
54. Stoddart, 'Cricket's Imperial Crisis', 136.
55. Data from the Racing Victoria website, www.racingvictoria.net.au.
56. McLean, 'Australian Economic Growth', 332.
57. A detailed state-by-state discussion of these inquiries is included in Lemon and Freedman, *History of Australian Thoroughbred Racing*, 431–93.
58. Ibid., 458.
59. Ibid., 426f (Queensland) and 450f (South Australia).
60. Victoria was the last state to get a totalizator, in 1930.
61. Lemon and Freedman, *History of Australian Thoroughbred Racing*, 423.
62. Ibid., 426f (Queensland) and 450f (South Australia).
63. Ibid., 429 (Queensland) and 497 (NSW).
64. Cashman, Headon, and Kinross-Smith eds, *The Oxford Book of Australian Sporting Anecdotes*, 228.
65. Lemon and Freedman, *History of Australian Thoroughbred Racing*, 500.
66. This and subsequent paragraphs draw mainly on Inglis, *This is the ABC*, especially 8–9.
67. Ibid., 37.
68. Ibid., 35.
69. Royal Commission on Wireless 1927, 'Report', 15.
70. For example, the Commission was keen on examples 'to the listener of how the English language should be pronounced'. Ibid., 15–16.
71. Inglis, *This is the ABC*, 75–6, 150.
72. Ibid., 36.
73. Ibid., 60.
74. Cashman, *'Ave a Go, Yer Mug'*, 93.
75. Harte, *History of Australian Cricket*, 288 notes radio coverage helped increase the popularity of cricket in this period.
76. Inglis, *This is the ABC*, 36.
77. Lemon and Freedman, *History of Australian Thoroughbred Racing*, 499; Victoria Park Racing and Recreation Grounds Company Limited v Taylor and Others [1937] HCA 45; (1937) 58 CLR 479 (26 August 1937).
78. Gallup poll summary, Feb.–March 1947. The listener figures may have been inflated somewhat by a feeling that listening to the cricket was the 'right' thing to do.

References

Armstrong, Geoff, and Peter Thompson. *Melbourne Cup 1930: How Phar Lap won Australia's Greatest Race*. Crows Nest, NSW, Allen and Unwin, 2005.
Blackman, Julian, and Bruce Chapman. 'The Value of Don Bradman: Additional Revenue in Australian Ashes Tests'. *Economic Papers* 23 (December 2004): 369–85.
Blainey, Geoffrey. *Black Kettle and Full Moon*. Camberwell Victoria: Penguin, 2003.
Blair, David. 'War and Peace 1915–1924'. In *More than a Game: An Unauthorised History of Australian Rules Football*, ed. Rob Hess and Bob Stewart, 114–38. Carton Vic: Melbourne University Press, 1998.
Cashman, Richard. *'Ave a Go, Yer Mug': Australian Cricket Crowds from Larrikin to Ocker*. Sydney: Collins, 1984.
Cashman, Richard. *Australian Cricket Crowds: The Attendance Cycle Daily Figures 1877–1984*. Sydney: University of NSW. Bicentennial History Project, Statistical Monograph No.5, 1984.
Cashman, Richard, David Headon, and Graeme Kinross-Smith, eds. *The Oxford Book of Australian Sporting Anecdotes*. Oxford: Oxford University Press, 1993.

Cathcart, Michael. *Defending the National Tuckshop: Australia's Secret Army Intrigue of 1931*. Fitzroy Vic: McPhee Gribble/Penguin, 1988.

Clark, Manning. 'LarriKins – The Context'.

Connell, R.W., and T.H. Irving. *Class Structure in Australian History*. Melbourne: Longman Cheshire, 1980.

Friedman, Benjamin. *The Moral Consequences of Economic Growth*. New York: Knopf, 2005.

Gallup Poll Summaries, every 2–3 months, 1941–1973, mimeo sheets held by State Library of Victoria SLTF 301.154 AU7GAL. In *The Larrikin Streak: Australian Writers Look at the Legend*, ed. Clem Gorman, 37–9. Sydney: Sun, 1990.

Gorman, Clem. *Larrikin Streak: Australian Writers Look at the Legend*. Sydney: Sun, 1990.

Harte, Chris. *A History of Australian Cricket*. London: Andre Deutsch, 1993.

Horne, Donald. *In Search of Billy Hughes*. Melbourne: Macmillan, 1979.

Hughes, Robert. *Things I Didn't Know*. Milsons Point NSW: Random House Australia, 2006.

Inglis, K.S. *This is the ABC*. 2nd ed. Melbourne: Black, 2006.

Larwood, Harold, with K. Perkins. *The Larwood Story*. 2nd ed. Sydney: Bonpara, 1982.

Lemon, Andrew, and Harold Freedman. *History of Australian Thoroughbred Racing Volume 2: The Golden Years 1862 to 1939*. Melbourne: Southbank Communications, 1990.

Macintyre, Stuart. *A Concise History of Australia*. 2nd ed. Cambridge and Port Melbourne: Cambridge University Press, 2004.

McKernan, Michael. 'Sport War and Society in Australia 1914–18'. In *Sport in History: The Making of Modern Sporting History,* ed. Richard Cashman and Michael McKernan, 1–20. Queensland: University of Queensland Press, 1979.

McLean, Ian. 'Australian Economic Growth in Historical Perspective'. *Economic Record* 80 (September 2004): 330–45.

Molony, John. *Australia: Our Heritage*. Melbourne: Australian Scholary Publishing, 2005.

O'Reilly, W.J. *Tiger*. Sydney: Fontana/Collins, 1986.

Phillips, A.A. *A.A. Phillips on the Cultural Cringe*. Melbourne: Melbourne University Press Masterworks Series 2006 (reprinted from Meanjin in 1950).

Phillips, Murray. 'Football, Class and War: The Rugby Codes in New South Wales, 1907–1918'. In *Making Men: Rugby and Masculine Identity,* ed. John Nauright and Timothy J.L. Chandler, 158–80. London, Portland OR: Frank Cass, 1996.

Phillips, Murray. 'Sport, War and Gender Images: the Australian Sportsmen's Battalions and the First World War'. *International Journal of the History of Sport* 14, no. 1 (April 1997): 78–96.

Rickard, John. *Australia: A Cultural History*. 2nd ed. London: Longman, 1996.

Royal Commission on Wireless. 'Report'. *Parliamentary Paper 1926–8 Session,* vol. 4. Canberra: Government Printer.

Serle, Geoffrey. *The Creative Spirit in Australia*. Melbourne: Heinemann, 1987.

Stoddart, Brian. 'Cricket's Imperial Crisis: the 1932–33 MCC Tour of Australia'. In *Sport in History: The Making of Modern Sporting History,* ed. Richard Cashman and Michael McKernan, 124–47. Queensland: University of Queensland Press, 1979.

Vamplew, Wray, ed. *Australian Historical Statistics*. Broadway NSW: Fairfax, Syme & Weldon Associates, 1987.

Vamplew, Wray. 'Australians and Sport'. In *Sport in Australia: A Social History,* ed. Wray Vamplew and Brian Stoddart, 1–18. Melbourne: Cambridge University Press, 1994.

White, Richard. *Inventing Australia*. Sydney: George Allen and Unwin, 1981.

Yallop, Colin. 'A.G. Mitchell and the Development of Australian Pronunciation'. *Australian Journal of Linguistics* 23, no. 2 (2003): 129–41.

Zogbaum, Heidi. *Kisch in Australia*. Melbourne: Scribe, 2004.

Heyday of the amateur? – 1950s

In one of the first of a remarkable string of Australian international sporting successes, Don Bradman's 'invincibles' won the 1948 Ashes cricket test series in England 4–0. During the final test, a non-cricket fan wrote to English captain Norman Yardley:

> Dear Mr Yardley, I have no interest whatever in cricket and do not care who wins. But the other day, quite by accident, I listened for a few moments to a Test match broadcaster. He said that something or someone called Lindwall was bowling. It sounded a peculiar name to me, but when the commentator proceeded to say that this bowler had two long legs, one fine short leg and a square leg, I was shocked. Tell me, Mr Yardley, what kind of creatures are these Australian cricketers? No wonder we can't win. [1]

By the end of the 1950s bemused observers around the world seemed to be acknowledging Australia as indeed the golden sporting country. In team sports, it held the Davis Cup for amateur tennis, the Eisenhower Cup for amateur golf, the Canada Cup for professional golf, and the Ashes in cricket.[2] Australia was also home to the fastest female swimmers, the fastest middle distance male runner, the World Championship Racing Driver and from 1962 the world's best female squash player. And it had hosted the very successful Melbourne Olympics in 1956.

As we saw in paper 2, and from Norman Yardley's correspondent, several interesting explanations were advanced for this dominance, a number of which don't stand much scrutiny. But there is no doubting that sport was a key ingredient in the new image of the 'Australian way of life'. That image was a more inclusive and democratic one than the sectarianism of the 1920s and 1930s discussed in the last paper. In the post-war boom, some of the successes were due to a broader social reach of sport, and this paper discusses that for tennis, the most popular participation sport of the decade. But there were some gaps between the image and reality as well – most notably in the ways some sports pushed the boundaries of what could be termed 'amateur'. The paper looks at some of the conflicting visions of sport that lay beneath the image of the Melbourne Olympics, and then shows how particular visions had an especially strong hold amongst some sporting officials of the time.

The Australian way of life

Governor General William McKell informed the Jubilee Citizenship Convention in 1951:

> Australia has been working out during the last hundred years a distinctive culture and way of life which, while sharing fully the traditions and way of life of the great British

family of nations, has its own characteristics. In the nineteenth century period of rapid growth, a sense of 'mateship', fair play, independence of spirit and self-reliance was engendered which forms a vital part of our tradition of nationhood.[3]

Despite the wide usage of this national image in the 1940s and 1950s, McKell was somewhat fanciful to trace the term 'Australian way of life' back very far. Historian Richard White has shown the term itself was little used before 1940.[4] As discussed in the previous paper, rather than one coherent image, Australia had different sectarian images in the interwar years, with many conservatives holding fast to the imperial ties and the British, not Australian, flag.

After the devastation of the Second World War, and the preceding Depression, most around the world yearned for something better in the post-war period. In Australia, as in other western countries, the years after 1945 saw the highly popular extension of the welfare state and increased state management of the economy – both of which had been controversial politically in the interwar years. Opinion polls in Australia showed strong support for increased Government control of industry, and for the contention that trade unions were 'a good thing'.[5]

Despite agreement on some things, political controversies still existed, for example in the Cold War around 1950 when the Menzies Government attempted to ban the communist party.[6] Supporting Menzies, the Institute of Public Affairs in 1949 attacked communists as threatening the Australian way of life.[7]

The new consensus on the 'way of life' was stronger outside political attitudes – for instance, the *Australian Women's Weekly* with a conservative orientation in the late 1930s sold some 400,000 copies a week to a largely middle-class audience. By 1950 the *Weekly* was reaching many working-class households as well, doubling its circulation to 800,000, with a less overtly political orientation – although stories about the royal family were still popular.[8]

And while sport had an important role in this way of life image, there were, as with the sportsmen's battalions in 1917, limits on how far appeals to sporting instincts could go. In 1952, the anti-communist Call to Australia organized ministers to give half-time addresses to Australian rules matches in Victoria. A prominent Methodist preacher found one audience at the Lakeside Oval in South Melbourne unreceptive and appealed to common ground with the claim that 'After all, we are all Christians'. A reply from the outer queried 'What about the bloody umpire?'[9]

The Australian way of life seemed to get more successful as Australia entered the long post-war boom. From 7.4 million in 1945, Australia's population almost doubled to 13.1 million in 1971. This population was increasingly urbanized, with the numbers living in the major capital cities increasing from half in 1945, to almost two thirds in 1971. And Australia shared in the remarkable western post-war economic boom of these years. National income per head doubled between 1945 and 1974, an unparalleled growth rate.[10]

Living standards climbed considerably, symbolized by the rapid expansion of suburban homes, and even more rapid expansion of household equipment. Fridges and TV sets (introduced for the 1956 Melbourne Olympics) became common, as did the ownership of motor cars. The proportion of people in Sydney owning their own home soared from 40% of the population in 1947 to 71% in 1961. In Melbourne, one household in three in 1951 owned a car, while by 1964 the figure was two in three (although drivers were still overwhelmingly male).[11] Alongside such private achievements, social facilities grew as well. In particular, there was a rapid expansion of sporting facilities, associated with the building of new schools, expansion of parks and sports grounds by local government, and (as we will see in discussion in Paper 12 of lawn bowls) remarkable volunteer efforts.[12]

The post-war boom created some challenges for existing social patterns. Australia's traditional business and political leaders had been strongly imperial, even to the extent of being antagonistic to domestic industry. The post-war boom gave strength to that local industry, which grew rapidly, and was often considered to be more 'American' in temperament. Some petrol retailers described their competitors who were using more American service standards as 'Un-Australian, undemocratic and socially immoral'.[13] As we will see below, those tensions were clearly in evidence at the Melbourne Olympics.

Such tensions were however downplayed as the way of life was urged as a goal for the 1.2 million migrants settling in Australia in the 15 years after the war as 'new Australians'.[14] While this 'way of life' was never very clearly defined, sport often loomed large. When Wanda Jamrozik's father came to Australia in 1950,

> he realised quickly that an understanding of cricket was the hallmark of successful assimilation. Being a Pole recently extracted from the wreckage of post-war Europe, he knew nothing of the game [and] stuck as he was, by Government order, in an open cut coal mine in Leigh Creek, 450 kilometres north of Adelaide, there wasn't much opportunity to observe the white-flannelled ritual ... Books were the thing. He ordered dozens of them, and spent his evenings pouring over the difference between a leg glance and a cover drive. His friends thought he was mad ... but before long he was able to sidle up to the managerial gatherings where the fate of the Australian XI was a regular topic of conversation. 'I would have brought in a third slip at least an hour earlier' he might say. Or 'Why didn't they take the new ball when they had a chance?' Within weeks he had been promoted to an administrative position, the first 'New Australian' to make the grade.[15]

If cricket was a useful social lubricant for some, it had two stronger sporting contenders in the Australian way of life in the 1950s and 1960s – tennis and swimming. Both were massively popular participation sports, and both produced widely celebrated world champions. Those successes, and the images and realities that accompanied them, are central to the rest of this paper.

What lay behind the remarkable Australian sporting achievements in the 1950s? As noted in Paper 2, many at the time supported the views summarized by sports historian Brian Stoddart: 'Most of the successes sprang from natural talent, an overwhelming belief in sport as a social metaphor for national development, and a reluctance to see an expansion in the economic dimensions of sport.'[16] But there was always something ingenuous, something of myth creation, about this emphasis on Australian 'natural talent'. In fact one of the most 'naturally talented' Australians, Don Bradman, rejected it: 'I don't care who the player is or how great his skill, there is no substitute for practice.'[17]

And 'natural talent' was certainly not enough for Australian sports administrators in the preparation for the Melbourne Olympics. When Bill Uren, manager of the Australian Olympic team in 1952, returned from Helsinki, he noted that both Hungary and Sweden, with similar population sizes, had higher medal counts than Australia. Uren warned

> The average standard of physical fitness of the Australian team was much inferior to that of many other countries. I would recommend that no man or women should be selected

in future teams who is not prepared to undergo the Spartan-like period of self-denial and rigorous training as practised by successful athletes of other countries.[18]

The successes of the 1956 Australian swimming team owed much to an intensive training regime. Two years earlier, the Amateur Swimming Union (ASU) had agreed to a detailed training programme which drew considerably on American Bob Kiphuth's coaching techniques, which stressed conditioning. Former US swim great Johnny Weissmuller later commented that the Australian women's training regime was harder than that of the men in the US.[19] Selected early in 1956, the team had eight weeks of mid-year callisthenics in Melbourne and Sydney. At the end of July, they travelled to the warm weather of Townsville, Queensland to start intensive swimming training. For 12 weeks, the swimmers worked out every day, and in a single carnival towards the end of this training they broke 13 Australian and six world records.[20]

In Townsville the ASU covered all training and accommodation costs, paid coaches and provided a small allowance for toiletries and other expenses. Yet despite the training schedule requiring them to be full-time athletes, the ASU maintained the aura that the swimmers were still amateurs. Swimming bodies from other countries were less impressed, protesting that the 'preparations were too intense and professional to suit the amateur sports'. Consequently, prior to the 1960 Rome Olympics, the ASU reduced the length of time swimmers spent in Townsville.[21]

In tennis too, some interesting things occurred underneath the 'amateur' image.

Tennis

Sports fans sometimes have to make difficult choices. The cricket writer for the Melbourne *Herald* lamented on 30 December 1953 that it was impossible to follow the cricket at the Melbourne Cricket Ground. Three miles away, the Kooyong tennis courts were hosting the Davis Cup Final – the cricket scoreboard posted progress scores, and many radios in the crowd tuned in.[22]

One of Australia's most remarkable periods of dominance in any world sport was in men's tennis in the 1950s. A remarkable number of champions won more than half of the decade's grand slam championships (the Wimbledon, French, Australian and US titles). In the Davis Cup, the international challenge trophy, Australia won eight of the ten contests in the decade.[23] The following decade saw Margaret Smith/Court and Evonne Goolagong/Cawley reach similar heights in women's tennis, alongside male stars such as Rod Laver.

This series of wins encouraged mass enthusiasm for tennis, and particularly for the Davis Cup. The world record for a tennis crowd was held for more than 30 years by the 25,578 spectators at White City, Sydney, on 27 December 1954, with thousands more being turned away.[24]

As well as natural talent, common explanations for this success pointed to the warm climate and the abundance of tennis courts, especially in country areas. Both undoubtedly played a part, but also existed prior to 1950, and after 1970, when Australia had less tennis success. Some commentators added the lower damage suffered by Australia in the Second World War compared with Europe – but this does not help explain success over the even less damaged Americans.[25]

One important factor was the wider social reach of tennis, drawing on a greater talent pool than was available in other countries. When he first visited the US in 1952, Lew Hoad described the game there as 'a socially conscious game, played mainly by the sons of wealthy parents'.[26] In contrast, the Souvenir Programme of the 1957 Davis Cup Challenge Round claimed that Australia had the highest ratio of tennis courts to population in the world. While the statistical basis for this might be doubtful, the claim seems plausible.[27]

In the early years of the twentieth century, tennis was the preserve of the well-off. Australia's first two Wimbledon champions were Norman Brookes (in 1907 and 1914) and Gerald Patterson (1919, 1922). Both came from Melbourne business families wealthy enough to have tennis courts at home.[28] A broader social expansion of the sport occurred from the 1930s. Jack Crawford, who won Wimbledon in 1933, grew up on a farm near Albury, on the NSW-Victoria border. And popular interest was such that the tennis supplies market was very competitive, with four reasonably sized firms.

Post war, tennis spread even further. A Gallup survey in 1948 reported 15% of Australians playing tennis regularly, the highest of any sport. A survey of wheat farms in north-western Victoria in 1940 found that 20% of women, and 7% of men, played tennis regularly during the summer. Sydney adolescents in the early 1950s averaged 1.5 hours a week playing tennis – half the total hours they averaged playing all other sports combined. Participation was spread fairly evenly across social classes, with more girls than boys playing.[29] One feature of both the Sydney adolescents and north-western Victorians at this time was that tennis was a major form of socializing. Indeed, for many Sydney teenagers, tennis was a socially-approved opportunity to meet members of the opposite sex.[30]

Whatever their initial motivation, the greater social spread of tennis was evident in the background of the Australian tennis stars who won individual titles at Wimbledon in the 1950s and 1960s.[31] While some still came from fairly well-off backgrounds, Frank Sedgman's father was a carpenter, Lew Hoad's a tramways employee, and Margaret Smith's father worked in an ice cream factory. She later reminisced:

> We didn't have any money. I always remember my first racquet … was a paling off a fence. And then I remember [aged eight or nine] a friend of my mum's came around and she said 'Margaret's got quite a good eye for a ball. I think I've got an old tennis racquet at home there that nobody ever uses. Maybe she'd like it' … And I thought that was the best thing I ever had in my life.[32]

And the tennis infrastructure helped develop young players who might otherwise not have seen their talent flourish. In his book on Australia's Wimbledon champions, Allan Kendall refers to oft-cited reasons for this dominance:

> In many ways, Australia was, indeed, the perfect tennis factory. Cheap land. Cheap sun. Cheap equipment. The poorest farmer could afford to clear a bit of land, cover it with soil plundered from the nearest ant-bed and there you had it. A beautiful court! Tennis was within the reach of all.[33]

Many key players did indeed have access to nearby courts – either private or public. Both the winners of the Wimbledon's women's crown received substantial financial support: from an early age, Margaret Smith was not charged for her coaching, and Evonne Goolagong was sponsored by local retired grazier Bill Kurtzman, and her coach Vic Edwards.

But while the broader social reach of tennis in Australia helped identify and support new talent, there was another reason why those players stayed in the amateur game – the way Australia interpreted the rules of amateurism. In the late 1940s, the world's two leading amateur players were both Americans from less well-off backgrounds – Jack Kramer and Pancho Gonzales. But after remarkable Grand Slam and David Cup success, neither could afford to continue as amateurs under the USLTA rules, and both became professional players.[34]

The US Lawn Tennis Association (USLTA), reflecting the game's wealthy background in America, was the most conservative of the world tennis organizations. Indeed, it gradually tightened eligibility rules in the interwar years. In 1919, when sporting goods manufacturers employed ten of the leading American amateur players, the USLTA introduced a rule forbidding such employment for players under 35 who wished to retain amateur status. In 1925, when America's leading player, Bill Tilden, was receiving some US\$25,000 each year to write for the press, the USLTA banned this as well. In 1941, when some players were receiving as many as 40 free racquets a year, the USLTA set a limit of four free racquets a year (raised to six in 1946) and required players to pay for strings and stringing.[35]

The Lawn Tennis Association of Australia (LTAA) had a more relaxed interpretation of the amateur rules than its US counterpart. From the mid-1930s, the Australian sporting goods manufacturers, Slazenger, Dunlop, Spalding and Alexanders provided jobs for the country's best young tennis players, with generous time off for practice and exhibition games. Adrian Quist, who played in Davis Cup teams in the 1930s and 1940s, and was Australian Open doubles champion ten times between 1935 and 1950, said, 'if we are completely honest with ourselves, we must say that players were employed to play tennis. They were almost professionals.' Most of the tennis stars did eventually turn fully professional, playing with Jack Kramer's troupe in the United States. After several such signings in 1958, the NSWLTA met with the sporting goods manufacturers to see what additional incentives could stem the flow of defections. By then, one Australian company was supposedly paying £80,000 annually to amateur players.[36]

Such financial advantages also influenced younger players. In the United States, as Jack Kramer reflected in his autobiography, 'so long as tennis remained the only amateur game in a sea of professional sport, it was only natural that natural athletes sought sports other than tennis'.[37] In contrast, Jack Fingleton, a former Australian test cricketer and leading cricket writer, saw tennis as doing much better in Australia than cricket: 'The money lure is one of the chief reasons why tennis has pushed cricket from public favour in Australia ... I do know many parents realise the advantages of a well-paid career and encourage their gifted sons to play tennis.'[38]

Specifically in the Davis Cup competition, which was the strongest source of funds for the LTAA, the organization was again adept at managing the rules. It organized and paid for lengthy overseas tours to give players match competition, and appointed Harry Hopman as non-playing captain to all Australian Davis Cup squads in the 1950s and early 1960s. In contrast American captains, due at least partly to tighter rules, rarely lasted more than two years. Hopman implemented vigorous training schedules, emphasizing physical fitness, and was able to lead most of the lengthy overseas tours, due primarily to generous expenses he received from the LTAA and income as tennis writer for the Melbourne *Herald*.[39]

While differing in interpretations of amateur status, both Australia and the US consistently used the rules of the Davis Cup to choose surfaces that assisted them in the competition. Until 1970, the Davis Cup was an international team competition, restricted to amateurs, in which the previous year's cup holder would play the final against the winner from an elimination series for challenging nations. The final was held on the holder's home turf, with the holder choosing both venue and the surface for the contests. From 1945 to 1960, the Cup was always held by the United States or Australia. Both were exponents of the serve and volley game on grass – and chose accordingly for the matches. Other countries, with fewer grass courts and used to the spin and slower pace of clay, were disadvantaged. One exasperated Italian player noted that most top tennis was played on clay, but 'Australia and America don't care who wins the Davis Cup, just so long as it is one of them ... Until somebody busts the Australian-American monopoly and the Cup is played on hardcourts, we have no hope.'[40]

In the late 1960s, the era of amateur tennis came to an end, with professionals able to enter the main tournaments. While Australia still maintained an impressive record in women's tennis in the 1970s, and in men's doubles for longer than that, a number of commentators publicly wondered why the wheels had fallen off Australian tennis supremacy. The change was not really that mysterious. A key Australian advantage – the differing interpretations of amateur rules – was no longer a factor. And the numbers of tennis players in Australia generally also shrank. By 2006, 712,000 Australians aged 15 and over (4.4% of the population) played tennis regularly, only one third of the proportion playing in 1950. From the social composition of the audience at tennis events, these players are predominantly well-off.[41]

The reasons for such declines in sporting participation are discussed further in Paper 12. The remainder of this paper follows the LTAA's trail of managing sports rules into other sports, firstly for the Melbourne Olympics, and then for amateur sport more generally.

Organizing the Melbourne Olympics

In a decade of sporting successes for Australia, perhaps the most enduring image of the 1950s is of the Closing Ceremony of the Melbourne Olympics on 8 December 1956. For the first time, athletes mingled and strolled together around the arena, rather than marching in their team formations – a fitting end, it is often thought, to the 'friendly games'.[42] The Melbourne Olympics were certainly highly successful, both in sporting achievements and public involvement. At least in popular mythology, the attendances in Melbourne remained records for several decades.

But the much-cherished image of the Closing Ceremony conflicts with other, more complex, images. One, confirming that sport was not so immune from political developments, was a bloody water polo match between Hungary and the Soviet team, just weeks after the Soviet Union had invaded Hungary. A second came with the Opening Ceremony, which had a much more conservative hew than the closing. Despite the ecumenical and international principles of the Games, the organizing committee ensured the ceremony both started *and* finished with the playing of 'God Save the Queen' and the Hallelujah Chorus. The Anglican Archbishop read a dedicatory address.[43]

The successes of the Games also overshadowed in public memory the fact that the city had come very close to losing the games only 18 months before they started. In April 1955, Avery Brundage, President of the International Olympic Committee (IOC), visited Melbourne to monitor progress. He was unimpressed, telling a media conference on 11 April:

A group of pretty smart Melbourne citizens attended the Rome meeting six years ago, at which the Games were awarded to Melbourne. I don't know how they did it ... [But] for six years we have had nothing but squabbling, changes of management and bickering. Melbourne has a deplorable record in its preparations for the games – promises and promises.[44]

The IOC revealed it had received an alternative hosting offer from Philadelphia, which it would consider seriously unless the Melbourne organizers dramatically improved their operations. The wrangling Brundage criticized arose from two different groups involved in organising and managing the Games. Historian Graeme Davison summed up the groups:

Throughout the long tussle to win and keep the Games, two wings of the Melbourne establishment and two visions of national and civic progress contended for mastery. One, entrepreneurial, futuristic and international in outlook, looked to business models of organisation and American know-how ... But the official guardians of the Olympic spirit were more militaristic, traditional and imperial in outlook. Its leaders were ex-service-men and amateur athletics officials.[45]

The civic group was led by businessmen Sir Frank Beaurepaire, former swimming champion, former Lord Mayor, and head of Olympic tyres, and Maurice Nathan, a furniture retailer. Former athletes and ex-servicemen Wilfred Kent Hughes and Edgar Tanner led the amateur sports group. Kent Hughes had been a State minister in the 1930s, managed the Australian Empire Games team in 1938, was a prominent supporter of the Empire Youth movement, and from 1949 was a minister in the national Menzies Government. Tanner had been an Olympic boxer, and became secretary of the Victorian Olympic Council (VOC).

While sports organizations had earlier harboured ideas of an Olympic bid, Beaurepaire orchestrated the post-war impetus to present a formal proposal to the IOC. As president of the VOC, in May 1947 Beaurepaire set up an 'invitation committee' of prominent citizens to prepare the submission. Sports groups expressed considerable ill-feeling that they had no formal representation on this committee.

The committee raised funds from 150 leading citizens, each of whom paid 100 guineas. But rather than from Melbourne's traditional business elite, in finance, mining and commerce, the 'leading citizens' were largely from new manufacturing industries and city retailers.

As well as an expensive book promoting Melbourne as the formal submission to the IOC, Beaurepaire and his committee paid for a lavish banquet in London in 1948, including a special consignment of Australian food and wine, at a time when London still had food rationing. For the IOC final decision at its Rome meeting in 1949, the Melbourne committee prepared a 13-minute colour film to promote Melbourne. Images were carefully created, stressing fine dining and wining in Melbourne without mentioning the six o'clock closing time for bars, and somehow including pictures of rolling surf, which is unusual in the sheltered waters of Port Phillip Bay.

Despite low AOC expectations for the bid, Melbourne won the final ballot for the 1956 Games, beating rival Buenos Aires by a margin of one vote. But, as Brundage complained in 1955, gaps soon appeared in the carefully presented images.

In ensuing tensions, both the business and sports-oriented groups briefed journalists sympathetic to their view, and leaked information to Australian and International Olympic bodies. Athletic officials raised doubts about the amateur credentials of the business figures including Beaurepaire, while the civic group complained about the officials' poor business organization.[46] Although the sporting groups were unsuccessful in early attempts to increase their numbers on the organizing committee, Kent Hughes replaced Beaurepaire as president of the VOC, and subsequently as chair of the organizing committee in May 1951.[47]

Further conflict occurred on whether the Games should be organized on business or military lines. The sporting groups consolidated control when retailer Arthur Coles resigned as Chairman of the Executive Committee in May 1953, and General Bridgeford became Chief Executive.

The most visible sign of the in-fighting was the location of the main stadium. In the official bid documents, the civic and sporting groups had agreed on a redeveloped Olympic Park, alongside the Yarra River. However, the dreams faded with realization of extremely poor ground conditions. Kent Hughes and many in the sports group favoured the Melbourne Cricket Ground, but they were stymied by the opposition of the Melbourne Cricket Club and the Victorian Football League, both jealously protecting their own interests. Beaurepaire and many in the business group supported a proposal from the Country Party, influential in State politics, to use the Flemington Showgrounds.

Acknowledging the soil problems at Olympic Park, the Invitation Committee sent a supplementary book to the IOC, listing the Showgrounds as the main arena, and claiming that the venue was located in one of Melbourne's most attractive areas. The outraged VOC drafted a circular pointing out that the Showgrounds were surrounded by 'Melbourne's noxious trades such as cattle yards, glue works, abattoirs, boiling down works, skin and hide stores ... From the city the rail route traverses railway yards, unkempt swamp area ... and finally runs through cattle and sheep yards with a vista of small allotment back yards'.[48] Continuing opposition to the Showgrounds from the sports groups, and with further negotiations with the MCC failing, the organizing committee was forced to look elsewhere. In July 1952 they advised the IOC that the venue was now the Carlton Cricket Ground, a site long preferred by some in the business group. Businessman Kenneth Luke, who was also Chairman of Carlton Football Club and President of the VFL, strongly supported the Princes Park option.

However, an incoming Labor State Government found that the costs at Carlton would have been prohibitive. At the end of January 1953, Premier John Cain Snr convened a three-day summit involving the Prime Minister, Deputy Leader of Opposition, all Victorian political leaders, the lord mayor, organizing officials and the MCC. The Premier announced the Government would not contribute towards the costs of Carlton, but would contribute to expansion of the MCG from 85,000 to 120,000 seats. The summit finally reached agreement on the MCG as the main venue for the Games.[49]

While subsequently confounded by the event's success, many were concerned prior to the Olympics about the images Melbourne would create internationally. But a change was occurring in the comparator. The overseas judge of Melbourne's image was now much more likely to be an American expert – from the home of modernism – rather than the English gentleman who had previously been the touchstone.[50] This change in the overseas reference point accompanied other changes at the time, for example with Beaurepaire's invitation committee dominated by a new business elite.

But a major exception to this change was in the administration of sports. The traditionally imperial and more militaristic amateur sports groups had been victorious in the struggle to control the organizing bodies for the Games. The massive success of the Games, and especially the medals won by Australian athletes, gave considerable social cachet to these groups.

Officials and the cult of amateurism

This collection has often referred to the role of sporting officials both in creating images of sports and in shaping the ways sports develop. Decisions have ranged across the spectrum from reaching out to new audiences and interests, such as in country football in Paper 5 and the Stawell Gift in Paper 9, to efforts to control particular sports, even narrowing social involvement, as in cricket and especially racing in Paper 8.

While amateur sporting officials basked in the successful images of the Melbourne Olympics, inside the sports many athletes joined champion runner Herb Elliott in seeing an 'unhappy blend of bureaucracy/autocracy in athletics officials'. He suspected many

> had been relatively unsuccessful in other walks of life, and had not learnt to deal with power. When they obtained power, they misused it ... Perhaps because sport was amateur and the vast majority of the population were not prepared to spend the hours in mundane tasks ... you ended up with relatively small people getting to the top.[51]

As late as 1980, a survey of sporting officials showed many executives and coaches had previously been successful athletes themselves. But most had an overwhelmingly conservative background: 36% of the sports leaders had been to private schools, and 38% had completed tertiary studies, at a time when only 7% of the working population had degrees.[52]

An example of the efforts from officials and administrators keen to cement their control over sport came when future politician Don Chipp had ambitions for the athletic sprint events in Melbourne:

> In attempting to register with the Victorian Amateur Athletics Association I received a rude shock. I was informed that because I was a professional footballer (I was with Fitzroy at the time) I could not be admitted as an athlete. I stoutly complained that I had deliberately maintained my amateur status and not taken any money for my games with the club. The amateur official retorted that that did not matter, I had taken football knickers and a football guernsey and therefore had lost my lily white status; however, if I cared to fill in the required number of forms, wait a period of up to a year, the stain on my blemished record could, as an act of grace, be wiped clean.[53]

A more remarkable story came in 1949. A 12-year-old girl, competing in an amateur swimming carnival in Western Sydney, won a 55-yard race, upsetting another swimmer who was considered a future star. Officials promptly checked the winner's background, discovering she had swum with a non-amateur group. Worse, she had received two shillings as a Christmas gift at a sporting function when she was 8 years old. The swimmer felt her background from 'the wrong side of the tracks' had also been a factor. For such unseemly behaviour the officials banned her from amateur competitions for two years. The official who told the 12-year-old the news later became a member of the Australian Olympic Committee and president of the international swimming body FINA.[54]

Such pettiness may seem extreme, but officials in many amateur sports had similar reputations. Early in her tennis career, Margaret Smith had several offers to switch her athletic prowess to other sports: 'At times I was tempted, especially when I was having trouble with the Lawn Tennis Association bureaucrats. But I realised that the officials who ran other sports in Australia were just as narrow minded.'[55] Smith had sound grounds for her antipathy. In 1961, she participated in the LTAA international tour, which received a handsome profit from the tour. Smith complained that much of the profit came from chaperon Mrs Nell Hopman's tight budgetary insistence on 'dreary, third class hotels'. The players also lacked an adequate diet, and proper medical attention: Smith contracted glandular fever but it was not diagnosed for five weeks.[56]

The following year, when the LTAA again appointed Nell Hopman as team manager, Smith refused to tour, and proposed alternative tour arrangements. After unsuccessfully trying to prevent Smith's private tour, the LTAA issued two edicts. First, in contrast to the arrangements for its own group, the LTAA threatened to cancel Smith's amateur status if she accepted any reimbursements of expenses for the tour. Second, all members of the official Australian team were forbidden to practice with Smith. Smith's career only continued thanks to support from a private sponsor.

But the episode that illustrated most vividly the lengths to which sports official-dom would go to protect their positions came in March 1965, when the Australian Swimming Union (ASU) fully justified swimming coach Forbes Carlile's criticisms of 'an inflexible, iron-fisted oligarchy'.[57] At its annual meeting in Hobart, the ASU had considered a report on the behaviour of the women swimmers at the Tokyo Olympics. On 1 March, the ASU announced.

> the union is very jealous of its good name and the reputation of the members of its team, both in and out of the water ... It is determined that it will maintain a strong discipline, especially amongst the members of its teams who represent Australia. It is with deep regret that the union thinks it necessary to take strong action arising out of incidents which occurred in Tokyo.[58]

The 'strong action' banned Dawn Fraser from amateur competition for ten years, and three other swimmers for three to four years. The bans effectively ended each of the women's swimming careers.[59] The ASU refused to announce the full details of the charges on the interesting grounds that 'young girls are involved and they should be protected'. The only charges mentioned publicly were disputes over swimmers marching in the opening ceremony, and disagreement with Fraser over an unofficial swimsuit.

Ann Hatton, team chaperon in Tokyo, said she was appalled at the 'unbelievably savage' sentences, which were 'imposed undemocratically, allowing the girls no right of appeal'.[60] Indeed, the ASU had only sent letters on 16 February, when two of the swimmers were overseas, advising of the misconduct hearing at the end of the month. While written responses were possible, the swimmers had no opportunity to address the meeting.

Despite informing the swimmers only of the opening ceremony charge (plus the additional offence specific to Fraser), the ASU disciplinary hearing seems to have considered other matters in the several hours they spent on the matter. A subsequent effort by writer Harry Gordon to check the Olympic archives for details found the key report to the ASU 'has been mutilated with scissors, with the entire reference to Dawn Fraser's behaviour deleted ... The scissor-work, evocative of wartime censorship of soldiers' mail, was applied to all copies of the report after the ASU met'.[61]

But if the ASU would not formally release details, it leaked information to the press, especially *The Sun* in Sydney, suggesting that the women involved had attended drinks parties and sneaked into the men's quarters.[62] Further, a leading official sent letters to FINA officials overseas hinting that there were other transgressions, and that Dawn Fraser 'was her own worst enemy'. Fraser later successfully sued for defamation, winning in March 1968 a full apology, an out-of-court financial settlement and removal of her ASU ban.[63]

At the time, the ASU's actions received widespread condemnation. In an editorial, *The Age* described the charges as serious, but 'Justice cannot yet be seen to be done, or seem to be done, because all the charges against the girls have not been made public … But it is surely beyond belief that mere official pettiness is the basis for the ASU's drastic action'.[64] UK papers described them as 'lunatic', 'shamefully humiliating' and 'high handed and autocratic', with the *Daily Mirror* in London commenting, 'Australian athletes of every kind have raised the standard of Australia in the four corners of the world, proving that with regard to population, they are perhaps the greatest [sporting] nation of all. What a pity they do not have officials to match.'[65]

More generally amongst sporting officials, there was some dissension about how sports were organized. In 1964, fencer David McKenzie was a delegate to the Australian Olympic federation, and was appalled at its organization. 'We had a magnificent public body, in effect, and it was being run like a church tennis group. It really was very poor.'[66]

The amateur sporting groups had won the day in the battles over the organization of the Melbourne Olympics. Riding on the success of Australian athletes, they had also developed a high public image for the amateur ethos. But the reality behind the successful images gave a darker side – a willingness to stretch the rules when necessary, and jealous efforts to maintain control of sports. And, as we will see in the next paper, the traditional and conservative orientation of the sporting bodies meant they were ill-prepared for the challenges of changing times in the 1960s and 1970s.

Notes

1. Smart, ed., *Penguin Book of Australian Sporting Anecdotes*, 17–18.
2. Bloomfield, *Australia's Sporting Success*, 30.
3. Cathcart and Darian-Smith, *Stirring Australian Speeches*, 239.
4. White, 'The Australian Way of Life'; and White, *Inventing Australia*, especially Chap. 10 'Every Man and his Holden'.
5. Gallup poll summary, October 1943, showed one quarter of conservative voters supported increased government ownership of factories, and in April–June 1951 80% of conservative voters supported trades unions. Support for each contention was even stronger amongst Labor voters.
6. The Menzies government proposed a 1951 constitutional amendment banning the Communist party in Cold War terms, while ALP leader Evatt argued the proposal was a general threat to civil liberties. The ALP arguments quickly made inroads: Gallup polls recorded the following percentages supporting the referendum: June 80%, Aug. 73%, Sept. pre referendum 57% – the actual vote was 49.4%. A subsequent Gallup poll, in Feb.–March 1952 showed 64% support for using existing powers to ban the Communist party.
7. White, 'Australian Way of Life', 537.
8. See Ward, 'Development of Melbourne', 488–9.
9. Macintyre, *Concise History of Australia*, 214.
10. McLean, 'Australian Economic Growth', 332.
11. Australian Bureau of Statistics (ABS, www.abs.gov.au), *Australian Social Trends*, 1996, 4102.0; White, *Inventing Australia*, 164; Davison, *Car Wars*: households owning a car in

1951, 8, in 1964, 22 and driving licence statistics, 43 – in 1964, 85% of licensed drivers were male.

12. Bloomfield, *Australia's Sporting Success*, 27.
13. Davison, *Car Wars*, 94.
14. White, 'Australian Way of Life', 537.
15. Smart, *Penguin Book of Australian Sporting Anecdotes*, 20–1.
16. Stoddart, *Saturday Afternoon Fever*, 27.
17. Cited by Hutchins, *Don Bradman*, 51.
18. Cited by Gordon, *Australia and the Olympic Games*, 191.
19. Fraser, *Dawn*, 91–2.
20. Gordon, *Australia and the Olympic Games*, 212.
21. Fraser, *Dawn*, 117.
22. *Herald*, December 30, 1953, 4.
23. Fewster, 'Advantage Australia', 49.
24. Ibid., 50–1.
25. Ibid., 52.
26. Cited by ibid., 64. A MRI Consumer survey in the US in 2004 confirmed the well-off background of most tennis players there. Readers of *Tennis* Magazine had median household incomes of $80,000, compared with an overall US median household income of $ 51,000. See http://www.mediamark.com/mri/techguide/fall2004/tg_f04_age_hhi.htm
27. Cited by Fewster, 'Advantage Australia', 53.
28. Kendall, *Australia's Wimbledon Champions*, 10–11 summarized Brooks' and Patterson's backgrounds. The exclusive social patterns of tennis in the early part of the twentieth century are outlined in O'Farrell, 'Unasked Questions'; Kinross-Smith, 'Privilege in Tennis'; and Kinross-Smith, 'Lawn Tennis'.
29. Gallup poll summary 1948, cited in McGregor, *Profile of Australia*, 135; the 1940 Victorian survey in Senyard, 'The Tennis Court'; and the study of Sydney adolescents is Connell *et al.*, *Growing Up in an Australian City*, 126–9.
30. Senyard, 'The Tennis Court'; and Connell *et al.*, *Growing Up in an Australian City*.
31. Kendall gives the background to each of *Australia's Wimbledon Champions*, and Fewster, 'Advantage Australia', 58–9.
32. Oral history collection of the Australian National Archive, printed in Cliff, *A Sporting Nation*, 87; and Court, *Court on Court*, 4.
33. Kendall, *Australia's Wimbledon Champions*, 13.
34. Fewster, 'Advantage Australia', 57.
35. Ibid., 57–8.
36. Quist's quote is from the oral history collection of the Australian National Archive, Cliff, *A Sporting Nation*, 91; and Margaret Court made the same point in *Court on Court*, 12. Other details from Fewster, 'Advantage Australia', 59–60.
37. Kramer. *My Forty Years in Tennis*, 244, cited by Fewster, 'Advantage Australia', 57.
38. Fingleton, *Masters of Cricket,* 212–13, 217, cited by Fewster, 'Advantage Australia', 60.
39. Harry Hopman's role is discussed by both Fewster, 'Advantage Australia', 61 and Kendall, *Australia's Wimbledon Champions*, e.g. 79; and Court, *Court on Court*, 24–43 and Kendall, 215 note the disagreements between Margaret Smith and Nell Hopman.
40. *Sun Herald* (Sydney), August 9, 1959, 2, cited by Fewster, 'Advantage Australia', 54. Fewster also discussed the common explanations for Australian tennis prowess, and the specific features of the Davis Cup.
41. ABS, *Participation in Sport and Physical Recreation 2006* (4177.0), Table 8, with 'regular' players those that played monthly or more. The social composition of tennis watchers is from ABS, *Sports Attendance 2006* (4174.0), discussed above in Paper 5.
42. The following discussion draws mainly from Davison, 'Welcoming the World', and Gordon, *Australia and the Olympic Games*, 194–225.
43. Davison, 'Welcoming the World', 73.
44. Cited by Gordon, *Australia and the Olympic Games*, 199.
45. Ibid., 66.
46. Ibid., 69–70.
47. Ibid., 197.
48. Ibid., 196.
49. Ibid., 199; Davison, 'Welcoming the World', 70.
50. Davison, 'Welcoming the World', 71.

51. Cited by Booth and Tatz, *One-eyed*, 144.
52. McKay, 'Sport, Leisure and Social Inequality', especially, 141–3. Its survey covered the 89 sports listed in the Australian sports directory, most of which would have been amateur bodies. The 7% figure for degrees comes from ABS, *Social Indicators 1984* (4101.0), 140–1. The numbers with degrees grew from 3% in 1969 to 7% in 1982 and to 11% in 1991 (the latter figure from ABS, *Social Indicators 1992* [4101.0], 131). In addition to degrees, a further group had completed certificates or diplomas – although it is unlikely that many of these would report themselves as having 'completed tertiary studies'. Numbers in this group were 9% in 1969, 19% in 1982 and 21% in 1991 (same sources).
53. Cited by Cashman, *Paradise of Sport*, 60.
54. Fraser, *Dawn*, 36–8; Gordon, *Australia and the Olympic Games*, 269.
55. Court, *Court on Court*, 23.
56. Ibid., 33–5.
57. Cited by Booth and Tatz, *One-eyed*, 145.
58. *The Age*, March 2, 1965, 24.
59. Gordon, *Australia and the Olympic Games*, 253–5, 262–3; reports in *The Age*, March 2, 1965, 1, 24; March 3, 1965, 1, 2, 3, 26; and March 4, 1965, 1; and Fraser, *Dawn*, 209–16.
60. *The Age*, March 3, 1965, 3.
61. Gordon, *Australia and the Olympic Games*, 262–3.
62. Fraser, *Dawn*, 210–11.
63. Ibid., 231.
64. *The Age*, March 3, 1965, 2.
65. Cited in ibid., 26; other comments cited in Fraser, *Dawn*, 212.
66. Gordon, *Australia and the Olympic Games*, 250.

References
Bloomfield, John. *Australia's Sporting Success: The Inside Story*. Sydney: UNSW Press, 2003.
Booth, Douglas, and Colin Tatz. *One eyed: A View of Australian Sport*. Sydney: Allen and Unwin, 2000.
Cashman, Richard. *Paradise of Sport: The Rise of Organised Sport in Australia*. Melbourne: Oxford University Press, 1995.
Cathcart, Michael, and Kate Darian-Smith, eds. *Stirring Australian Speeches*. Carlton Vic: Melbourne University Press, 2003.
Cliff, Paul, ed. *A Sporting Nation: Celebrating Australia's Sporting Life*. Canberra: National Library of Australia, 1999.
Connell, W.F., E.P. Francis, E.E. Skilbeck, and a group of Sydney University Students. *Growing up in an Australian City: A Study of Adolescents in Sydney*. Melbourne: Australian Council for Educational Research, 1957.
Court, Margaret. *Court on Court: A Life in Tennis*. London: Allen, 1975.
Davison, Graeme. 'Welcoming the World: the 1956 Olympics and the Re-presentation of Melbourne'. *Australian Historical Studies* 109 (1997): 64–76.
Davison, Graeme. *Car Wars: How the Car Won our Hearts and Conquered our Cities*. NSW: Allen and Unwin, 2004.
Fewster, Kevin. 'Advantage Australia: Davis Cup Tennis 1950–59'. *Sporting Traditions* 2, no. 1 (November 1985): 47–68.
Fraser, Dawn. *Dawn: One Hell of a Life*. NSW: Hodder Headline Australia, 2001.
Gallup Poll Summaries, every 2–3 months, 1941–1973, mineo sheets held by State Library of Victoria SLTF 301.154 AU7GAL.
Gordon, Harry. *Australia and the Olympic Games*. Brisbane: University of Queensland Press, 1994.
Hutchins, Brett. *Don Bradman: Challenging the Myth*. Melbourne: Cambridge University Press, 2002.
Kendall, Allen. *Australia's Wimbledon Champions*. Sydney: ABC Books, 1995.
Kinross-Smith Graeme. 'Privilege in Tennis and Lawn Tennis'. *Sporting Traditions* 3, no. 2 (May 1987): 189–216.
Kinross-Smith Graeme. 'Lawn Tennis'. In *Sport in Australia: A Social History,* ed. Wray Vamplew and Brian Stoddart, 133–53. Melbourne: Cambridge University Press, 1994.

McGregor, Craig. *Profile of Australia*. London: Hodder and Stoughton, 1966.

Macintyre, Stuart. *A Concise History of Australia*. 2nd ed. Cambridge and Port Melbourne: Cambridge University Press, 2004.

McKay, Jim. 'Sport, Leisure and Social Inequality in Australia'. In *Sport and Leisure: Trends in Australian National Culture,* ed. David Rowe and Geoff Lawrence, 125–60. Sydney: Harcourt Brace Jovanovich, 1990.

McLean, Ian. 'Australian Economic Growth in Historical Perspective'. *Economic Record* 80 (September 2004): 330–45.

O'Farrell, Virginia. 'The Unasked Questions in Australian Tennis'. *Sporting Traditions* 1, no. 2 (May 1985): 67–86.

Senyard, June. 'The Tennis Court: A Country Woman's Window to the Modern World'. *Sporting Traditions* 13, no. 1 (November 1996): 25–42.

Smart, Richard, ed. *The Penguin Book of Australian Sporting Anecdotes*. Ringwood Vic: Penguin Books, 1996.

Stoddart, Brian. *Saturday Afternoon Fever*. North Ryde NSW: Angus and Robertson, 1986.

Ward, Tony. 'The Development of Melbourne in the Interwar Years'. PhD diss., Monash University Melbourne, 1984.

White, Richard. 'The Australian Way of Life'. *Historical Studies* 18 (1979): 528–45.

White, Richard. *Inventing Australia*. Sydney: George Allen and Unwin, 1981.

Changing times 1960–75

Western Suburbs played Mosman in a Sydney first grade cricket match on Saturday 23 October 1976, the day of a solar eclipse. In the weeks before, health authorities had warned of the dangers of looking directly at the sun during the eclipse, and the two captains, Bob Simpson and David Colley, heeded those warnings. They agreed to play during the normal tea interval, and then draw stumps early so that everyone would be indoors for the eclipse. Wests eventually won the game, but the NSW Cricket Association declared the contest a 'no match' because of the unauthorized alteration of normal playing hours. Wests lost their points and all performances – including Simpson's 104 and Allan Border's 83 – were struck from the records. Wests' veteran bowler Wally Wellham called it 'one of the darkest days in the history of Sydney grade cricket'.[1]

To many in 1976, the failure of a rule-bound NSWCA to give any ground for exceptional circumstances was symptomatic of most sporting bodies. This image was a long way from the success that sport enjoyed in the 1950s as part of the Australian way of life. This paper traces that change in image.

Sport initially benefited from the economic boom enjoyed by all developed countries in the years after the Second World War. In Australia, most people, whether participating or attending, had more money and time to spend on sports. Both sporting clubs and local governments contributed to the rapid expansion of sporting facilities such as tennis courts and memorial swimming pools across Australia. And a high social and media profile was given to numerous Australian world champions.

However, the boom also produced other social changes, less favourable for sport. Higher incomes and greater car ownership gave access to alternative leisure opportunities. Changes in working hours, especially with more women working part time, affected the time people could devote especially to the practice schedules of organized sport. During the 1960s, sports started to lose their golden aura, and seemed increasingly inflexible in the face of changes such as solar eclipses.

By the mid-1970s, newspapers in Australia and overseas were lamenting the 'decline of a sporting super race' and seeking reasons why Australians were now 'middle-aged athletes gone flabby'.[2] Sports attendances, while many were still impressive, were in decline, and participation levels, particularly amongst young adults, had fallen considerably. In addition, and not totally unrelated, emphases in the Australian national image changed. Images apart from sport now dominated, for example, through Australian films such as the 'Adventures of Bazza McKenzie' and the international success of music groups such as the Bee Gees, Air Supply and Men at Work. In this new image, sports and sporting organizers were often seen as hide-bound conservatives.

Tracing the changes to sports and the sporting image through the 1960s and 1970s, this paper continues the collection's general theme that neither the image nor the underlying reality is static. And in looking at the image we need to consider both its relationship with the realities, and the social dynamics surrounding the images.

Many have drawn parallels between devotion to sport and religion, not least in examples such as the zealot last seen in Paper 2 writing 'Essendon Football Club' when the Census asked for religion. The first section of this paper looks at the interaction between sports and religion in our period, and what the trends tell us of more general social changes. The following section documents how sport became associated with a more conservative image in these years, and the final section discusses the experience of women's lawn bowls in Victoria and its relationship with the sporting image.

Sport and other religions

In the early 1970s the vicar posted a notice outside his church in Hawthorn, Melbourne: 'What would you do if God came to Hawthorn today?' Graffiti under the sign responded: 'Move Peter Hudson to centre half forward.'[3]

Such a laconic approach to picking the Hawthorn team, and possibly replacing the star full forward, sits well with the no-nonsense Australian sporting image. Paper 3 discussed the common image of the 'ocker', little interested in cultural or spiritual things.[4] That has been a long-standing image: D.H. Lawrence in the 1920s commented, 'They don't set much store on deepness over here. It's easy come, easy go, as a rule.'[5] In the early 1960s, an American Professor of Journalism referred to Australian sports journalists as 'not merely reporters, heralds and chroniclers of muscular events; they are priests of a national cult'.[6]

This image of sport replacing religion does not, however, sit well with the fact that around 1960 almost half of adult Australians went to church regularly (at least once a month), with one third attending services once a week.[7] Neither does the idea of a constant image fit with marked changes in attendance levels since then.

Many commentators worldwide have often described sport as a secular religion. One such was English Lord Mancroft, possibly with his tongue in his stiff upper lip: 'The English are not a spiritual people, and so they invented cricket in order to have some conception of eternity.'

And many have suggested that as Australian religious attendances have declined since the 1950s, people have found their 'conception of eternity' in sport. There are, however, two surprising twists to this idea. First, between 1960 and 1975 at least, sports participation and attendance rates fell at the same time that religious attendance fell. And secondly, visions of sport differed between congregations, symbolized in attitudes to Sunday afternoon sport. Catholics, with the highest rates of religious observance, had few problems with spectator sports on Sundays. Non-conformist Protestant churches, also with high attendance at church, were convinced such events would profane the Lord's day. These patterns pick up our general theme of the diversity of attitudes towards sport, complicating any idea of a standard sports culture. They also provide useful illustration of the broad social trends in these years, affecting involvement in sports as well as numerous other social activities.

As major social institutions, churches had long had significant influence beyond their pews. Paper 10 noted the antagonistic stands on the war conscription referendums of the Protestant churches (for) and the Catholic (against). As late as 1955 a referendum in Victoria to allow pubs to stay open later than six o'clock was defeated after a major campaign by non-conformist Protestant churches.[8]

Churches also played important roles in the development of sports. Many local tennis clubs were on church land, as were some bowling clubs. Two of the seven bowling clubs in the Victorian country town of Warrnambool, Christ Church and St John's were on church land – the former Anglican, the latter Presbyterian.[9] And many suburban cricket and football teams bore the name of their local church.

But here too there was a dynamic between the aims of organizers and how people responded. From 1947 to 1951 in the northern suburbs of Melbourne, the Prince of Wales Park Methodist Football Club won consecutive premierships in the regional Methodist Football Association. After their fourth flag, club president Reverend Bailey complained that the players were celebrating too hard. Many players objected to the imposition of the church's standards on their carousing, and by 1952 had set up the breakaway Northcote Park football club.[10]

So if the extent of the religious attendance challenges part of the established Aussie image, some complicating factors also need attention. First, as with many of the nationwide figures discussed in this collection, and as Reverend Bailey found, there were considerable variations lying underneath the averages. Secondly, affected by some of the similar patterns that affected sport, church attendances fell considerably from 1960 onwards. Thirdly, there was no one simple relationship between church-going and attitudes to sport.

Even just with the attendance figures, some marked differences occurred. Women have always been more likely to go to church than men, and older people more often than younger people, but these differences fade in comparison with those between denominations. In the late 1950s, Catholics were by far the most observant, with 75% regular attendance (and some 60% each week). About half of Presbyterians and Baptists went regularly, while the figure for Anglicans was just under one third. For all denominations, attendances climbed a little in the 1950s, possibly reflecting increased leisure time and the advent of the car making getting to church easier. In contrast, the figures fell dramatically after 1960. By the early 1970s, regular attendees were one-third of the population, and by 2002 the figure had fallen below 20%.[11] The pattern of decline varied a little by age: enrolments in Presbyterian and Methodist Sunday Schools were still growing well into the 1960s for example. After doubling from 1956 to 1966, enrolments then slumped: 'By the mid 1970s, enrolments had more than halved, and by the 1980s a once-powerful institution was all but extinct.'[12]

The strong growth of car ownership in these years affected these trends. In 1951, only one household in three owned a car, by 1961 it was about half, and by 1971 the vast majority of households.[13] Up to the mid-1960s, cars seem to have made it easier for families to transport children to Sunday School – but after that date, the greater general social flexibility cars allowed worked against such institutions.

Across these years there were also changing attitudes towards spectator sport on Sunday afternoon. In the late 1940s, one third supported such sport, while two-thirds opposed – with the strongest rationale being to preserve the sanctity of Sundays. By the early 1960s, the figures had reversed, and by 1966 three-quarters supported Sunday afternoon sport, with only one quarter opposed. But even in the 1960s there was a clear distinction between football and cricket on one hand, and horse racing on the other. Despite the support for Sunday afternoon cricket or football, two thirds of adults were opposed to race meetings and associated gambling on Sundays.

But these patterns were not simply a mirror of the decline in church attendance. As early as 1950, a majority of Catholics (as noted above, the most regular church attendees) supported Sunday afternoon sport. And by the mid 1960s, despite the general trend, a majority of Methodists (also strong attendees) were still opposed.[14] A legacy from the views during the First World War still persisted, with Catholics more likely to be working class and support sport as entertainment, while the more middle-class Methodists had firmer views on the morality associated with sport. Linked to these social class views, ALP voters had higher support for Sunday afternoon sport than the average, while conservative voters were less interested.

The decline of church attendances in the 1960s accompanied a general loosening of sectarian feelings in sport. In the 1950s, some VFL clubs in Melbourne and League clubs in Sydney had been resolutely either Protestant or Catholic, and while the speed of change differed between clubs, that had largely gone by the 1970s. Indeed, the strength of the Catholic links of the Collingwood football club already meant little in the mid-1960s to one parish priest in St Kilda. Shortly after the Saints beat the Magpies by a point to win the 1966 flag, one of his parishioners died. The deceased had been a strong Collingwood supporter, so the relatives nervously approached the priest, who was known as a passionate Saints follower.

'Would you refuse to bury a Collingwood supporter?'
'Refuse? Of course not. I just wish I could be burying them all day.'[15]

Other rites of passage usually celebrated in church also changed. Historian Graeme Davison's team analysed the addresses of couples getting engaged in Melbourne, comparing the early 1950s and the early 1970s. In 1950, almost 60% of couples getting engaged were from the same or an immediately adjoining suburb. Twenty years later, cars meant that the 'geographically possible' bounds of courtship had greatly widened. Now more than 60% of couples getting engaged came from suburbs well beyond walking or biking distance, while the proportion coming from the same suburb had halved.[16]

Australia was far from alone in seeing such impacts on social patterns from the post-war economic boom and new technologies such as widespread car ownership, or the contraceptive pill. Nor was it alone in seeing a multitude of new ways opening up in which people could spend their leisure time. And the widespread 'youth rebellion' of the late 1960s and 1970s also occurred across the western world.

But these international trends played out in differing ways in different countries. In Australia it especially affected the strong British element in the national culture. As discussed in Paper 4, until the mid-1960s there was still strong support for God Save the Queen as the national anthem – a support that collapsed by the early 1970s.

The general changes were particularly hastened by changes in Australia's relationship with Britain. A primary element was economic. From the mid-1950s, Australian exports to Asia (especially Japan) and to the United States were becoming more important, and in the early 1960s the United Kingdom applied to join the European Common Market. Rather than the previous imperial preference for Australian goods in Britain, the prospect was for tariffs against Australian products.[17] On 25 September 1962 the *Australian Financial Review* commented, 'We may have to stop thinking about Britain as "Home" and start thinking urgently about getting to know very much more of our Asian neighbours' needs.'[18]

Fuelled both by the changing economic fortunes, and the general social dislocations, Australia changed in many ways in the late 1960s and 1970s. As the next section will argue, sport failed to change much, and was increasingly seen by many as conservative, out of touch and, possibly most importantly, unsuccessful.

Sport in eclipse

In 1970, tennis star Margaret Court won the Grand Slam: the tennis championships of Australia, France, Wimbledon and the United States in one year. Despite the fact that she was only the second woman to achieve the feat, she found little recognition in an Australia still reeling from tennis becoming professional:

> When I got home to Australia no-one paid much attention to my Grand Slam. There were no big civic welcomes, as there had been after my first Wimbledon victory ... As supposed amateurs, we had more recognition from the public than we got for a long while after being acknowledged for what we really were: true professionals. The hypocrisy was so deep-seated in tennis and had reached out so widely – through not only the officials but the general public as well – that it took a long while before our true status was recognized.[19]

Court's suspicions about the amateur bias of the 'general public'were well founded, at least as judged by sports coverage in *The Age*. In the United States, media attention was overwhelmingly on professional sports by 1970. In Australia, though, two-fifths of media coverage in 1975 was of amateur sport, with another one-fifth on the then semi-professional sports of cricket and football. The two-fifths coverage on professional sport, a share which had changed little since 1950, was dominated by horse racing.[20]

Earlier papers have discussed the range of Australian sports from fully professional, such as horse racing, to the fully (if sometimes dubiously) amateur, such as athletics and swimming. And there was a flourishing subculture which supported the Stawell Gift. But most of the key sports organizations of the 1960s were adept at publicizing the undoubted attractions of the amateur ideal, and in the process cementing themselves as the keepers of the holy grail. As noted in the previous paper, the organizations were also characterized by imperial and militaristic links, even by the standards of most conservatives in Australia. The strength of the image was attested to by in a letter Don Bradman wrote in February 1987. Despite making a good income whilst a cricketer through media contracts, Bradman claimed,

> Not that I would ever have pursued a professional sporting career – it was always against my instincts. I have no objection to professional sportsmen but I don't think they derive the same pleasure from their exertions as the people who play sport primarily for enjoyment.[21]

This orientation was singularly poorly positioned to adapt to the changing times. In fact, most saw little need to adapt. Yes, the glory days of 1960 had perhaps started to fade in some sports, but Australia was still a sporting power – and the old organization and methods would surely win through again in the near future.

In fact, behind the continuing façade of the Australian sporting image, things were already crumbling by the early 1970s. In the flagship of sporting attendances, the weekly turnout for VFL games in Melbourne, total attendances fell a little, in contrast to the strong growth of both population and incomes. In consequence, weekly VFL attendees dropped from 8% of Melbourne's population in the late 1950s to 5% in the early 1970s.

At least as recorded in racing, the decline in proportions attending sports occurred amongst both the die-hard fans and the event goers. Numbers going to the races fell from 27% of the population in 1951 to 20% in 1966, and further to 16% in 1995.[22] The proportion of regulars – those coming six or more times a year – was falling even faster than the total figures. Regular race goers formed 9% of the total population in 1951, but this fell to 6% by 1966 and further to 3% in 1995. Amidst the overall declining numbers, attendances were static at iconic race meetings such as the Derby and Oaks Day in Melbourne. As discussed further in Paper 14, such meetings gave the basis for recovery, emphasizing occasional fans, in the 1990s.

One analysis of the trends in football attendances in Melbourne has produced both expected and surprising results.[23] Attendances declined as incomes grew, with alternative leisure options becoming available. Attendances also declined when the VFL or clubs raised ticket prices. But, contrary to what might be expected, total attendances were less in years when the club with the largest supporter base, Collingwood, did well. The reason for this goes back to the discussion in Paper 5 of the different motivations of sports fans. Collingwood had the largest number of die-hard fans – but space limits on the number who could attend home games at Victoria Park. Consequently, Magpie attendances were fairly constant, no matter how the club was doing. Other clubs had larger numbers of fair-weather supporters, and sufficient grandstand space to accommodate their generally smaller numbers. So when those clubs did well (meaning poorer results for Collingwood) total attendances rose.

But in the longer term variations between club support levels were less important than the general downward trend. One factor here was the lack of improvement in facilities for fans, at a time when community standards generally were increasing with rising living standards. One Magpie fan remembered with distaste conditions at Victoria Park around 1970:

> The toilet conditions were non-existent. You'd just urinate where you could. Often the urine would be flowing all over the floor. When we played the big games like against Essendon or Carlton, it was so packed. I remember two Carlton games vividly in 1970 and 1971 where you couldn't move, so after we'd drunk from our cans we'd just urinate in the cans because you couldn't move. It was pretty basic stuff.[24]

Nor were things totally rosy on the sports participation front either, although differing groups had divergent trends in the 1960s and 1970s. School children's participation in organized sport was remarkably high around 1980, and that may indeed have been the high point. Certainly for lawn bowls, as we will see in the final section of this paper, peak participation figures occurred around 1980. But, for adults overall, participation in organized sport fell from about one third in 1950 to just over one quarter by 1975.[25] As discussed in Paper 6, the overall changes in sporting participation varied by age group, with people aged over 60 increasingly active, as youngsters in their 20s turned away from organized sport. Even amongst the group in their 20s there were differences by gender and especially by income. In 1950, due to both income and the availability of leisure time, sporting participation was much stronger amongst higher income families. Although some disparity still existed in 1975, the figures had become more democratic – which means that the overall fall in participation was strongest amongst the better off. Indeed, the strongest fall was among higher income women, whose participation rate close to halved over these years. The general

Table 1.   Estimates of participation in organised sport by Australians in their twenties, 1950–2000, by gender and income.

		1951	1975	2000
Men	Higher income	72	51	46
	Lower income	51	38	39
Women	Higher income	67	37	45
	Lower income	18	17	31
All		52	36	40

decline was reinforced by the trend for earlier marriage and start of child rearing for especially middle-class women. Working-class women of this age were already marrying in their early 20s in 1950 – and reported then little time to pursue sports. Unlike men, and their better off sisters, lower income women saw little change in sports participation between 1950 and 1975.[26] This collection has emphasized that 'one size fits all' images often obscure considerable diversity. This was clearly the case in these participation rates for people in their 20s, with the overall fall in rates complicated by trends in child rearing, and by the increase in incomes during the period enhancing the access to sport of especially lower income households.

Nonetheless, there was still a strong overall fall in participation rates for those in their 20s. This was influenced by a number of factors. We have already noted above the increasing leisure opportunities in post-war years, and the rapid growth in car ownership. There also seems to have been an influence from the image of sports. In a new youth culture emphasizing individuality and self-expression, the conservative and regimented image of many team sports was no longer a good look.

In 2004, writer Michael Gurr, shortly after moving to Footscray in inner Melbourne, started supporting the local team, The Bulldogs.

I'm on thin ice with football – a game I love but have only been able to arrive at late. Team sports were always run by bully-teachers, excelled at by bully-kids. At some point I pulled down the roll-a-door and said: They can have it, let them have it.

But he now appreciates

what good serious fun a game of football can be. I'm sad about the years of enjoyment I missed, how shallow men stood between me and the game – consequently I know very little about the mechanics of it. But sometimes it's good to be ignorant and just let those intense conversations that dissect football wash over you.[27]

These issues, and their implications for the image of sport in Australia, came to a head with the 1971 Springbok rugby tour of Australia.

In the late 1960s, Australia took a number of steps to improve race relations. A constitutional referendum in 1967 passed with an overwhelming vote, extending recognition of Aborigines. The following year, when Aboriginal boxer Lionel Rose won the world bantamweight title in Tokyo, some 250,000 people turned out for his triumphal homecoming from Melbourne Airport to the Town Hall, shouting, 'Good on ya Lionel, you beaut little Aussie!'[28]

Such changes did not however extend as far as broad opposition to the all-white South African rugby team, when it arrived in Australia in June 1971 for a six-week tour. The tour was controversial, and most games were marked by anti-apartheid demonstrations, occasionally with violence erupting. The intensity of feelings moved quickly into hyperbole. The relatively small number of protesters was a threat to 'the rule of law' according to one newspaper, and threatened 'the principles of responsible government' according to the Prime Minister.[29] The Premier of Queensland felt justified declaring a State of Emergency, a step that had previously only been taken on four occasions, each during bitter industrial disputes. From the other side of the fence, historian Manning Clark reckoned, 'our society was as deeply divided as it was during the Spanish Civil War and the Strikes of 1890–93'.[30] And in the aftermath, when the Australian Cricket Board cancelled the proposed 1971–72 South African cricket tour, ex-cricketer-turned-writer Jack Fingleton termed the announcement, 'the biggest decision in Australian cricket history'[31]

Australia was not alone in battles between rugby followers and anti-apartheid demonstrators. The 1971 tour followed similar tussles in Britain in 1969, and was later overshadowed by the Springbok tour of New Zealand in 1981. But the extent of the hyperbole indicated both sides in Australia felt that the battles here said something about the national character.

Key Sydney organizer Meredith Burgmann wrote six weeks after the tour:

> Not only did we, the demonstrators, feel very emotional about the subject, but our opponents did also. The vehemence with which contrary opinions were expressed can only be attributed to one thing and that is the position which sport plays in Australian life. By attacking sporting teams we had chosen something even more important to the average Australian than the red bogey.[32]

At the start of the tour, Perth demonstrator Rupert Gerritsen said, 'we think that the elevation of sport into a sacred cow in Australia, which transcends all other issues, is pitiful'.[33]

Supporter of the tour, Liberal Prime Minister McMahon asked Australians to show their 'fine sporting instincts and sense of fair play'.[34] A day later he stated his belief that the Australian public would jealously guard its worldwide reputation as sportsmen.[35] A key rallying cry for supporters of the tour was the desire to 'keep politics out of sport'. On 25 June McMahon said the government regarded the visits of sporting teams as a non-political matter, to be arranged between the sporting bodies concerned. With the Australian Council of Trade Unions (ACTU) imposing a ban on transporting the visitors, the Prime Minister announced that the Air Force would, if necessary, fly them between cities: 'Australians wanted the Springboks to come here. Australians wanted to divorce sport from politics. And they do not like being intimidated by the small group within the ACTU.'[36]

Opponents of the tour argued that, rather than the demonstrators, it was the South African government that had put politics into sport with its apartheid policies. Both Leader of the Opposition Whitlam and head of the ACTU Hawke attacked McMahon for (in Hawke's phrase) the 'absurd lengths the Australian government was prepared to go to identify itself with the racist government of South Africa'.[37]

Halfway through the tour, the *Sydney Morning Herald* argued a more pragmatic view that, 'sport which has to be conducted behind barbed wire is an ugly absurdity and we can do better without it. The sooner this dreary tour is over the better.' But this line was not popular with the paper's proprietor, and only three days later, another editorial attacked the demonstrators as 'louts and peddlers of hatred and violence', with 'larrikin tactics' that 'are quite deliberately challenging the rule of law'.[38]

While the demonstrations did not disrupt the completion of any of the rugby matches (all of which the Springboks won, generally by wide margins), they did forcibly raise the political issues. Post-tour, Burgmann reflected, 'The public opinion polls revealed that by the end of our campaign nearly one in three Australians did not want sporting ties with South Africa. This compares very favourably with the earlier figure of seven per cent.'[39]

Soon after the tour, on 8 September, the Australian Cricket Board announced that it was cancelling the South African cricket tour proposed for the end of 1971:

> Whilst there was substantial evidence that very many Australians felt the tour should go on, the board was equally made aware of the widespread disapproval of the South African government's racial policy which restricted selection of South Africa's team.[40]

The board had no doubt that the tour would set up 'internal bitterness between rival groups' and large demonstrations – with attendant large demands on police. Making the announcement, board chairman Don Bradman said he was disappointed that the government had left it up to the board to make the decision. 'Our board is not interested in politics in sport. We cannot deny that the South African government is.'[41] Neither the government nor the Australian Rugby Union made any similar statement acknowledging that it was the South African government which made a mockery of their wish to keep politics out of sport. In that, the ARU typified many sporting organizations of the time – doggedly maintaining their position, despite the world changing around them. And despite situations like eclipses of the sun.

But sports differed, and so did both organizers' actions and others' responses. While the cricket board was more attuned than the Rugby Union to changing political times in the early 1970s, it was itself slow to react to other changes in its sport – as is discussed in the next paper. And in another sport, resilient attachment to older ways of doing things did not seem to have much of an impact on the sport's popularity until 10 to 15 years later. We now turn to that sport, lawn bowls, seen through the prism of the experiences of member clubs of the Victorian Ladies' Bowls Association.

Bowls

Samantha Warren attracted media attention in February 2007 when she played in the Australian women's bowls Open. Not least, this was due to her challenging two key images of the sport. First, as opposed to the typical age of over 50 for bowlers, Warren is a teenager. Secondly, as opposed to a lingering image of rigorous all-white uniforms, she played in a 'hot pink fitted top and contemporary khaki three-quarter pants'. Warren commented: 'it's great to get out there in something that looks great, and I feel really comfortable in it. A lot of my friends have seen the different clothes I have worn at the Open this week and they love it'.[42] As noted in the discussion of leading sports in Paper 6, bowls is one of the most popular participation sports in Australia, and has been for the past 60 years. For most of this period, women's bowls in particular has often reflected the images that Warren challenged.

The first aspect was a predominantly older age group for bowls. Paper 2 noted that lawn bowls is the key reason why sports participation in Australia for ages over 55 is much higher than in the United States. An Australian Bureau of Statistics survey in 2002 calculated that more than half of Australia's 275,000 bowlers were aged 65 or over, with another quarter aged between 55 and 65.[43] This age emphasis is also reflected in the strength of bowls clubs in retirement areas – such as the Ocean Grove Club, which in 2003 reported it was one of Victoria's biggest clubs, with 410 members.[44]

The second, associated with those age groups, was of traditional (and often more regional rather than big city) Australian names. An illustration is the first names of the nine Life members of the Belmont Club in Geelong: Glad, Joan, Thelma, Connie, Doreen, Alice, Al, Frances and Coral. At Ballan the only Life member, Edna Muhlhan, was Club Champion for seven years, President for eight and Secretary for seven.

The third part of the image was illustrated at a Pennant match at Wallan Club, north of Melbourne, when one bowler celebrated by performing a head stand. Most members thought this unique, but the President was less impressed, walking up and shouting 'more decorum ladies, please!' In the common image, this emphasis on decorum was linked to a rigid adherence to rules, including fussy dress standards.

But if clubs could be determined in their adherence to dress rules, they were also determined in the efforts they put in to building their sport and facilities. At the beginning of December 1956, Australia's Official War Historian C.E.W. Bean suggested why Australian women in particular had been so successful in the Melbourne Olympics:

> the outstanding strength of our sportswomen has lain in their morale. Anyone who knows the self-reliant energy and unselfishness of some of their organisations raising funds for their grounds and equipment, and even for overseas tours, by vigorous voluntary effort, must be impressed by their enterprise and good citizenship.[45]

Women's bowls gave plenty of examples of the 'vigorous voluntary effort', 'self-reliant energy and unselfishness' which flourished across Australia in the years after the Second World War. And few examples of 'outstanding strength of morale' could match Betty Stewart, in Ararat in western Victoria. She dressed in whites each Saturday for two years and watched the men play bowls until they eventually allowed her to form a ladies' section in 1954. She became the first president.

The number of registered women bowlers in Victoria increased dramatically from a miniscule 1,400 in 1945 to peak at some 38,000 in the late 1980s, although the overall number of bowlers has fallen since then by about a third. The number of clubs also grew dramatically. From an initial six clubs in 1907, the Victorian Ladies' Bowling Association (VLBA) had 79 registered clubs in 1947, and 559 clubs in the late 1980s.[46]

The number of clubs grew rapidly after the Second World War, strongly linked to economic fortunes. Prior to 1930, most clubs were in the better-off suburbs of inner Melbourne. Both immediately before and just after the Second World War, the strongest growth was in the north west of Victoria, then prospering from booms in wheat and especially wool. As the post-war boom continued and general living standards rose into the 1960s, growth occurred across the state, with an emphasis in the developing suburbs of Melbourne. More recently, new clubs are most often found in retirement areas – either along the coast, or in retirement villages. The growth in Victoria was replicated in other states. The number of women bowlers in NSW increased in the 1950s alone from 4,000 to 24,000. Men's bowls started its growth a little earlier, in the 1930s, but also had phenomenal expansion in the post-war years.[47]

Especially in the 20 years after World War II, many new clubs were initially housed in surplus army or air force huts, with Bright starting life in a former fish hatchery. Such flimsiness had its dangers: 16 clubs reported that at some stage their clubhouses had been consumed by fire (Camperdown suffering twice), and the Clayton clubhouse was destroyed in a storm[48].

Other facilities were primitive too, typified by two clubs in north-west Victoria. Early members at Pyramid Hill had to take a footbridge across a water channel to use the toilets at nearby tennis courts. Upon joining the Rainbow Club, each member had to contribute a cup, saucer and plate. But the prize for perseverance probably goes to the long-suffering women of the Warragul Club, as they did not ask men to put a tap into the kitchen from their foundation in 1939 until 1947.

Clubs overwhelmingly had to rely on their own efforts to raise money for such improvements. The Mordialloc Club raised money by holding garden fêtes, and approaching local market gardeners for produce to sell. Cohuna raised money in the 1940s from euchre parties and catering at 6d a head. Timboon estimated that since inception in 1961 it raised $72,000 through catering, dress parades, card nights and many other activities. Chirnside Park built its bowling pavilion in the late 1980s in five months at a cost of $188,000 – $38,500 in debentures, the rest from contributed labour.

Many club summaries noted such volunteer efforts of 'dedicated fundraising' and 'hard work', and the camaraderie they created for the club. They also reported the pride at the development of new facilities – with Mordialloc noting the benefits of new toilets, 'an improvement on the toilets discretely placed a good distance from the greens, with hazards such as dashing through rain and watching out for snakes!'

Some Clubs did receive assistance in developing their facilities. The Aradale Club, located at a major mental hospital, started up with a donation from the grateful family of a former patient. Cobram boosted its early funds through a 1/- raffle, with the main prize a sheep donated by local farmer. And some clubs were located on land provided by the local church, Returned Services League club, or the local council. Some of the gifts of land came with strings attached: when local Mr Every donated the land for the White Hills Club in 1950, it was with a caveat that forbade play on Sundays.

Any rules coming from land tenure operated alongside strict rules the clubs imposed on themselves. In 1958, novice members of the new Mansfield Club encountered a foundation president described as a 'strict adviser on etiquette'. A State Council member launched the Fawkner Club in April 1964 with a stern talk on protocol and dress standards. And the Drouin Club has memories of a game against Moe one very hot day when a member turned up without stockings. She was sent home by the opposition captain and the game commenced only when she returned correctly attired.

The list of the dress requirements does indeed appear daunting.[49] Rules adopted in 1925 specified cream or white dress, with hems no more than 13 inches (32 cm) from the ground. From 1930, only white was acceptable, although flesh coloured stockings were approved in 1959. From 1960, no necklaces or earrings could be worn. Standards relaxed slightly from 1972, when hems could be 15 inches (36 cm) from the ground. In 1980 discrete earrings were allowed, and in the 1990s hats, sun visors and stockings became optional, with two piece outfits and navy blazers now allowed. In 2000 neat casual attire was allowed for all club social games below Pennant.

While the rules were largely in place prior to the Second World War, it appears policing of them became more rigid over time. Alphington Club reported that in 1934 a lady was approached while playing in a non-regulation dress with a V-shaped neckline at the back. She promptly took it off and put it back on back-to-front. It was not until the 1960s that the VLBA asked the City Oval Club in Ballarat to cease using the red blazers or cardigans they had used since 1931. And soon after Elsternwick Park was established in 1956, the ladies gained the nickname 'White leghorns' because of their all-white outfits – suggesting that other clubs were not yet in all-whites. So it appears the rules were most tightly enforced in the 1960s, alongside perhaps the fastest growth in the numbers of members.

What gave rise to the remarkable growth in popularity of bowls from 1950 to 1990? As noted above, many of the clubs started small, and reached peak numbers later in this period. Even late in the 1960s, some new clubs reported enthusiasm but little previous experience amongst foundation members. When the Dandenong Workers Club started a Ladies' Bowls Club in 1970, only one of 20 members had played bowls before; the new Lindenow Club in 1971 had only two out of 40.

One feature was the accessibility of the sport to older people keen on remaining physically active – as noted above, participation rates since 1951 have increased most strongly for the older age groups. This accessibility grew as car ownership became more common. Prior to this, many clubs reported transport difficulties. Not all could adopt the innovative approach of Leitchville Club where, to take part in the 'marathon' Murray Valley Champion of Champion matches held at Elmore, the ladies persuaded the local train driver to stop his train behind the green to pick them up. The second was the wide social appeal of bowls. From an upper-class cachet prior to the Second World War, the clubs reached out to a wider social pool as they grew rapidly in the post-war years.[50] A third factor was undoubtedly the camaraderie it offered women – which was sometimes hard-won, as Betty Stewart found in Ararat. Most women's clubs shared facilities with men's clubs. Most of the new clubs in the post-war boom opened men's and women's clubs within a year or so of each other. In contrast, many men's clubs of longer standing were slow to recognize the women's game. The Hawthorn Club allowed women associates from 1930, but restricted them to looking after the men's meals until 1950, when they started bowling. The Mulgrave country club's first concession to women in July 1963 was to allow admission as 'social fundraising ladies'.

Other aspects of the sport also started to change. Beaufort 'following a stormy debate' in 1962, decided that 'beer was not a suitable refreshment to be purchased for the tournament'. In contrast, in 1982, nervous, inexperienced bowlers from Hampton RSL were so over-awed at their first visit to another club that they stopped at the local supermarket and sent the 'most demure and prettiest lady' in for four cans of brandy and dry which were gulped down before continuing.

A more serious change for the sport came with rapid declines in numbers in the 1990s, affecting both the men's and women's games. Bowls Australia figures showed total registrations of 270,000 for the 2004–05 financial year. These were over 40% down on figures of 480,000 in 1992.[51] This trend was seen in local women's clubs across Victoria. In the north west, the Terang club started in 1952 at 25, and peaked in 1986 at 101, but now has 55 women members.

As discussed in Paper 6 and noted above, for those in their 20s, participation in organized sport generally in Australia had fallen considerably by the 1970s. While this fall did not occur for older age groups until the 1990s, it seems that some of the same factors, especially alternative leisure options with higher incomes, were involved. One factor particularly affecting the precipitous decline in bowls numbers was the image of the sport, especially based on the uniform code, as being somewhat regimented, even authoritarian.[52] That image, as Bowls Australia publications noted, contributed to less interest from potential new members from 1990 on. Despite less rigorous standards, Bowls Australia research still finds 'that a lot of women believe that dress regulations are too stringent in bowls'. The organization has

> recently eased the regulations at a national level. We are looking to implement a whole new range of fashion for women bowlers, including shorter shorts and singlet-style tops without collars ... the feedback we have received this week indicates that the players and fans appreciate the new look.[53]

From the Australian national image of irreverence and distrust of authority, it is perhaps not surprising that a sport seen by many as somewhat authoritarian has had trouble attracting new members in the last decade. Indeed, a more pertinent question may be why an authoritarian sport was so successful in gaining members in the first place. As outlined here, the sport seemed to get stricter with uniforms even as it grew the fastest.

The key seems to be what the sport offered older women. For the first time, large numbers of older women were reasonably fit, had spare time, had access to transport, and could take advantage of the game and its socializing opportunities. Faced with a massive increase in numbers, and across a much wider social cross section, the sport responded as if it saw itself on a civilizing mission, insisting on strict standards. Those attitudes were not limited to bowls – indeed they reflected attitudes common in the ranks of amateur athletics and other organizations, as discussed in Paper 11.

The remarkable rise in popularity of the game, and then subsequent decline, provide an illustration of some of the factors in the patterns of sports participation in Australia. It also gives a more complete picture of what lay behind the common image of women's bowls. That image was specific to a particular time, and does not reflect either the rapid growth of the sport from 1945 to 1990, nor the efforts that clubs have taken since then to attract more members. And both trends depended massively on how women responded.

But in the 1980s bowls organizations, at the peak of their success, had few drivers for change, despite the conservative image they had amongst many in the population. The situation was very different for some other sports though. And the national image of the sporting Australian was invoked in a number of ways to encourage new interest in sport. The leading examples of this are discussed in our next paper.

Notes

1. NSWCA, *Making the Grade*, 39. The book dates the eclipse as occurring in 'November 1976', but other records date it at 23 October.
2. The 'decline of a sporting super race' was in an editorial in *The Australian* – see Australian Sports Commission, *Australian Sport: A Profile* 1985, 17; the 'middle-aged athletes gone flabby' were described by Kaye, *The Guardian*, July 28, 1976, 1.
3. Cashman, Headon, and Kinross-Smith, eds. *The Oxford Book of Australian Sporting Anecdotes*, 249–50, citing Hutchinson, *The Great Australian Book of Football Stories*, 297. The same story has appeared in locations overseas, for example with Liverpool and centre forward Ian St John.
4. Oxley, 'Ockerism, the Cultural Rabbit', 193.
5. Lawrence, *Kangaroo*, 157. While a comment by one of Lawrence's characters, this is a recurring theme of the book, and seems to reflect Lawrence's view.
6. Cited by Jobling, 'Australian Sporting Heroes', 92.
7. Data for this and subsequent paragraphs from various Gallup polls. The polls sometimes asked for weekly attendances, and sometimes monthly (or 'regularly'). The text uses

monthly figures, estimated from weekly data when necessary, using patterns in polls that asked for both periods.

8. Davison, *Car Wars*, 159.
9. Data from Victorian Ladies' Bowling Association (VLBA), *The VLBA: a History from 1907 to the Present*, club histories in the Appendix. As an out-reach activity the sports links were not always successful – the current author made his only cricket century batting for a suburban Uniting Church cricket club, without ever visiting the associated church!
10. Paul Daffey, 'There's No Song and Dance about this Club'. *The Age*, April 10, 2007, Sport, 6.
11. Data from various Gallup polls, with 2002 from Australian Bureau of Statistics (ABS, www.abs.gov.au), *General Social Survey 2002* (as reported in Australian Social trends 2004, 4102.0, 183). That survey asked for attendance in the last three months (23%) – the one month number was estimated from this.
12. Davison, *Car Wars*, 51.
13. Ibid., 8, 22.
14. Gallup Poll summaries Feb.–March 1946, May–June 1949, July–Aug. 1952, July–Sept. 1964, Nov. 1966–Feb. 1967.
15. Walker and Doyle, *Sports Jokes*, 104.
16. Davison, *Car Wars*, 52.
17. Historian Stuart Ward has documented how Britain-centric Australian commercial policies were well into the 1950s – Ward, 'Sentiment and Self-Interest'.
18. Ibid., 104.
19. Court, *Court on Court*, 139.
20. Shellcot, 'Reading Sport in Melbourne', 67. In 1925, the first of the three years Shellcot studied, amateur sport was even more dominant, at 63%, semi-professional sport 20%, and the 17% for professional sport was virtually all on horse racing.
21. Letter to Bruce Chapman, quoted in Blackman and Chapman, 'The Value of Don Bradman', 371
22. Gallup poll summaries in July 1951 and Nov. 1966–Feb. 1967; ABS, *Sports Attendance 1995* (4174.0). The 1951 survey gave average attendances per year, while the other two gave percentages attending in various ranges (1–2, 3–5, 6+ etc): the other figures in the text have been estimated from the available data. The estimates are sensitive to some assumptions, but give a robust overall picture.
23. Morley and Wilson, 'Fluctuating VFL Attendances'.
24. Cited in Senyard, 'Mining the Barracker Archive', 27.
25. The calculation and background of these figures are discussed in paper 6.
26. The following estimates of percentage participation rates in organized sport amongst people in their 20s were calculated from data discussed in Paper 6. Overall participation rates for higher and lower income households were applied to the age-specific participation rates given in various surveys. The estimates for each income/gender group and the trends between the years were checked for reasonable consistency.
27. Gurr, *Days Like These*, 248–9.
28. Tatz, *Aborigines in Sport*, 50.
29. Cited by Harris, *Political Football*, 67.
30. Manning Clark, 'Foreword', to Harris, *Political Football*, 6.
31. Fingleton, article in *The Australian*, cited by Harris, *Political Football*, 239.
32. Meredith Burgmann, 'What the Demos Won'. *The Nation*, September 18, 1971, cited by Harris, *Political Football*, 245.
33. Cited by Harris *Political Football*, 64.
34. Ibid., 21.
35. Ibid., 67.
36. Ibid., 21.
37. Ibid., 63.
38. Ibid., 99.
39. Burgmann 'What the Demos Won', in ibid., 244.
40. Harris, *Political Football*, 239.
41. Ibid., 240.
42. Reported in *The Age*, February 22, 2007, Sport, 12.
43. ABS, *Participation in Sport and Physical Activities* 2002 (4177.0).

44. Victorian Ladies' Bowling Association, *The VLBA*, Appendix, summaries from Ocean Grove, Belmont and Ballan Clubs. This appendix records stories from most of the 540 bowls clubs across Victoria, providing a remarkable case study of involvement in community-based sport in Australia.
45. *Sydney Morning Herald*, December 4, 1956, 2.
46. VLBA, *The VLBA*, 14, and Appendix.
47. McGregor, *Profile of Australia*, 137. In comparison, New South Wales had 85 men's bowls clubs in 1926, and while this had more than doubled to 199 by 1946, the most rapid growth came after the Second World War – by 1961 there were 612 men's bowls clubs in the State. McCarthy, 'Lawn Bowls', 126, 127, 129. Victoria had similar growth in men's bowling: from 84 clubs in 1913, to 160 by 1926, and then 529 clubs in 1979 with 48,900 members: Royal Victorian Bowls Association, *First One Hundred Years*, 82, 33.
48. VLBA, *The VLBA*, Appendix. The impact of the sports image and declining numbers was noted in McCarthy, 'Lawn Bowls', 132.
49. VLBA, *The VLBA*, 53.
50. Guttmann, *From Ritual to Record*, 30 gave early details of the upper-class cachet of bowls in England.
51. 1992 numbers from Bowls Australia figures cited by McCarthy, 'Lawn Bowls', 132, and Bowls Australia provided the 2004–05 figures in an email to the author on 25 July 2005.
52. McCarthy, 'Lawn Bowls', 132.
53. Bowls Australia spokeswoman Sally West, reported in *The Age*, February 22, 2007, Sport, 12.

References

Australian Sports Commission and Department of Sport, Recreation and Tourism. *Australian Sport, a Profile*. Canberra: Australian Government Publishing Service, 1985.
Blackman, Julian, and Bruce Chapman. 'The Value of Don Bradman: Additional Revenue in Australian Ashes Tests'. *Economic Papers* 23 (December 2004): 369–85.
Cashman, Richard, David Headon, and Graeme Kinross-Smith, eds. *The Oxford Book of Australian Sporting Anecdotes*. Oxford: Oxford University Press, 1993.
Court, Margaret. *Court on Court: A Life in Tennis*. London: Allen, 1975.
Davison, Graeme. *Car Wars: How the Car Won our Hearts and Conquered our Cities*. NSW: Allen and Unwin, 2004.
Gallup Poll Summaries, every 2–3 months, 1941–1973, mimeo sheets held by State Library of Victoria SLTF 301.154 AU7GAL.
Gurr, Michael. *Days Like These*. Melbourne: Melbourne University Press, 2006.
Guttmann, Allen. *From Ritual to Record: the Nature of Modern Sports*. New York: Columbia University Press, 1978.
Harris, Stewart. *Political Football: The Springbok Tour of Australia 1971*. Melbourne: Gold Star Publications, 1972.
Jobling, Ian. 'Australian Sporting Heroes'. In *Sport: Nationalism and Internationalism,* ed. Wray Vamplew, 91–118. Melbourne: Australian Society for Sports History. ASSH Studies: No. 2, 1987.
Lawrence, D.H. *Kangaroo*. Harmondsworth: Penguin in association with Heinemann, 1950.
McCarthy, Louella. 'Lawn Bowls'. In *Sport in Australia: A Social History,* ed. Wray Vamplew and Brian Stoddart, 112–32. Melbourne: Cambridge University Press, 1994.
McGregor, Craig. *Profile of Australia*. London: Hodder and Stoughton, 1966.
Morley, Clive, and K.G. Wilson. 'Fluctuating VFL Attendances: Some Insights from an Economic Analysis'. *Sporting Traditions* 3, no. 1 (November 1986): 69–81.
New South Wales Cricket Association. *Making the Grade: 100 Years of Grade Cricket in Sydney 1893/94 to 1993/94*. Sydney: New South Wales Cricket Association, 1994.
Oxley, Harry. 'Ockerism, the Cultural Rabbit'. In *Australian Popular Culture*, ed. Peter Spearitt and David Walker, 190–209. Sydney: Allen & Unwin, 1979.
Royal Victorian Bowls Association. *First One Hundred Years of the Royal Victorian Bowls Association*. Melbourne: Royal Victorian Bowls Association, 1979.
Senyard, June. 'Mining the Barracker Archive'. In *Football Fever: Grassroots,* ed. Bob Stewart, Rob Hess and Matthew Nicholson, 19–30. Melbourne: Maribyrnong Press, 2004.

Shellcot, Tim. 'Reading Sport in Melbourne: Analysis of 50 years of Sports Coverage in The Age Newspaper'. In *Making History, Making Memories,* ed. Rob Hess, 57–74. Melbourne: Australian Society for Sports History. ASSH Studies: No. 20, 2006.

Tatz, Colin. *Aborigines in Sport.* Adelaide: Australian Society for Sports History. ASSH Studies: No. 3, 1987.

Victorian Ladies' Bowling Association. *The VLBA: a History from 1907 to the Present.* Melbourne: VLBA, 2003.

Walker, Max, and Brian Doyle. *Sports Jokes.* Carlton, Vic.: Allen and Unwin, 1997.

Ward, Stuart. 'Sentiment and Self-Interest: The Imperial Idea in Anglo-Australian Commercial Culture'. *Australian Historical Studies* 116 (2001): 91–108.

Marketing sports nationalism 1975–85

Early in the morning of 27 September 1983, some six million Australians gathered around TV sets to watch two 12 metre yachts battle out the final of a seven-race match series for the America's Cup. To the booming pop sounds of Men at Work's song 'Down Under', and beneath multitudes of green and gold boxing kangaroo flags, Australia II beat the American defender Liberty 83.[1]

Following the win, many exuberant Australians emerged 'from their homes before breakfast, unwashed and in dressing gowns, to pass glasses of champagne over the fence to neighbours'.[2] Recently elected Prime Minister Bob Hawke, resplendent in a jacket variously described as 'gaudy' and 'appalling', described the win as 'one of the great moments of Australian history' and memorably declared 'any boss who sacks anyone for not turning up today is a bum'.[3]

To some, the euphoria over the America's Cup win was confirmation that Australians are sports mad. For others, 'mad' by itself seemed a more apt description. Especially since only 1% of Australians sail, and in a typical year only 5% watch any yachting on television – with most of that for just one race, the post-Christmas Sydney–Hobart.[4] Even most of those who do watch keep some distance from the sport, summed up in the popular description of off-shore yachting as 'standing in a cold shower tearing up $50 notes'.

Such was the unlikely basis for record television ratings. The social euphoria was also surprising as a major change from the trend of sport becoming a markedly less significant part of the national image during the 1970s, as noted in the last paper. The America's Cup win was one of three high profile sporting developments that wrapped themselves in the Australian flag at this time. The two others were: the 'cricket war' with World Series Cricket taking on the establishment in 1977–79; and the creation of the Australian Institute of Sport in 1981.

Both the yachting and the cricket broke new ground in using modern marketing techniques for sports events. They were also innovative in the markets they targeted. Paper 12 noted that the overall decline in sports attendances occurred among both regular and occasional fans – but with sporting organizations taking on increasingly conservative hues, it often appeared they were focussing primarily on their diehard fans. In contrast, the new marketing campaigns tried to bring in wider audiences.

As has been discussed already, the national image had frequently been used previously to help hype interest in sporting events – and to help achieve other agendas, from selling more tickets to cementing the status of the Australian Broadcasting Commission. This paper discusses the very specific agendas for using national rhetoric in the three sporting developments, which together helped reassert the national sporting image.

Cricket

The image of Australian cricket, and with it the more general image of the Australian sports lover, changed considerably in the 1970s. Many agreed with cricket historian Richard Cashman's words:

> The reputation of the Australian crowd as a good-natured, fair minded and knowledge-able assembly began to nosedive, and the Hills of the country became synonymous with cheap jingoism, boorishness, partisan barracking, intimidation, vulgar abuse and, to many, ugly ockerism.[5]

Most cricket purists blamed this decline on the 'Packer revolution' in cricket in the late 1970s. In this view, the gentlemanly game, waxing and waning over several days, was pushed aside by raucous commercialized one-day 'circuses', with players clad in coloured 'pyjamas' rather than the traditional whites. But it is wrong to see a simple battle between traditional cricket and the Packer commercialized version. Cashman's words in fact described comments on cricket crowds between 1970 and 1975, well before Packer's World Series Cricket (WSC) started in 1977. The form of cricket was already changing. One-day cricket matches started in 1970, and the first one-day World Cup was held in London in 1975. The final, between Australia and the West Indies, was the first overseas cricket match broadcast in its entirety on television in Australia, with broadcaster ABC celebrating it as 'probably the most popular sporting telecast ever undertaken'.[6]

And when WSC started in late 1977, it was much more than just one-day games. There were a variety of games: several day 'Supertests' and a series of matches in country Australia as well as the one-day games. None of these formats were initially that successful, with only lukewarm attendances in the first year. In addition, early WSC matches were played in the traditional all-whites, with coloured apparel only starting in January 1979. Indeed, the pattern of cricket's development could have taken a quite different path with some different decisions at various points along the way.

There is a common view that cricket experienced two fairly lacklustre decades from 1950 to 1970. As with a number of images in this collection, a look at the cricket attendance statistics (detailed in Figure 1 below) suggests a rather different story. The 1946–47 season had set an unusually high standard – Don Bradman's last Ashes series in Australia attracted a total of 1.35 million attendances to all first class cricket matches. Nonetheless, attractive cricket in the 1958–59 and 1962–63 Ashes series came close to those numbers, each attracting 1.3 million. But those attendances were not keeping pace with the growth in population, and actual attendance numbers fell in the late 1960s with many drawn matches giving the game a 'boring' image.

The game revived in the early 1970s. Some closely-fought series and a new aggressive Australian captain in Ian Chappell encouraged more interest. The Australian Cricket Board reinforced the trends with heavy promotion of the fast bowling duo of Lillee and Thompson. Attendances soared from the beginning of the decade, with the 1974–75 Ashes series against England the most popular since 1946–47. Even the inter-state Sheffield Shield competition benefited, with atten-dances of 350,000 in 1973–74, well above the 235,000 average for the previous two decades.[7]

The growing popularity of the game increased television interest as well as ground attendances. This also led to adverse comments form some purists. In

January 1975, some wrote to the *Sydney Morning Herald* complaining about the 'verbose drivel' of cricket commentators on television and appealed for 'more silence and less talk'. Acknowledging these views, former captain and commentator Richie Benaud replied that the commentary had to cater 'for the benefit of all classes of viewers':

> Those viewers range through those who have played cricket well, moderately or badly, housewives peering at the screen through a mist of washing up, children wanting to be educated in the game, those through some physical handicap or employment have been unable to get to the ground, and some who have never before seen a cricket match on television.[8]

Along with the growth in crowd sizes came growth of the 'ocker' element described by Cashman. Cricket authorities introduced more controls on alcohol. While some banned alcohol coming into the ground, others such as the MCG and SCG set limits on how much fans, with the new portable 'eskies', could bring in (the MCG started with a limit of 24 cans of beer per person).[9]

But amidst the success, the cricket authorities had several blind spots. They underestimated the significance of broadcasting rights to commercial television. In extending the audience for the game, they proved inept at managing crowd behaviour, and then overestimated how loyal the newcomers would be. Most of all, they failed to deal effectively with players' demands for an increased share of the monies flowing into cricket.

Relative to the average wage, match payments had been falling since the 1930s, and the situation did not change much with the buoyant times of the 1970s. From gate receipts and sponsorships, the ACB earned $900,000 from the 1974–75 Test series. From this the 12 players were paid, in total, $40,000, under 5% of the overall profit.[10] Such returns were pitiful in comparison with other professional sports players, and discouraged some players from pursuing cricket careers for so little financial reward.[11]

In 1975, Australian captain Chappell met with the board on pay, demanding that players should be contracted and paid $25,000 to $30,000 per annum. The Board refused, stating: 'The players are not professional. They are all invited to play cricket and if they don't like the conditions there are 500,000 other cricketers in Australia who would love to take their place.'[12] While the board did increase salaries after 1975, for most players it was too little, too late. In addition, the board still restricted cricketers from making money from other sources, such as writing for the media.[13]

Player dissatisfaction with pay met a change in the commercial landscape for televising cricket. The ABC had long been associated with cricket coverage, and by 1974–75 the broadcaster claimed to have some 80% of the TV cricket audience. This was despite various initiatives by commercial broadcasters: for instance Richie Benaud's commentary could be heard on Channel 7 in 1974–75 and 1975–76, then Channel 10 in 1976–77, before Benaud moved to Channel 9.[14]

The landscape changed because the Federal Government increased the Australian content requirements for TV channels. Kerry Packer and Channel 9 realized the potential for sport to fill this extra requirement. With his golfing coverage already expanding, in 1976 Packer offered the ACB $1.5 million for exclusive rights to national and international cricket. Despite this being seven times their income under the current contract with the ABC, the ACB refused.[15] One reason may have been

Packer's confronting language, reportedly asking the Board, 'Come on now, we're all harlots ... What is your price?'[16]

Packer's offer was to take over broadcasting existing cricket games. If the ACB had agreed to this, undoubtedly cricket would have changed to some degree. Channel 9's interest in greater ratings and advertising revenues would surely have encouraged some innovations in live broadcasting, such as the use of several cameras, and more detailed commentary. But other changes, such as the level of increases in payments to players, Channel 9's intensive marketing, and the importance of one-day games, may well not have occurred, at least to the same extent. These came more from the competition between the ACB and Packer than they did from some 'grand plan'. While some of his players testified to Packer's personal interest in the game, Packer himself acknowledged his motivation was primarily commercial. To a suggestion in June 1977 that his support for the game was 'half-philanthropic', Packer replied, 'That makes me sound more generous than I am'.[17]

In response to the ACB's rebuff, Packer announced in early May 1977 that World Series Cricket would start in the 1977–78 season. Over the two previous months, he had signed nearly all of the Australian Test team, most of the West Indies team, and other leading world players. The fact that the negotiations had been kept secret prior to the announcement was an indicator in itself of the ill feelings many cricketers had for the Board.[18]

The ACB was shocked at the exodus. One board member lamented, 'what we did at the time we thought was the best for Australian cricket. We just had no idea of the depth of feeling of the players.' Another demonstrated how out of touch the Board was: 'When I first started to play we were paid £1 a day for first-class matches. The players [in 1977] were just downright greedy. If it was good enough for us, why not them?'[19]

As well as better salaries for the players, WSC put considerable money into improving TV coverage of the game, and trying to broaden its appeal. Even critics applauded its use of more cameras at each ground, giving better visual coverage of the games. And new commentary styles were tried, especially trying to interest the women who make up a substantial part of the potential day-time audience for cricket. One WSC broadcaster put a special phone connection in, so his mum could ring his control booth at the cricket if she had trouble following the commentary:

> So the little light would come on the Mum phone, and he'd pick it up and his mother would say, 'David, what's the position backward of deep backward square?' And he'd turned to the commentator and say, 'Mum doesn't know what the hell you're talking about.' So came drawing on the screen, so came various kind of graphic analyses of the game itself.[20]

Not all of the WSC initiatives worked. Reminiscing on the 30th anniversary of WSC, bowler Max Walker remembered one effort to interview players on the boundary as they came in off the field. One interviewer asked questions of the Chappell brothers, with the response 'getting five adjectives in the one sentence. The network cut the cord and pulled the pin.'[21]

But most purists were not swayed by the WSC innovations. Many supported the ACB in its reaction to Packer's initiative, and agreed with writer Eric Beecher deploring 'a band of money-hungry mercenaries' and 'shrewd commercial manipulators' who were 'holding the game to ransom'. He confidently predicted failure: 'Do they honestly believe such trumped-up exhibition will interest cricket watchers ... fattened on a diet of real Test matches?'[22] As we will see below, this overestimated the number of frequent fans already among the cricket audience.

In fact, WSC did not do well in its first season, making a $3 million loss in 1977–78. Its Supertests attracted little interest, averaging 5,300 fans per day, while the ACB's closely fought five tests with India averaged 11,500 per day. Nor was the Country Cup competition in regional Australia a great success. But numbers were better for the WSC one-day matches, and 25,000 turned up for the innovation of a day-night one-day match in Sydney on 24 January 1978.[23]

At the start of the 1978–79 season, WSC realized it faced even tougher competition from the ACB, with an Ashes tour. WSC decided to build on what success it had in the first season, by emphasizing Sydney and Melbourne and the day-night one-day games. It also launched a big marketing push, identifying a new target market: 'Our audience will increasingly be one which chooses the Bee Gees instead of ABC concerts.' Key executives suggested the best way to reach this market was baseball's success in the US marketing itself as a 'family day out'. Packer rejected this proposal in favour of nationalism, wanting people turning up to see Australia win. Creative advertising consultancy Mojo turned this goal into the hugely successful 'C'mon Aussie C'mon' campaign.[24] The first WSC day-night game at the SCG in the 1978–79 season, on 28 November, attracted 50,000 people.[25] Bill O'Reilly, not a fan of the one-day game, still described the match as an incredible performance, with the atmosphere of a football final afternoon.[26]

But if WSC had grounds for optimism, traditional cricket was in a parlous state. While the ACB Test attendance numbers for the 1977–78 season had been twice those for the Supertests, the competition clearly hurt: the ACB had Test takings of $0.4 million to support its activities – less than half the $1.1 million it had made in 1975–76.[27] The State cricket associations reported losses in June 1978, especially heavy for NSW and Queensland.[28]

Even worse came for the ACB in the summer of 1978–79. The new Australian test team, depleted of WSC players, was soundly beaten by England in the Ashes series. Faced with one-sided games, audiences stayed away in droves, with the fourth test attracting the smallest test crowd in quarter of a century, and the ABC television ratings declining dramatically.[29] By the end of the summer, the ACB had made a profit of only $127,000 from the Ashes tour, and most state cricket authorities were facing massive losses. The NSWCA had to sell Cricket House, its home for 47 years, to stay afloat.[30]

Losing crowds and money, the ACB announced a deal with Packer on 30 April 1979, with Channel 9 gaining exclusive rights to all cricket games for the next ten years.[31] Despite the deal, and the reunification of the Australian team, rancour continued for some years afterwards, alongside operational disputes between the Board and PBL.[32]

The new cricket schedule included both annual Test series and the one-day matches that had been the saviour of WSC. As noted above, many saw a change in cricket audiences, 'between the long-term, traditional and usually high brow followers of the game and the newer, often younger, more low-brow fans'.[33]

PBL marketing claimed they were trying to reach a wider audience for cricket, including women and families. Once again, there was a gap between this image and the reality in the grandstands. For one example, in early 1980s family tickets in Adelaide comprised only 2–4% of total ticket sales.[34] For another, in 1995 women comprised only 29% of those going to cricket games, one of the lowest proportions of any sport.[35]

A look at total cricket attendance data suggests that the increased audience was very similar to that attracted to the excitement of establishment cricket in the mid-1970s, with traditional fans being supplemented by young males more in the 'ocker' mode.[36]

1.3 million people attended all first class matches in 1978–79, the successful second year of WSC, and 1.35 million attended in 1982–83 with an Ashes series and a popular one-day international series. These figures were only slightly higher than total attendances of 1.2 million in 1974–75, when there was very little one-day cricket.

Going back further in time, it seems that the oft-touted image of the traditional cricket fan needs revision, recognizing some differing motivations as discussed in Paper 5. From the year-to-year variations in attendances in the 1950s and 1960s, it appears there were at least two broad groups attending. The first, conforming to the traditional fan image, was the bedrock of support for annual Sheffield Shield games, who also attended international games when they occurred. Even here there was some variability – Sheffield Shield attendances fell considerably in summers of international tours. But even if these traditional cricket fans doubled their average number of attendances in years when other countries visited, they would still have provided less than half the total attendances recorded for the Ashes in 1958–59 or the 1962–63. This indicates a substantial second audience, of 'event-goers' predominantly attending for the excitement of international tussles.[37] The numbers of event-goers especially varied considerably depending on the attractiveness of the cricket – the closely fought 1960–61 series against the West Indies for example attracted many more than did the 'dreary' Ashes series in the late 1960s.

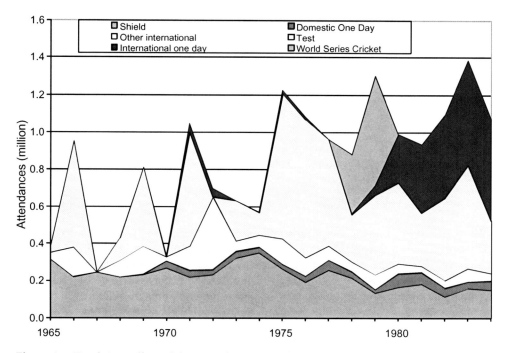

Figure 1.   Total Australian cricket attendances 1964/5–1983/4.

The new schedules after 1980, with more one-day matches and annual Test series, lifted average annual attendance numbers. But in the peak years of Ashes tours, total numbers did not change much – what changed was the games fans attended. The Ashes in 1982–83 had much smaller attendances than those eight years earlier. With a choice of game styles now available, it seems many of the event-goers attracted to Tests in 1974–75 by the excitement of Lillee and Thompson chose the one-day games rather than Tests in 1982–83. And now, with regular international tours and one-day matches in non-Ashes years, they were much more likely to come along to the cricket every year.

Cricket traditionalists found plenty to moan about with the new arrangements. The downplaying of Tests in favour of one-day matches, the lure of money, and descriptions of deteriorating behaviour, both off and on the field as exemplified by the infamous underarm bowling incident in 1981.[38] But on this analysis, the crowds attending cricket had not changed much from that in the mid-1970s – although it seems the marketing and one-day matches did attract larger television audiences.

The nationalism of 'C'mon Aussie C'mon' certainly contributed to the success of World Series Cricket's second year, but so did a change in the type of matches, with more one-day day-night games. And it seems that World Series and the subsequent jointly administered games succeeded largely through consolidating an audience that was already occasionally coming to the cricket, when the national stakes were high and when an air of excitement was created.

A couple of years later, another marketing effort stressing nationalism in sports managed to create a massive, if temporary, interest in a little-followed sport.

Bond and Australia II

When Australia II won the America's Cup in September 1983, boat owner Alan Bond said the win was 'the greatest thing that has ever happened to Australia'. Writer Philip Derriman reckoned such hype seemed almost reasonable amongst the sports-mad euphoria, although he himself took a more sceptical view. Noting the small numbers yachting attracts, Derriman stressed the image-creation process rather than the underlying reality: 'Australians would not have rejoiced so much about Australia II's success if there was not so little else in sport to rejoice about these days.' He asked,

> Would we have got nearly so excited about the win had it occurred at Newport 20 years ago when Herb Elliott was running, Dawn Fraser swimming, Peter Thompson golfing, Jack Brabham driving, Norm O'Neill batting, Heather McKay playing squash and Rod Laver playing tennis? Probably not.[39]

The team's flag, showing a boxing kangaroo, became a national symbol – so much so that the Sydney Olympics bought the rights to the flag from Alan Bond, and the kangaroo boxed its way around Stadium Australia for the 2000 Olympics.[40] The strength of that symbol was a lasting testimony to the success of Bond's marketing campaigns, campaigns that drew heavily, and somewhat indiscriminately, on national icons. As noted in Paper 4, at the tightest point of the 1983 challenge Bond declaimed, 'we will win and win gloriously, just like our boys did at Gallipoli'.[41]

Nor was Bond reticent in proclaiming the commercial agendas behind his bids. In 1974, announcing the first of his four tilts at the America's Cup, Bond stated,

Anyone who considers racing for the America's Cup isn't a business proposition is a bloody fool. There can be no other justification for spending six million dollars on the Australian challenge unless the return is going to involve something more than just an ornate silver pitcher.[42]

In 1974, in the midst of a crisis in the construction industry in Australia, Bond's ambitious Yanchep development north of Perth was in serious financial trouble. But Bond was confident that the banks lending him money wouldn't dare start to foreclose on his debts while he was representing Australia in Newport. Bond threatened one key banker, Citibank, that any moves against him during the racing would mean a lot of front page publicity the bank would not like to see.[43]

The PR on the 1974 trip was not as sophisticated or as successful as it was in the later contests. Bond antagonized many with uncooperative behaviour – for example, describing the Cup's 100 year history as 'sentimental nonsense'.[44] Back home however, Bond's salesman skills, already wrapping the challenge in the national flag, encouraged the Australian media to extol the virtues of the challenger.[45]

Three years later, the team returned to Newport with another challenge. At a press conference, Bond claimed:

All we want to do is to win some races. Last time we were here to promote Yanchep. We achieved that purpose and now we're here to sail ... I'll enjoy it much more this time. There was too much tension before.[46]

Despite the disclaimer, the business connections were still there. In 1980, on his third challenge, Bond won agreement from US bankers he met in Newport to fund his take-over of Australian mining company Santos. Australian banks had previously declined the deal as too risky, but by 1983 it had turned into massive profits for Bond. Author Doug Riggs noted that in purely business terms, 'Bond's decade and $16 million investment in the Cup had gained him $400 million profit' by 1983.[47]

By 1983, when the challengers and defenders between them spent the then staggering sum of $50 million on the challenges, the New York Yacht Club seemed caught in its old patrician ways by the aggressive challenger.[48] Bond's team had a number of technical innovations, including the boat's controversial winged keel, and detailed work with the crew by sports psychologists.[49] But it especially excelled in PR, with the team, including a full time PR and media relations officer,[50] putting out a blizzard of media releases. In contrast, the NYYC proved clumsy at handling even fairly simple PR efforts such as licensing mementos.[51]

When a technical dispute arose over Australia II's winged keel, the Bond team were adept at explaining their side to the some 1,300 journalists covering the America's Cup – while the NYYC was by then hardly on speaking terms with the media.[52] And Bond's media campaign targeted separate markets. In the States a clear distinction was drawn between the NYYC and everyone else, through for example bumper stickers reading 'I love New York, it's the club I hate'.[53] In the Australian media campaign, the dislike was spread more widely, with widespread reminiscences of two previous examples of supposed American sporting perfidy: the deaths of champion Australian boxer Les Darcy of septicaemia in the US in 1916, and racehorse Phar Lap in 1932.[54]

Australia had other sporting heroes at the time: marathoner Robert de Castella, ultra long distance runner Cliff Young, and the tennis players who won back the Davis Cup.[55] But none were promoted as assiduously as Bond's America's Cup win – and none had the business links that underpinned that PR effort. *The Australian* told its readers, 'the crew of Australia II had shown all Australians that we can still do anything if we try'.[56] And Alan Bond was not backward in his use of the triumph to build increasingly grandiose business plans[57].

Such was the power of successfully creating national images for a boat race. Also in these years sporting organizations were successfully dwelling on themes of national pride to gain government funding for new sports programmes.

Australian Institute of Sport

In the 1950s and 1960s, virtually all government help for sports came from local government, especially through the provision of facilities such as sports fields. Apart from some direct support for high profile events such as the Melbourne Olympics, State and Federal Governments took virtually no part.

After the 1972 election, as part of a broad social reform programme, the new ALP Whitlam Government established a Department of Tourism and Recreation, which administered subsidies for travel and coaching, and from 1975 grants towards sports facilities. It also commissioned two influential reports – the Bloomfield report in 1973, which gave an overview of the development of sport and recreation in Australia, and the Coles report in 1974–75 which gave detailed recommendations for a National Institute of Sport.[58]

After the 1975 election the incoming conservative Fraser Government scrapped a range of Whitlam programmes, including those in the sports area. The Department was abolished, and funding severely scaled back. Within months however the media highlighted the poor Australian performance at the Montreal Olympics in July 1976, when the team did not win one gold medal. In response to the public furore, Prime Minister Fraser promised both additional funding and an inquiry into improving sport. These were very much immediate responses to an embarrassing situation – neither actually happened in the next two years.[59]

Following the Montreal Olympics, John Daly, Chief Coach of the Australian track and field team, wrote an open letter to *The Australian*.[60] Noting the decline in Olympic medals since the early 1960s, he argued, 'For a decade now we seem to have been heading for sporting oblivion. In these Olympic Games we have been struggling to compete for minor placings and even to make finals.' Daly extolled the abilities of Australian athletes who 'could bring success and pride to the nation if given a chance', and 'have always provided role models for the youth of the country'. But 'unless there is a radical change in the philosophy of sport development in Australia they will be courageous but unsuccessful amateurs in an arena of competent professionals'. Daly noted successful 'national systems of sport such as exist in Canada and Europe'. Foreshadowing the efforts of many lobbyists in the next few years, he concluded with a wrapping in the national flag: 'If success is demanded then Australia must pick up the bill'.

While the Federal Government cut sports programmes in the late 1970s, a number of initiatives took place at state and local level. These included the Victorian Government's Life Be In It campaign – which responded to research findings that only 20% of Victorians saw positive benefits from physical activity, with 60% confident there was no need to work on their fitness. Several states joined with local government to jointly fund Community Recreation centres.[61]

In January 1980 the Fraser Government finally bowed to the pressure and agreed to establish a National Institute of Sport. The Institute opened a year later, with 153 athletes awarded scholarships in eight sports. The eight sports chosen represented a balance between sports in which Australia was expected to do well, and sports with particularly adept and powerful sports officials.[62]

Both the AIS and sports programmes more generally were boosted by the Hawke ALP Government, elected in 1983. New Sports Minister John Brown published a strategy document, 'Sport and Recreation: Australia on the Move', which argued that by assisting sport and recreation, the Government was helping unify the nation.[63] In February 1988, Brown's successor as Minister, Graeme Richardson, took a character-istically more pragmatic view, viewing it as 'good political mileage for relatively modest expenditure'.[64]

As noted in the discussion of medal tallies in Paper 2, Australia's performance at the Olympics improved strongly from 1980. Commonwealth Games results also improved, with the *Canberra Times* arguing in early 1990, after good results in the Commonwealth Games in Christchurch, that Australia had regained its international competitiveness.[65] The AIS played a large part in this recovery: almost all of the 240-strong team at Barcelona in 1992 had either attended the AIS or been supported by the Australian Sports Commission.[66] Successes also came in several non-Olympic sports.

Along with the successes, the AIS had its problems. Some reflected worldwide concerns, such as a highly publicized inquiry into drugs in sport in the late 1980s. Others were the teething troubles of any new organization finding its feet. An early CEO left under clouds of too much expenditure on hospitality, appointments of friends and relatives to staff positions, and budget overspending. In the mid-1990s a 'sports rorts' controversy over funding of sports facilities in marginal electorates claimed the scalp of the then Minister.[67] And some antagonism developed between the AIS in Canberra and state government initiatives – tensions which a more decentralized approach for key sporting facilities helped diminish.

But in two areas the tensions reflected more deep-seated differences over visions of sport. The first was battles by the leading sports organizations to maintain their positions, and the second was the balance between support for medal-winning elite sport versus community-based sports programmes.

In 1984–85 the Hawke government set up the Australian Sports Commission, with objectives to improve Australia's international performance, to increase sports participation, and to maximize funding from the private sector. However, the Confederation of Australian Sport (CAS), the peak body of membership-based sports organizations, saw this as an intrusion into their activities. In 1985, they unsuccess-fully lobbied the opposition parties in Parliament to oppose the Bill for the new statutory authority.[68]

By 2000, as discussed in Paper 6, a big change had occurred in the structure of sports participation. In earlier years, most sports participants did so as members of organized sports. In 2002, 4.5 million adult Australians enjoyed sport but without being part of any club – the same number as those participating in organized sport.[69] By 2006, the non-organized sport group was well ahead, 6.1 million to 4.4 million in organized sport.[70] The CAS, which claimed total membership in its organizations of 6 million in 1980, saw its numbers shrink to 4.5 million by 1999 – a drop from 40% to 24% of the Australian population.[71] *Shaping Up,* an influential study into sport in Australia saw this as disturbing, warning, 'Sports can anticipate a declining financial base, fewer volunteers, and declining membership at senior competition level which will flow on to international competitiveness'.[72]

Despite the drop in memberships, and the popularity of non-organized sport and recreation, national sporting organizations still argued that they should have a central role in sports administration. This was especially evident in attitudes to Active Australia, a Sports Commission programme aiming at increased participation in all types of physical activity. Some submissions to the *Shaping Up* report fully supported the programme, Parks and Leisure Australia, arguing: 'In order to both maximise participation and encourage active lifestyles, the traditional club sport base must be supported through a parallel participation infrastructure which allows for recognition and encouragement of the individual.' In contrast, many sports organizations supported the Australian Swimming comments that a national sports organization:

> should be the only body/organisation funded to deliver sport participation. Strategic National programs such as Active Australia should be conducted solely through sporting bodies, therefore eliminating the promotion and provision of services to organizations operating outside the context of sport, including those associated with private enterprise.[73]

This adverse comment in 1999 about private enterprise in sport seems remarkably dated!

The other area of ongoing debate was whether Commonwealth Government funding should take a broad or narrower focus. In the mid-1970s, the early Whitlam government programmes had funded both elite and broad participation programmes. But when the Fraser government eventually restored some sports funding, it concentrated on elite sports and the Australian Institute of Sport. Under subsequent Labor governments 1983–96, Olympic sports were the big winners in increased budgets from $41 million in 1985 to $86 million in 1993, although there was still some funding for grass roots sport. From 1996, the conservative Howard government kept funding for the elite programmes, especially Sydney 2000, while heavily reducing the broader participation programmes.[74]

By 2000 there was broad agreement with Ross Oakley's comments as Chair of the *Shaping Up* study:

> In the year 2000, Australians will have cause to celebrate one of the most successful sporting systems in the world. The success of our athletes and sporting teams has given Australia international recognition and our citizens great national pride. It has returned both tangible and intangible benefits to the nation, and established itself as an integral part of Australian culture[75].

A further measure of the success of the 'successful sporting system' came from the mid 1990s with the number of Australian coaches and sports administrators hired by international sporting teams and bodies.[76]

But while the marketing of sports nationalism had widespread success, there were still strong differences in vision. On one hand, a broad inclusive view of sport supported general participation. On the other, both the Commonwealth Government and the entrenched sporting organizations took a narrower focus, on elite and organized sport. As we will see in the final paper, these visions were linked to differences in views of Australian nationalism.

But at the same time as sports organizations were pushing their narrower focus, commercial sports were taking the other tack. The image created by World Series Cricket, of attracting larger crowds and broader cross-sections, encouraged other sports to try to move beyond their diehard fans and attract more occasional supporters. We look at examples in three key sports in the next paper.

Notes

1. Barry, *Rise and Fall of Alan Bond*, 136.
2. Phillip Derriman, 'Australia II Euphoria is a Sign of Lean Times'. *Sydney Morning Herald*, September 29, 1983, 30.
3. Thompson, 'Boats, Bondy and the Boxing Kangaroo', 106.
4. Statistics cited by ibid., 77.
5. Cashman, *'Ave a Go, Yer Mug'*, 135.
6. Ibid., 132.
7. Ibid., 130.
8. Cited by ibid.,134.
9. Ibid., 142.
10. Harte, *History of Australian Cricket*, 560.
11. Ibid., 569.
12. Ibid., 561.
13. Ibid., 565.
14. Cashman, *'Ave a Go, Yer Mug'*, 132–3.
15. Cashman, *Paradise of Sport*, 197.
16. Haigh, *Cricket War*, 34.
17. Ibid., 323.
18. Harte, *History of Australian Cricket*, 579–82.
19. Ibid., 585.
20. John Clarke interviewed by Warwick Hadfield, 'Stop being serious, this is funny!' *The Sports Factor*, ABC Radio National, 1 August 2003.
21. Max Walker, interviewed in Warwick Green, 'It was 30 Years Ago'. *The Age*, December 6, 2007, Sport, 12.
22. Cited by Haigh, *Cricket War*, 65.
23. Ibid., 174, 153.
24. Ibid., 211.
25. Ibid., 225.
26. Cashman, *'Ave a Go, Yer Mug'*, 163.
27. Haigh, *Cricket War*, 174.
28. Harte, *History of Australian Cricket*, 594–5.
29. Ibid., 602; Haigh, *Cricket War*, 232.
30. Haigh, *Cricket War*, 279, and also 246–7.
31. Harte, *History of Australian Cricket*, 606.
32. Ibid., 621.
33. Cashman, *'Ave a Go, Yer Mug'*, 133.
34. Ibid., 165–6, 173.
35. Australian Bureau of Statistics (ABS, www.abs.gov.au), *Sports Attendance 1995* (4174.0) Table 5.
36. Source of data: Cashman, *Australian Cricket Crowds*, 300.
37. On speculative but plausible reasoning, it is likely the number of 'event-goers' was at least double the number of the traditional fans. This was calculated by assuming that the traditional fans who made up 300,000 attendances in a non-Ashes year would each double their days at the cricket when the English visited, giving a total of 600,000 attendances. This leaves another 600,000 attendances for the event-goers. Assuming that traditional fans averaged twice the number of days at the cricket than did event-goers (which seems a conservative assumption) the number of event goers who attended cricket in Ashes years was twice the number of traditional fans.
38. Booth and Tatz, *One-Eyed*, 171, who note that the incident, on the last ball of a one-day final between Australia and New Zealand, 'parked a furore between the two countries' and 'has lingered longer in the national sporting psyche than most other sporting events'.
39. Derriman, 'Australia II Euphoria is a Sign of Lean Times'.
40. Thompson 'Boats, Bondy and the Boxing Kangaroo', 115.
41. Barry, *Rise and Fall of Alan Bond*, 135.

42. Ibid., 64.
43. Ibid., 73.
44. Riggs, *Keelhauled*, 130.
45. Barry, *Rise and Fall of Alan Bond*, 65–7.
46. Riggs, *Keelhauled*, 125.
47. Ibid., 126.
48. Ibid., 138.
49. Ibid., 257.
50. Thompson, 'Boats, Bondy and the Boxing Kangaroo', 93.
51. Riggs, *Keelhauled*, 135, 173.
52. Ibid., 179.
53. Ibid., 173.
54. As with all successful media campaigns, this was not just a one-sided media concoction, but built on a popular chord. Ten years before the 1983 challenge, when the author's wife moved from the US to start teaching in Australia, she met several students who blamed Americans for the death of 'our horse' Phar Lap.
55. Thompson, 'Boats, Bondy and the Boxing Kangaroo', 101.
56. Editorial, *The Australian*, September 28, 1983, cited by ibid., 95.
57. Barry *Rise and Fall of Alan Bond,* 141.
58. Bloomfield, *Australia's Sporting Success*, 38–43.
59. Ibid., 45.
60. John Daly, 'Courageous Amateurs Must Fail'. *The Australian*, August 3, 1976.
61. Bloomfield, *Australia's Sporting Success*, 49–54.
62. Ibid., 55–7.
63. Ibid., 69–70.
64. Ibid., 91.
65. Cited by ibid., 99.
66. Ibid., 100.
67. The controversy was popularly referred to as the 'sports rorts' affair. Rort is Australian vernacular for taking a financial advantage which borders on the illegal.
68. Ibid., 84–6, 174–5.
69. ABS, *Sports Participation 2002* (4177.0), Table 3. The 'organized sport' group included 1.7 million whose sport was solely with organized clubs, and 2.8 million who participated in both organized and non-organized sport.
70. ABS, *Sports Participation 2006* (4177.0), Table 3.
71. Australian Sports Commission, *Shaping Up*, 86. The number of organizations affiliated with CAS had increased slightly, from 107 to 120. While the 4.5 million affiliated with CAS seems consistent with the 4.5 million reporting membership in organized sport in the 2002 ABS survey, this equivalence is indicative but not accurate. The CAS numbers include double counting; for example, someone who is a member of both a cricket club and a football club would be counted twice by the CAS. However, a detailed list of CAS sports (*Shaping Up*, 113–14) does not include aerobics, so large numbers of aerobics/gym members who would report themselves as in organized sport for the ABS would not be in the CAS data.
72. Australian Sports Commission, *Shaping Up*, 86.
73. Ibid., 86–7.
74. Booth and Tatz, *One Eyed*, 199.
75. Ross Oakley, Chair Sport 2000 Task Force, Foreword to *Shaping Up.*
76. Bloomfield, *Australia's Sporting Success*, 209–11. In addition, many of the people who worked on Sydney 2000 subsequently worked with the Athens Olympics in 2004, and with the preparations for the Beijing Olympics in 2008.

References

Australian Sports Commission. *Shaping Up: A Review of Commonwealth Involvement in Sport and Recreation in Australia*. Report of Sports 2000 Task Force, November 1999.
Barry, Paul. *The Rise and Fall of Alan Bond*. Sydney: Transworld Publishers/ABC, 1990.
Bloomfield, John. *Australia's Sporting Success: The Inside Story*. Sydney: UNSW Press, 2003.

Booth, Douglas, and Colin Tatz. *One eyed: A View of Australian Sport.* Sydney: Allen and Unwin, 2000.

Cashman, Richard. *'Ave a Go, Yer Mug': Australian Cricket Crowds from Larrikin to Ocker.* Sydney: Collins, 1984.

Cashman, Richard. *Australian Cricket Crowds: The Attendance Cycle Daily Figures 1877– 1984.* Sydney: University of NSW. Bicentennial History Project, Statistical Monograph No. 5, 1984.

Cashman, Richard. *Paradise of Sport: The Rise of Organised Sport in Australia.* Melbourne: Oxford University Press, 1995.

Haigh, Gideon. *Cricket War: The Inside Story of Kerry Packer's World Series Cricket.* Melbourne: Text Publishing, 1993

Harte, Chris. *A History of Australian Cricket.* London: Andre Deutsch, 1993.

Riggs, Doug. *Keelhauled: Unsportsmanlike Conduct and the America's Cup.* Australian ed. North Ryde NSW: Angus and Robertson, 1986.

Thompson, Christopher. 'Boats, Bondy and the Boxing Kangaroo'. In *Buoyant Nationalism: Australian Identity, Sport and the World Stage 1982–83,* ed. Ian Warren, 59–130. Melbourne: Australian Society for Sports History. ASSH Studies: No. 14, 2004.

Take the money and run, 1985–2007

In the 1990s, many professional sports players saw dramatic increases in salaries, allowing one Rugby League player to say, 'I know I'm living beyond my means, but I can afford it'.[1]

One of the most important changes in Australian sport in the past four decades has been a massive injection of money into the game – initially from corporate sponsorship, and then from television rights. As with many of the trends discussed in this collection, similar changes occurred overseas. But the way they worked out, and the particular impacts they had on each sport, had some particular features in Australia, and indeed, differed between sports, depending on actions taken by a range of people.

Frequently, the patterns included tensions between the corporate and television interests – who wanted to gain as wide as possible a market for their products – and those running sports clubs, who were much more comfortable with their traditional fans. The changes also had implications for the sporting image of Australia. This paper illustrates these trends with accounts of changes in three major sports: Australian rules, rugby league, and horse racing.

Show me the money

Worldwide, sports have become big business, through sponsorship, free-to-air television and pay TV. Revenues for the 1998 soccer World Cup totalled some €60m, increased ten-fold by Germany 2006 to reach €700m, and in 2007 were expected to grow further to 1 billion for the 2010 event in South Africa.[2]

In the United States, which led this trend, the TV programmes with the top five all-time highest ratings are consistently Super Bowl football matches: 138 million viewers, half of all Americans, watched at least some of the January 2003 television coverage of the Super Bowl, enabling the network to charge $2.1 million for a 30-second advertising slot.[3]

The three major professional sports in the US had always paid good money to stars. Around 1930, Babe Ruth was paid more than US President Herbert Hoover, famously justifying it with the line, 'Why not? I had a better year than he did'.[4] However, in the last 20 years, and especially from the advent of pay TV, player salaries in major league baseball have soared. The average in 1985 was $371,000; by 1995 it had close to trebled to $1.1 million; and in the next ten years it doubled again, to $2.31 million in 2004.[5]

Even before the most recent stratospheric rises, one player admitted:

> Don't think for a moment that any player is under the slightest illusion that, in any absolute sense, his performance is worth the money he receives. The point is that we are

members of the entertainment industry, a particularly crazy enterprise. What we do generates this money, primarily through TV and radio contracts. Either we get it or the owners get it; and since we are doing the playing, we might as well get our fair share.[6]

This is not just a matter of the commercial rights for sport – it is also affected by particular situations in individual sports, and decisions both owners and players made. By 2005, the 'fair share' received by players differed between the major sports codes. Players in both the US National Football League and Major League baseball received in total just over 60% of their League's total revenues, while in the National Hockey League the figure was 75%, and in the National Basketball League it was 50%.[7]

While salaries have soared for Australian team sports as well, players' shares of total revenues are much lower, between 25% and 30% for cricket, the two rugby codes and the AFL. The structure of sports here differs in a number of respects. Pay TV is less extensive in Australia than the US, and as discussed in Paper 2, the total value of TV rights is less. Also, travelling distances and costs are greater relative to market size.

Even so, the scale of the commercial changes in the last 35 years is impressive. In 1971, the Victorian Football League received $230,000 from broadcasting and television rights. Club incomes were also modest: the St Kilda club received that year $35,000 from gate receipts, $41,000 from club membership and $50,000 from VFL pooled income. The regular match payment for players was $30, just over half the minimum adult weekly wage.

In marked contrast, by 2005, the AFL's total income was $204 million. St Kilda received $6.3 million from gate receipts and the AFL, $4.6 million from membership and reserved seats, $7 million from sponsorship and events, and $1.5 million from social and gaming activities. The average annual salary of players was $162,000 in 2006, more than seven times the minimum adult wage.[8]

Such changes have had big impacts on the ways sport relates to fans, and the reactions of fans. This can be illustrated briefly for two sports that changed their organization and marketing considerably in the decade after 1995. Somewhat later than other sports, the NSW Rugby Union acknowledged on 12 April 1995 that, 'Amateurism as a concept is outmoded and should be dispensed with in the modern game'.[9] Starting the following year, in conjunction with News Ltd, rugby union established two competitions: the Tri-Nations (between the Australian, New Zealand and South African national teams) and the 'Super 12' (subsequently 14) competition, between club sides based in major cities from the same countries.[10] In Australia, the changes were successful in building support for the game. In 1995, 330,000 Australians attended rugby union games – by 2005–06 this number had climbed to 648,000.[11] One group particularly attracted by the new format was rugby-loving expatriates from New Zealand and South Africa.

The second sport, soccer, had long been semi-professional, and many teams in the National Soccer league from 1977 to 2004 drew support from specific expatriate communities in Australia.[12] Its changes came in response to other commercial challenges – by the end of the 1990s, organizational disarray and rapid turnover of teams were threatening major corporate sponsorship. Australian soccer was revamped in 2005–06, with the new teams based on city-wide franchises. Statistics for 2005–06 show 516,000 people attending soccer – similar levels to the 503,000 in 1995. Strong growth followed in the 2006–07 season, especially in Melbourne with the successes of the Melbourne Victory team.

In their reorganizations, both sports aimed to reach beyond their traditional supporter base. Rugby union successfully appealed to both dedicated and occasional fans. It increased the number of fans attending six or more games a year by one third, and more than doubled the numbers of less frequent fans. In soccer, however, with fairly static total numbers attending, the increase in occasional fans (up 60,000 over the decade) was largely offset by fewer attendances from previously keen fans. The numbers attending six or more games fell by 50,000.[13]

The two sports differed markedly in two other trends. Rugby union saw no change in either the gender balance at games or the occupational patterns. In both 1995 and 2005, women formed one third of those attending, and the professional and managerial groups dominated the crowds. In contrast, soccer saw the female proportion growing from 32% to 36%, and a change from predominantly blue collar crowds to large numbers of the professional and managerial groups.

Paper 6 argued that the diversity of sports attendance makes any simple image of a sports fan problematic. These differing experiences of rugby union and soccer, as well as reinforcing this point, emphasize that there is also no simple process by which sports become commercialized. Rather, broad trends, such as increasing money from broadcasting rights, have different effects depending on the structure and the history of particular sports, the decisions sports organizers make, and how both frequent and occasional fans respond.

This paper illustrates these points by looking at three sports in more detail – the transition from the VFL to the AFL in Australian rules, the battle between broadcasters over rugby league, and the reorientation of the Melbourne Cup carnival.

Australian rules

From the 1970s to the 1990s, Australian rules football saw massive changes, primarily from the leading Victorian competition, run by the Victorian Football League changing itself into a national competition, under the brand of the Australian Football League. The changes were controversial, and took some time to take effect, with many fans initially becoming disenchanted with the game.

Paper 5 discussed the remarkable attendance levels for Australian rules in Melbourne from the 1920s onwards. By the end of the 1960s, attendance levels were still massive, with 5% of Melbourne's population typically turning out each weekend for home-and-away games. Saturday night replays of games drew top ratings throughout the 1960s, with all TV stations showing replays at some stage after 1965.[14]

However, the trends were not encouraging. The 5% figure was down from 7% in 1960, and despite a growing Melbourne population, total crowds were static at the three million level through the decade. This number grew in the 1970s, but solely due to increases in the numbers of both home and away and finals games. Average crowd size fell slightly from the early 1960s to the late 1970s.[15] One harbinger of a solution came in 1968, when cigarette manufacturers W.D. and H.O. Wills paid $12,000 for signage and promotional opportunities during the final series.[16]

Clubs faced increasing problems in the 1970s, from both competitive and financial pressures. The competitive pressures especially came from the success of the North Melbourne club. In the 1960s, North Melbourne had been one of the weakest clubs in the VFL competition, frequently coming last in the ladder.[17] That changed with a new commercial strategy instituted by club President Allen Aylett. With new commercial sponsorship, North Melbourne's annual income increased from $65,000 in 1968 to

$247,000 in 1974, allowing the club to purchase the best available players. A reinvigorated North Melbourne finished second in 1974 and won the premiership in 1975, and again in 1977.[18] The North example raised the financial stakes for all clubs, setting new standards of both commercialism and player payments that other clubs had to match. Many clubs signed commercial agreements, but these increased the gap between better off clubs, and those which had fewer resources, especially Fitzroy and South Melbourne.[19]

Aylett's success at North Melbourne led to his election as president of the VFL in 1975, with a mandate for commercial modernization. However, not everyone in the VFL was persuaded such developments were necessary. In their votes for the VFL president in 1975, the clubs split their votes between Aylett and his main opponent. Aylett was installed only on the casting vote of the outgoing president.[20]

The VFL now commenced a plan to 'modernize and commercialize'. VFL income increased dramatically through selling VFL endorsements, increasing commercial sponsorship and TV rights. The 1977 Grand Final was the first to be telecast live, with HSV7 paying $200,000 for the broadcast rights.[21] The VFL had previously developed plans for the future of the game, most notably with the construction of a massive new ground at VFL Park in Melbourne's south-eastern suburbs. In the late 1970s it started business-like corporate planning in earnest, adopting a plan in 1980 to rationalize grounds and the number of clubs in Melbourne, and to start a national competition with new clubs in Sydney and later Brisbane.[22]

The VFL also tried to strengthen its brand and television presence, in conjunction with Channel 7. This included televising reserves games on Sunday afternoon, in competition against Channel 0/10's coverage of the Victorian Football Association (VFA) and National Football League games. Admitting defeat, in 1982, Channel 10 dropped its coverage of the VFA apart from the final series.[23]

While the VFL was developing ambitious new plans, many clubs faced immediate financial difficulties. Player payments benefited from the competitive pressure, increasing from 30% of average weekly earnings in 1977 to 75% in 1980.[24] In addition, facilities at many grounds could not meet rising community standards – with some becoming dilapidated. Clubs such as South Melbourne (membership in 1980 of 1,500) and Fitzroy (3,200) were in no position to respond to such pressures.

In July 1979, the VFL approved an application from all-but-bankrupt South Melbourne to play in Sydney from 1982. A 'Keep South at South' campaign rallied members and unsuccessfully tried legal action to keep the club in Victoria. However, the move was clearly going ahead when the team's players threatened to walk out unless the move was approved.[25]

Other clubs were also in trouble. At a board meeting in 1982, Aylett warned that the VFL was at financial crossroads:

> It is not hard to conclude that unless our structural problems of player payments, player transfer regulations, grounds, club finances and the overall viability and structure of our competition are looked at seriously, and some real on-going solutions are found, our present competition will not exist in its present form for much longer.[26]

In 1983, the VFL was almost $2 million in debt. Clubs were faring even worse, with average debts of $500,000 each, and many facing Corporate Affairs Commission queries about why they were continuing to trade.[27] It took some time – and a considerable number of highly publicized disputes along the way – until the clubs and (now) AFL got their houses into order.

While the VFL attempted to deal with the financial crisis, considerable opposition grew to its corporate management style. Criticism came from state governments of both political persuasions, from several clubs, the Players Association and many fans.[28] An editorial in *The Age* in 1981 described a public view of the League as a 'dictatorial, money hungry, self-promoting organisation which is destroying the roots of football as a sport and catapulting the game into unwanted professionalism'. Paper 12 noted that earlier opposition to Sunday afternoon sport had faded by 1966, with three quarters of people now in favour. But in October 1981, antagonism to the VFL was such that more than 70% of Melburnians were opposed to VFL plans to extend games into Sunday afternoons.[29] And attendances at games in Melbourne fell through the 1980s.

For the clubs based in Melbourne, the VFL recognized the importance of strong member-based clubs, and tried to strike a balance between corporate management and fan bases. The initial ventures into Sydney and Brisbane however had few local fans, and in the mid-1980s the VFL approved private consortia buying the Sydney Swans and the Brisbane Bears. By the end of the decade, both clubs returned to public owner-ship, with the short-term owner of the Swans selling his team for $10, well short of his $6.5 million investment.[30]

But the strength of local feelings stymied a VFL effort to merge the financially struggling clubs of Fitzroy and Footscray. Footscray supporters built a 'Fight for Foot-scray' campaign, presenting their battle as one for local working-class and western suburbs' tradition against the corporate business groups now running the VFL.[31] Although both clubs survived the merger, Fitzroy was effectively being run by receiv-ers, and later, in 1996, merged with Brisbane.

Relying on the traditional fan base – especially when that base was becoming increasingly hostile to the VFL – was no longer sufficient. A report to the VFL in 1985 was one of the first to clearly distinguish between frequent fans and 'theatre goers'. It recommended that the VFL should take initiatives to attract the more occasional fans – and to build the interstate market.[32]

The VFL's next new teams were established in Perth and Adelaide, cities with strong Australian rules local competitions. Even here there was dissension, with

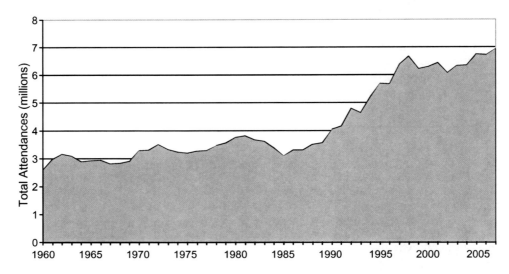

Figure 1.   Total attendances, VFL/AFL seasons (including finals).

criticism in those cities over the now AFL's imperial ambitions. And four of the 12 Melbourne clubs voted against the proposal to establish a Perth team – with the vote in favour relying on two clubs which needed their share of the licence fee money to stay financially afloat.[33] Perth joined the national competition in 1987, Adelaide in 1991, with second teams from the same two cities a few years later: Fremantle in 1995 and Port Adelaide in 1997. Other efforts to merge struggling Melbourne clubs – first Melbourne and Hawthorn, then Melbourne and North Melbourne – were derailed by local mobilization and support from wealthy businesspeople.[34]

One measure of fan discontent was falling attendance numbers. As indicated in Figure 1, total attendances of 3.6 million in 1989 were lower than the 3.8 million of 1980, despite the new interstate teams and an increase in the number of games played each season from 138 to 160. The average crowd size of 22,000 in 1989 was well below average numbers in the 1960s and 1970s.[35]

As Figure 1 shows, the AFL plans began to bear fruit in the early 1990s, with strong growth in attendance numbers. From the 3.6 million of 1989, numbers exceeded 5 million in 1994, and reached 6.7 million for the first time in 1998. Key in the increased numbers was the growing success of the interstate teams. Sydney and Brisbane recovered from inauspicious starts and became competitive, while the teams from Western and South Australia managed to build strong fans bases. In addition, the AFL consolidated Melbourne games into three and then two larger venues with much better facilities (the MCG and the Dome in Docklands).

This account of the transformation of the VFL into the national AFL emphasizes that there was no simple process of commercialization. While the strength of attendances at matches in Melbourne was a strong starting point for the League, the dedication of those fans also engendered a strong suspicion of the VFL's corporate agenda. In the 1970s, even the clubs themselves, well aware of difficult finances, did not agree on the need for some of the changes. And the initial efforts to establish teams in Sydney and Brisbane were little short of fiascos – with many years passing before strong teams in those cities built up supporter bases.

So, as with most of the trends discussed in this collection, there is no straightforward story of sports-mad fans adjusting to new social and commercial realities. Rather, the commercialization process created both new opportunities and new challenges. The eventual outcomes resulted from the ways sports organizers responded, and the reactions they got from fans.

Super League

In 1996, an expensive and bruising battle broke out between the New South Wales Rugby League, with television contracts with Channel 9, and Super League, a creation of media magnate Rupert Murdoch for Foxtel pay TV. The battle, and the reactions of some clubs and supporters, again emphasize the importance of specific situations and decisions in the development of sports and sporting images.

By 1995, the NSWRL had successfully navigated some of the commercialization challenges described for the AFL above and in the previous paper for cricket. The League had established new clubs in Brisbane and Canberra, and had lucrative broadcast and sponsorship deals. It had also tried to enhance its fan base with advertising, including successful campaigns starring Tina Turner, attracting more upmarket and female fans. In addition to club games, State of Origin matches between New South Wales and Queensland teams were successfully promoted.[36]

Despite this success, the NSWRL/ARL faced problems from both weaker and stronger clubs.[37] Some Sydney clubs were struggling to draw crowds of 10,000, and numerous clubs were also having problems sticking to their salary caps. Yet the leading club was probably the most disgruntled. The Brisbane Broncos entered the competition in 1988, won consecutive premierships in 1992 and 1993 and regularly attracted crowds of 50,000. But the Broncos felt that the board treated them unfairly in disputes over salary caps and conflicting sponsorship deals. After a battle over the location for the 1993 Grand Final, the ARL Chief Executive further antagonized the Broncos by remarking, 'They should be grateful we've given them a game at all'. On several occasions, the board seemed to threaten the Broncos with expulsion from the League, despite their success. Chief Executive of the Broncos, John Ribot said: 'We never really thought they would kick us out but right then the decisions they were making were so bad that we started thinking that they just might be silly enough to do it.'[38]

Such antagonism set the seeds for Super League. Ribot began preparing a plan for a new league, based on 'an elite ten team competition with the best players in the competition on top quality grounds'. Potential teams were from the major Australian cities, Auckland, two regional NSW teams, and some strong Sydney clubs. The traditional Sydney clubs of Souths, North Sydney, Wests and Balmain were not considered.[39]

The logical place for Ribot to go with his plan was to News Limited, run by Rupert Murdoch. News Limited companies were already the major sponsors of the Broncos, and Murdoch had proved how successful pay TV sport could be, with the Premier League soccer in England.[40] Indeed, he had international plans for the League, proposing a new rugby league competition in Britain and France, and signing players from New Zealand and in many Pacific Islands, such as Fiji and Tonga.[41]

News Limited discussed its plans for Super League with the ARL, offering what it proposed as a joint venture. The ARL rejected the proposal, fearing it would be little more than a figurehead for Foxtel Super League – and also because any deal would cut across its existing contracts with Kerry Packer and Channel 9. Packer owned both the free-to-air and pay-TV rights to the ARL until 2000, and threatened to sue anyone who tried break the contracts.[42] The ARL tried to pre-empt any defections in November 1994 by requiring clubs to sign loyalty agreements. Despite this, whole clubs and numerous players signed for much higher salaries with Super League on one night in March 1995.[43]

The ARL regarded Super League as an assault on the traditions and honour of the game, with the antagonism evident in Chairman Ken Arthurson's comparison of the coup with the Japanese attack on Pearl Harbour in the Second World War. A flurry of court battles, won first by the ARL but won eventually on appeal by the breakaway competition, meant Super League could not start in 1996 as it had planned.[44]

The 1997 rugby league season saw a 10-team Super League compete with a 12-team ARL competition for fans' interest and support. Other matches were also affected: the State of Origin series was lacklustre that year due to the ARL's refusal to consider Super League players for international or state duties. An article in *Inside Sport* in March 1997 summed up the mood: 'we've tested public enthusiasm for Rugby League and the results are in: the winner is apathy'.[45] George Piggins, former head of the South Sydney Rabbitohs, summed up the views of many about the stoush: 'they stuffed a bloody great game'.[46]

The poor crowd attendance and dwindling corporate sponsorship meant that many teams in both leagues were in financial crises by the end of 1997 – and both the ARL and News Limited were facing major losses.[47] A peace deal was announced at the end of 1997, with a new National Rugby League to include teams from both competitions, starting with 20 teams in 1998, but reducing to 14 by 2000. The broadcasting rights were split with Packer's Channel 9 retaining the free-to-air rights, and Murdoch's Foxtel retaining the pay-TV rights.

The decision to reduce the number of teams in the new competition recognized that many smaller teams would struggle financially. However, as had occurred in Melbourne with the VFL, the merger proposals reckoned without the widespread and passionate resistance campaigns from threatened club supporters – in the rugby league case, from the Rabbitohs. Early in 1999, South's President George Piggins issued an 'Open Letter to Rabbitoh Fans', which encapsulated many of the themes and arguments of clubs threatened with merger or exclusion. Piggins' 'heartfelt plea' urged all fans 'to help and send a powerful message to the NRL that you're not prepared to let South Sydney die without one hell of a battle'. For the match against the Bulldogs the following Saturday, 'the team needs a large and vociferous crowd':

> We need you to yell, wave banners, boo the ref and cheer our local heroes as they come from the field around 4 pm. Hopefully, as winners. We need each and every one of you to show solidarity with the proudest and most traditional club in rugby league history. We need all of our supporters there to tell those who want this mighty club wiped out of existence that it will take a Redfern dog fight to beat us ...

> The game's only a few days away and I promise you it will be a ripper. I know you'll all walk away with your heads held high, proud of the way the team played and the part you played in our fight for survival, just by being there.[48]

Not satisfied just with 'people power', South's also took legal action, and after a successful decision in the Federal Court, recommenced playing in the NRL in 2002. Despite that decision being overturned on appeal in the High Court in 2003, the NRL decided to keep the Rabbitohs in, running a 15-team competition from 2002 to 2006.

As with the AFL, the Super League experience indicates there was no simple transition of the sports culture and image into the commercialized world. Decisions of sports organizations, clubs and media bodies all played a part – as importantly, did reactions of fans. Similar factors affected changes in horse racing.

Horse racing

While its attendances are overshadowed now by Australian rules football, the statistics of horse racing in Australia are still impressive. In 1990, even after several decades of rationalization, more than 400 racecourses in Australia staged 3,700 meetings, with 25,000 races. Close to 40,000 starters in those races competed for $190 million in prize money.[49]

Despite such statistics, not all was healthy in 1990. The industry drew much of its attendances from blue collar men, and its key audience was ageing. In the early 1950s, buoyed by economic growth after the Second World War, more than a quarter of adults attended races at least once a year, and those that went averaged eight attendances a year. By the early 1990s, only one sixth of the population attended, and only averaged 4.3 times.[50] However, at least at Flemington in Melbourne Cup week, the long decline in attendances reversed dramatically from the early 1990s. The best race day to illustrate this is not the Melbourne Cup, 'the race that stops the nation', as that race day has consistently attracted crowds over 100,000 since the 1880s (peak capacity at the

Flemington race course is around 125,000). A better measure comes from the attendances at the two Flemington meetings either side of the Melbourne Cup: Derby Day (held on the Saturday before the Cup) and Oaks Day (held the following Thursday).[51]

As noted in Paper 12, attendances at these meetings had been largely stable since the 1950s, with the Oaks doing somewhat better than the Derby. This was a better result than the gradually falling attendances at most race meetings, but still represented a declining proportion of Melbourne's population, which more than doubled from 1.2 million to 3.1 million in the post-war years.

While the two meetings attracted similar numbers in the 1980s, growing slightly with economic good times, they targeted different audiences. The Derby was a more traditional race meeting, with large blue collar male attendances. Oaks Day, long marketed as 'Ladies Day', had an emphasis on fashion, and attracted somewhat more up-market women.

As Figure 2 shows, both meetings saw phenomenal growth in popularity in the 1990s. This success was little envisaged in the early 1990s, when the general problems of the racing industry became exacerbated in Victoria by economic recession. Bookies' turnover at Flemington almost halved between 1988 and 1994. The Victoria Racing Club (VRC), based at Flemington, reported losses in 1992 and 1993, and many other racecourses were in financial difficulties.

But a successful response to this situation required a new way of thinking about the potential market for racing. In particular, it needed a move from a concentration on traditional fans to attracting the event goers. In the late 1980s, the traditional mindset still dominated at the VRC. The 1987 Chairman's report to the VRC outlined the improvements in racing facilities at Flemington Racecourse, and contended, 'the best promotion any race can have is prize money'.[52]

Starting the following year, the VRC commenced a change in orientation, with very different promotions for key races. A new Spring Racing Carnival promotion, combining racing and tourism operators, commenced in 1989, and by 1994 VRC reports were talking of the need 'to be competitive in the ever-changing entertainment

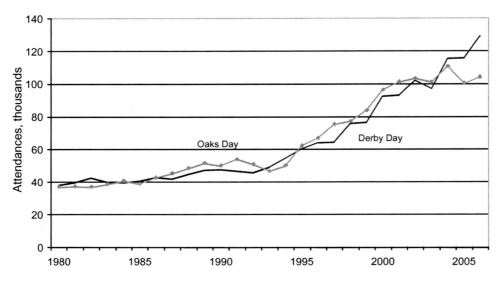

Figure 2.   Attendances at derby Day and Oaks Day 1980-2006.

and gambling markets'.[53] The club responded with a range of new activities, including more races in the evenings and on Sundays. A new 'Racing Victoria' marketing initiative aimed at 'introducing young people to the excitement of the sport'.[54] The marketing campaign especially targeted this excitement to young women, with the expectation that if the campaign worked and young women attended racing in large numbers, young men would only be a couple of lengths behind.

By 1993 the Annual Report could describe 'the social phenomenon that Oaks Day has become over the last few years'.[55] This became even more phenomenal later that decade, as noted in Figure 2 above. Attendances at Derby Day and Oaks Day increased from just under 50,000 in the early 1990s to consistently above 100,000 after 2000, with Derby Day reaching a massive (and very crowded) 129,000 in 2006.

As well as the overall increases, the campaign increased the proportion of women on Derby Day – and increased the proportion of men on Oaks Day! The change in the overall female proportion was marked. In 1951, a little over one third of race goers across Australia were women. By 2000, 45% of those attending races were women, with a big difference between the occasional attendees (almost half women) and those attending six or more meetings a year (only one third women).[56]

However, as with the other sports discussed in this paper, 'some initiatives are more successful than others', to use a VRC comment in 1995. The increase in attendances in the 1990s was largely limited to the Derby and Oaks Days. Attendances at the other meetings of the Spring Carnival grew little in the 1990s, and in the decade to 2002, attendances at other thoroughbred meetings in Victoria (excluding the Spring Carnival) declined from 1.4 million to 1.2 million.[57] The decline in the numbers of traditional fans continued, making even more important the marketing push to attract event-goers, even if to only a few meetings.

Despite such unevenness, by the end of the 1990s the VRC was very happy with the results of its efforts. Annual Reports reported much stronger interest across the community in racing, even amongst non race goers, and claimed Oaks Day was 'undisputed as Melbourne's social event of the year'. This was quite some distance from the 1987 mindset that 'the best promotion any race can have is prize money'. Possibly ironically, the change of tack to attract event-goers ended up substantially increasing prize money. With increased numbers, and greater sponsorship, by 1999 the VRC was paying 70% more in prize money than it had a decade earlier.[58]

Following some of the central themes of this collection, this paper discussed three sports in transition, with new opportunities and challenges from the growing amounts of broadcasting and sponsorship money in sport. There were many different reactions from sports administrators, players and fans to the changes. Some initiatives worked spectacularly, such as Derby and Oaks Days. Others took time to have an effect – such as the VFL's transition to the AFL. Others were less successful, such as the continuing decline in attendances at other racing meetings. And still others were expensive failures, such as Super League (which was estimated in 2005 to have cost News Limited $560 million[59]). And all required responses and support from fans, be they the traditional Rabbitohs fans or the party going set at Oaks Day.

However, the new national leagues threw up some other new challenges. Not least for the coach of a Melbourne football team who, facing a tough game in Adelaide, lambasted his players for all turning up 30 minutes late for a team meeting. After calling them unprofessional (and a few other things as well), the coach was interrupted by players saying, 'Wait on, we *are* all here on time'. And so they were – guess who had forgotten to turn his watch back half an hour to South Australia time?[60]

Notes

1. Walker and Doyle, *Sports Jokes*, 272.
2. 'Ambush Marketing: War Minus the Shooting'. *The Economist*, February 18, 2006, 59.
3. Mandelbaum, *Meaning of Sports*, 184.
4. Cited by Gould, *Triumph and Tragedy in Mudville*, 297.
5. *Statistical Abstract of the United States 2006*, 794, available from www.census.gov.
6. Cited by Gould, *Triumph and Tragedy in Mudville*, 287.
7. Players in Premier League soccer in England also receive about 60% of League revenues. Mark Hawthorne, 'Players Lose Out on Profits'. *The Age*, February 26, 2005, Sport, 5. Other stories about this time indicate that the estimates were prepared by the AFL players' association, prior to some salary talks with the AFL Commission.
8. Dabscheck, 'From Trickles of Silver to Rivers of Gold', 9–10.
9. Statement by NSW Rugby Union chairman Ian Ferrier, cited by Smart, ed., *Penguin Book of Australian Sporting Anecdotes*, 460.
10. Bushby and Hickie, 'The Making of Rugby History', 2.
11. Australian Bureau of Statistics (ABS, www.abs.gov.au) *Sports Attendance Australia 2005–06* (4174.0). ABS, *Sports Attendance Australia 1995*.
12. See Hay, 'Australian National Soccer League'.
13. Attendance and gender data from ABS, *Sports Attendance Australia 2005–06* (4174.0), Table 11. The frequency and occupational status data for 2005–06 is from Tables 10 and 8 respectively, with comparisons with the same ABS publication for 1995.
14. Stewart, 'Boom-time Football, 192.
15. Statistics from AFL website (www.afl.com.au) – see discussion below.
16. Stewart. 'Boom-time Football', 191.
17. Ibid., 197.
18. Ibid., 197–8.
19. Ibid., 198.
20. Nadel, 'Colour, Corporations and Commissioners', 202.
21. Ibid., 203–5.
22. Ibid., 207; and Booth and Tatz, *One-eyed*, 180.
23. Nadel, 'Colour, Corporations and Commissioners', 206.
24. Stewart, 'Boom-time Football', 196; and Nadel, 'Colour, Corporations and Commissioners', 211.
25. Nadel, 'Colour, Corporations and Commissioners', 215.
26. Ibid., 220.
27. Ibid., 221.
28. Ibid., 207.
29. Editorial and opinion poll cited by Sandercock and Turner, *Up Where, Cazaly?*, ix.
30. Booth and Tatz, *One Eyed*, 181. Nadel, 'Colour, Corporations and Commissioners', 215 commented: 'For all the talk about corporate planning in the Aylett years the Sydney Swans exercise represented ad-hoc decision making at its worst'.
31. Nadel, 'Colour, Corporations and Commissioners', 223; Dabscheck, 'From Trickles of Silver to Rivers of Gold', 17.
32. Nadel, 'Colour, Corporations and Commissioners', 223–4.
33. Nadel, 'The League goes National', 228.
34. See ibid.
35. Historical statistics on AFL website: www.afl.com.au.
36. Colman, *Super League*, 10–11, 17–21.
37. Ibid., 50–5.
38. Ibid., 8.
39. Ibid., 60.
40. Ibid., 53, 32.
41. Kelner, *To Jerusalem and Back*, 3.
42. Colman, *Super League*, 76–82.
43. Ibid., 3–5.
44. Booth and Tatz, *One-Eyed*, 189–90.
45. Ibid., 189.
46. Piggins, *Never Say Die*, 140.
47. Dabscheck, 'From Trickles of Silver to Rivers of Gold', 19.

48. 'Open Letter to Rabbitoh Fans', *The Daily Telegraph*, March 3, 1999. See Piggins, *Never Say Die.*
49. Vamplew, ed., *Oxford Companion to Australian Sport*, 182.
50. Gallup polls summary, July 1951 (and also in Nov. 1966–Feb. 1967); ABS, *Sports Attendance 1995.*
51. Data from the Racing Victoria website (www.racingvictoria.net.au).
52. Victoria Racing Club, *Annual Report* 1987, 1.
53. Victoria Racing Club, *Annual Report* 1994, 8.
54. Ibid., 17, and see also *Annual Report* 1995, 4.
55. Victoria Racing Club, *Annual Report* 1993, 1.
56. ABS, *Sports Attendance 2005–06* (4174.0), Table 10.
57. Victoria Racing Club, *Annual Report* 2002.
58. The research on community interest in racing was reported in VRC, *Annual Report* 1999, 27, the claim for Oaks Day, *Annual Report* 1996, 32, and the increase in prize money, *Annual Report* 1999, 3.
59. Dabscheck, 'From Trickles of Silver to Rivers of Gold', 19.
60. *The Age*, June 25, 2007, Sport, 16.

References

Booth, Douglas, and Colin Tatz. *One eyed: A View of Australian Sport.* Sydney: Allen and Unwin, 2000.

Bushby, Mary, and Thomas Hickie, eds. 'The Making of Rugby History'. Introduction to *Rugby History: the Remaking of the Class Game.* Melbourne: Australian Society for Sports History. ASSH Studies No. 22, 2007.

Colman, Mike. *Super League: The Inside Story.* Sydney: Pan Macmillan, 1996.

Dabscheck, Braham. 'From Trickles of Silver to Rivers of Gold: the Transformation of Australian Team Sports 1970 to 2007'. *Sporting Traditions* 23 (2007): 9–32.

Gallup Poll Summaries, every 2–3 months, 1941–1973, mimeo sheets held by State Library of Victoria SLTF 301. 154 AU7GAL.

Gould, Steven Jay. *Triumph and Tragedy in Mudville.* New York: W.W. Norton, 2003.

Hay, Roy. 'The Origins of the Australian National Soccer League'. In *The World Game Downunder,* ed. Murray and Hay, 113–32. Melbourne: Australian Society for Sports History. ASSH Studies No. 19, 2006.

Kelner, Simon. *To Jerusalem and Back.* London: Macmillan, 1996.

Mandelbaum, Michael. *The Meaning of Sports: Why Americans Watch Baseball, Football and Basketball and What They See When They Do.* New York: Public Affairs, 2004. 1976.

Nadel, Dave. 'Colour, Corporations and Commissioners'. In *More than a Game: An Unauthorised History of Australian Rules Football,* ed. Rob Hess and Bob Stewart, 200–24. Carton, Vic: Melbourne University Press, 1998.

Nadel, Dave. 'The League goes National'. In *More than a Game: An Unauthorised History of Australian Rules Football,* ed. Rob Hess and Bob Stewart, 225–55. Carton, Vic: Melbourne University Press, 1998.

Piggins, George. *Never Say Die: The Fight to Save the Rabbitohs.* Sydney: Pan Macmillan, 2002.

Sandercock, Leonie, and Ian Turner. *Up Where, Cazaly? The Great Australian Game.* Sydney: Granada, 1982.

Smart, Richard, ed. *The Penguin Book of Australian Sporting Anecdotes.* Ringwood, Vic: Penguin Books, 1996.

Stewart, Bob. 'Boom-time Football'. In *More than a Game: An Unauthorised History of Australian Rules Football,* ed. Rob Hess and Bob Stewart, 165–99. Carton, Vic: Melbourne University Press, 1998.

Vamplew, Wray, ed. *The Oxford Companion to Australian Sport.* Melbourne: Oxford University Press, 1992.

Victoria Racing Club. *Annual Report,* various. www.racingvictoria.net.au/p-Annual-Reprot.aspx. Earlier editions held by State Library of Victoria.

Walker, Max, and Brian Doyle. *Sports Jokes.* Carlton, Vic.: Allen and Unwin, 1997.

Conclusion

In 2000, two critics argued: 'We find little to celebrate in the Australian sporting character, propped up as it is by pampered and temperamental "stars", uncharitable and biased journalists, unprincipled, unscrupulous and over-indulged officials, and increasingly obnoxious crowds.'[1] John Clarke had more positive images in mind when he remembered a football match at the MCG. Melbourne was on top in the game, and Sydney full forward Tony Lockett had little to do:

> Now and again the football would look as if it was coming up our end and Lockett and the imposing fullback would verge on excitement for a moment, but they would then pull back to a more modulated position and stand around for another five minutes. And a bloke, no idea who he was, but he's a genius, got up, got himself to the end of the row and turned to go up the steps to go outside, and at exactly the right moment, audible by about 100,000 people sitting up our end of the ground, he yelled out, 'I'm going for a pie Tony, do you want one?' and everybody just erupted in applause, it was perfect.[2]

Both sides would probably agree that Australians love sport, even that it is a special part of our national identity, but the context and meaning of the statement vary considerably.

The central themes of this collection ask questions of Australia's sporting image, and its relation to national identity. First, how accurate is that image, in the realities of sports involvement and achievements? And second, how has the image changed over time in response to changes in those realities, and to changes in the agendas various parties have applied to that image?

International comparisons of sporting performance do show areas where Australia is ahead of the field in sports involvement – but this does not occur across the board, nor is it consistent across time. Australia does seem different in sports attendance levels, in receptiveness to sports satire and, at times, in international sports achievement. But in other areas, such as participation in organized sport, or TV ratings for sport, our performances are similar to or lower than, for example, in New Zealand or the US.

But, as this collection has emphasized, national images are much more than just reflections of realities. Indeed, there can often be a considerable gap between the images and social realities. This collection's investigation of some of the common images of sports in Australian national identity has encountered a number of surprises. These surprises include:

- Despite the 'sports mad' image of diehard fans, the wider social reach of sport in Australia is more due to the occasional fans, the 'event goers';

- Although the dominant sporting image is of the young, bronzed Australian male, international success has often been more due to Australian women, and participation in sports has been increasingly by women and older people;
- Despite the frequent image of a philistine ocker sports fan, people attending sports are more likely than the rest of the population to take part in cultural activities, and in physical exercise;
- Despite the one-eyed passions that usually accompany obsessions, one of the strongest characteristics of Australian sporting culture is a deprecatory sense of humour.

Such challenges to the established image, especially as their strength has varied, link to the collection's key argument. While most views see national images as long-standing, the sporting image, like other components of national identity, has seen quite marked changes over time. Further, while many claims link the sporting image to a broad Australian culture or psyche, those changing images have frequently been shaped by the agendas of specific groups or people manipulating the image to particular ends.

The diversity of images was illustrated in a *Sunday Age* editorial for Australia Day 2007. The paper was fairly typical in describing images 'of laid-back larrikins with zinc on their noses getting together for a barbie and a game of cricket'. The editorial went on:

> When we talk about national identity, we invariably make reference to the Anzac legend (particularly Gallipoli); of a harsh land historically riven by drought and fire that has to be tamed; of a larrikin spirit that thumbs its nose at authority and refuses to take itself too seriously; and of a sport-loving nation that knows how to win.[3]

This collection has shown that there have been considerable differences between people and over time in the ways people have put these images together into an overall national identity. The 'harsh land' was little referred to in the centennial celebrations in 1888, but certainly appeared for the bicentennial in 1988. The temperance movement in the first part of the twentieth century was not at all keen on the larrikin spirit. The 'sport-loving nation that knows how to win' was much less evident around 1980.

A central theme of the collection has investigated how and why such changes in the national image, and especially the sporting image, have occurred. Key factors in the underlying realities have been economic and technological developments. The early wealth of Australia, together with the opportunities taken by trades unions, was critical in this country being an early starter in massive attendances at sporting matches. The same forces created a much broader social market for sport than existed elsewhere. New technologies have had strong impacts – the radio in the 1930s, the car in the 1950s and 1960s, television and its impacts on broadcasting rights since the late 1970s. And the advent of cheap international airfares has affected how the country commemorates Anzac Day.

These economic factors created the basis – and some boundaries – for the sporting image. But within those constraints, advocates of different visions of sport had considerable room to manoeuvre. The collection has documented many examples of how differing visions affected both how sports developed and how the sporting image changed. On many occasions, significant tensions have existed between differing visions.

These differences, and their links to sport in the national image, continue in the present. Perhaps the key tension is between a fairly conservative, Anglo-centric view of national identity and a wider, more inclusive view. In sports crowd parlance, there are similarities here to the differing approaches taken by organizers, of whether to centre on the diehard fans or to try also to involve the event goers.

At the end of 2007, the conservative Liberal-National coalition lost the Federal election. In his concession speech, Prime Minister Howard said his 11-and-a-half years in government had left Australia 'prouder and stronger and more prosperous ... The Australian people are the greatest people on earth and this is the greatest country on earth'.[4]

This collection has argued that nationalism and ideas of national identity come in a variety of shapes and sizes. Certainly Howard portrayed a particular image of Australian nationalism. In his concession speech for his own seat of Bennelong, also lost in the November 2007 election, he reiterated a frequently used phrase: 'As I've often said throughout my political life, the things that unite us as Australians are far greater and more enduring than the things which divide us.'[5] But appeals to certain 'things that unite us' often mask a certain framing of the agenda. During his time in office, Howard encouraged particular viewpoints in the so-called 'culture wars', taking a more celebratory approach to Australian history and identity in preference to what he termed 'the black arm band' view.[6] Sport, and especially cricket, formed an important part of Howard's stated aim of a 'relaxed and comfortable' view of Australian identity. One critical commentator described this vision as 'the white-flannelled view of history'.[7]

The conservative framing of national images was also seen in the introduction of a new test for Australian citizenship, asking how well intending citizens understood 'Australian values'. Announcing proposals for the test in December 2006, Parliamentary secretary for immigration Andrew Robb MP explained the test as, 'trying to measure whether people have an understanding of what makes Australia tick. It might be something which indicates that people know a lot of Australians are obsessed by sport.' But Robb rejected any idea that the test might ask for 'Bradman's Test average, or who was the last Australian cricket captain'.[8] When the final details were revealed in August 2007, columnist Catherine Deveny called for 'a real test that requires real Australian qualities'. Deveny suggested several questions of her own, including:

Macca, Chooka and Wanger are driving to Surfers in their Torana. If they are travelling at 100 km/h while listening to Barnsey, Farnsey and Acca Dacca, how many slabs will each person on average consume between flashing a brown eye and having a slash?[9]

Whatever the attitudes to the citizenship test, or the view of Australian values and identity that underlies it, this collection has demonstrated there is considerable support for Robb's contention that 'a lot of Australians are obsessed by sport'. Indeed, it might well be an indicator of obsession with sport that anyone in 2006 would even consider that a citizenship quiz might ask the test average of Don Bradman, who retired from playing international cricket in 1948. Would anyone think of suggesting that a comparable US questionnaire ask about Babe Ruth's batting average? Or ask an aspiring citizen in the UK the names of the goal scorers in the 1966 World Cup victory?

While there are numerous examples illustrating the high profile of sport in Australia, this collection has demonstrated there are strong limits on how far this can be pushed. Paper 10 noted that efforts to recruit sportsmen's battalions in the First World War were largely failures, and mixed receptions have also attended recent efforts by politicians to bolster their popularity by adopting sporting images. Sydneysider Paul Keating, Prime Minister from 1991 to 1996, was much criticized when he adopted Melbourne AFL club Collingwood.[10] And John Howard was frequently booed when he appeared at the Melbourne 2006 Commonwealth Games.

Such limits on how far the sports image can be used are reinforced by the varying degrees of sports passions shown by different Australians. And, even for the sports mad (well, most of them anyway), sports passion is only one aspect of personality, emphasized at some times and less important at others.

Many commentators on Australian images, especially in sporting contexts, have recently noted the continuing changes and differing agendas. While Richard Neville was proud in 2000 of Sydney's 'good-natured piss-taking, the sense of fair play, and the barracking for the underdog', by November 2005, he felt 'all that seems long ago and in another country'.[11] Earlier that year, in a speech marking Australia Day, AFL Chief Executive Andrew Demetriou was concerned that recently 'we have become wary, looking inward rather than looking out. We have closed down, rather than opened up.'[12]

Researcher Laknath Jayasinghe also describes a marked change in the popular mood. In 1998–99, when he attended a number of cricket matches of the Ashes tour, he heard relatively few racist taunts: 'The overwhelming feeling in the outer was irreverence and ratbaggery and good fun ... the crowd was giving it to the Poms and the Barmy Army quite playfully'. In contrast, by January 2006, 'You don't have to sit in certain sections of a cricket crowd for too long to hear racial abuse'.[13]

The trend described by Neville, Demetriou and Jayasinghe (and many others) is associated with a worldwide increase in tensions since 11 September 2001. But, as this collection has shown more broadly, international social developments often take particular dimensions in Australia. In this case, the tensions were reinforced by a concerted political effort to build and appeal to a particular style of Australian nationalism. In this, there are strong elements of 'us' and 'them' polarization, of traditional Aussies versus the more diverse vision supported by Neville *et al.*

This has had impacts in sport. This collection has emphasized diversity – in visions of Australia, in the extent of sports madness, in the motivations of sports fans and participants. It has also demonstrated that Australia has been most successful at sports where it has celebrated and used this diversity. In spreading the social net wider than most competing countries for sporting talent, for early cricket teams, for tennis heroes in the 1950s, and for women swimmers in the 1950s and 1960s. And in the development of a self-deprecatory sports humour that reflects that wide social net, and doesn't let narrow groups take themselves too seriously.

But, as this collection has also demonstrated, there are continual tensions in both the development of sport and visions of Australian identity. Paper 12 discussed the increasingly conservative image of sports in the 1960s and 1970s, with many concentrating on their diehard fans. This image proved increasingly less attractive to event goers, who had growing numbers of other entertainment opportunities. In consequence, the proportions of people attending sports fell, as did the levels of participation in organized sport.

While there are dangers in judging too much from short term changes in statistics, the available data shows that many Australians are responding similarly now. In the late 1990s, encouraged by better marketing of sport towards event goers, numbers attending sports games grew, up from 42% of the adult population in 1995 to 45% in 2002.

The most recent data, from 2005–06, shows an abrupt reversal of this trend – the latest figure is now down to 40%, although different sports are seeing quite different trends.[14]

A similar pattern has occurred in involvement with organized sport. From 1996 to 2002, participant numbers grew slightly, from 29% to 31% of the population. After 2002, these figures also fell, down to 27.5%. These organized sports figures differ markedly from the numbers (especially women) involved in all forms of physical exercise, which actually went up, from 62% in 2002 to 66% in 2006.[15]

This collection has emphasized that such waxing and waning in sports involvement is not uncommon. Neither are changes in the ways different people and groups jostle to support the images they would like to see. Both elements have had impacts on the national sporting images – and indeed on the ways individual sports have developed.

And so it is with national identity more generally. Research discussed in this collection shows that there is much less difference between typical characteristics in different countries than is often thought, and that in each country there is considerable variation about supposedly common characteristics. Further, the elements that form a national identity are in fact far from fixed – proponents of various views of character have much raw material they can work with.

Depending on the preferences of the observer, such diverse raw material can be used to create quite different images – and quite different actions. Two examples are telling. In late 2005, fights occurred in the Sydney beach suburb of Cronulla between groups of flag-toting Anglo Australians and Lebanese Australians. As Laknath Jayasinghe noted, various political and social messages became associated with wearing the Australian flag at subsequent sporting events. A move in the opposite direction, from the sports field to wider society, occurred following racial taunts towards Aboriginal footballer Michael Long in 1995. Long publicized the incident on and off the field, saying, 'Aboriginal people have been copping it for too long and I wanted to make a stand – not just in relation to what happens on the football field but off the field in day to day life.'[16] Ten years later, AFL Chief Executive Andrew Demetriou saw the incident as a turning point for the AFL, which has subsequently developed policies for tackling on-field racism and introduced indigenous football programmes across the country. Demetriou saw these as a possible model for dealing with other issues confronting Australia.[17]

The extent to which such initiatives make a difference to national identity very much rests on how and why the national images are being presented. This collection has demonstrated that notions of national identity are very sensitive to the agendas various people have – and to the ways in which others respond. Above all, we are looking at a varied and continually changing pattern, as sports, other social patterns and agendas all change. As this collection has demonstrated, the overall national image results from an interaction between differing visions of sport and the country, and different takes on the sporting image.

On 17 April 2006, Sydney's Randwick racecourse hosted the $1.2 million Doncaster Handicap, one of its feature races. 83-year-old Second World War veteran Allan Inglis, blind and using a walking frame, flew in from Canberra for the meeting. Approaching a tote window before the Doncaster, Inglis produced a plastic bag and told the operator that he wanted $100,000 to win on racehorse Racing To Win, as well as a $10,000 quinella[18] on that and another horse. When the tote operator counted a total of $114,000 out of the bag, Inglis declined to take the extra $4,000 back, adding it to the win bet. Although the quinella was not successful, Racing To Win won, and paid the punter a total of $509,600.

Most Australian media covered the story, suggesting they thought there was something in it that would strike a chord with many Australians. Differing chords would have resonated for various of the characters and visions we have discussed in this collection. The wowser would deplore the extent of the gambling image, claiming most Australians do not in fact gamble or attend racing. In contrast, the larrikin would celebrate the win – and probably ask Inglis to observe a great Australian tradition and shout the bar. Many others shared a journalist's query that day, asking the veteran what he was doing betting so much.

Accepting his winnings cheque, Allan Inglis replied, 'I am doing bugger all except trying to stay alive'.[19]

Notes

1. Booth and Tatz, *One Eyed*, 210.
2. John Clarke, interview on Hadfield, 'Stop Being Serious, this is Funny!' *The Sports Factor*, ABC Radio National, August 1, 2003.
3. Editorial, 'Time for Clear Thinking on our National Identity'. *Sunday Age*, January 21, 2007, 14.
4. ABC news website, 'Defeated Howard thanks Australia'. Posted November 24, 2007 10:47pm, www.abc.net.au/news/stories/2007/11/24/2100335.htm.
5. Paul Bibby, 'Howard Out for Final Count'. *Sydney Morning Herald*, December 13, 2007.
6. For one overview of these debates, see Macintyre and Clark, *The History Wars*, and the extended review by Daryl Adair, 'Shooting the Messenger'.
7. The letter writer was historian and Adelaide Oval museum curator, Bernard Whimpress, cited by John Harms, 'More Than a Game'. *The Age*, March 11, 2006, Sport.
8. Jewel Topsfield and Michelle Grattan, 'Aspiring Citizens Should Know About Gallipoli: Robb'. *The Age*, December 13, 2006.
9. Catherine Deveny, 'We Don't Want Migrants Coming Here with their Rich Culture'. *The Age*, August 29, 2007. It's a daunting task, approaching such idiom. For a brief translation: Macca, Chooka and Wanger are not unusual nicknames for 20-something males. Surfers is Surfers Paradise, a holiday and party destination in south east Queensland. A Torana is a car made by Holden, frequently 'hotted-up'. Barnsey, Farnsey and Acca Dacca are three popular Australian rock signers/bands, respectively Jimmy Barnes, John Farnham, and AC-DC. A slab is a package of 24 cans of beer, 'flashing a brown eye' is displaying a naked bum, and 'having a slash' is urinating.
10. See Martin Flanagan, 'For Mine, PM's a Sports Pretender'. *The Age*, October 9, 2004.
11. Neville, 'Grandchildren of the Revolution'. *The Age*, November 5, 2005, A2, 5.
12. Andrew Demetriou, 'The Australia We Should Be'. *The Age*, January 25, 2005, an edited extract from his speech at the Australia Day lunch at Melbourne's Convention Centre. See also Sasha Shtargot, 'AFL Chief's Broadside at Australia'. *The Age*, January 22, 2005.
13. Cited by Harms, 'More than a Game'. Other commentary along these lines includes two opinion pieces in *The Age* on 27 January 2007: Jim Davidson, 'A Nation of Barrackers at the Expense of All Else', and Tracee Hutchison, 'Face it. Our Flag is a Divisive Symbol'.
14. See the discussion of data sources in Paper 5.
15. See the discussion of data sources in Paper 6, with the qualification on movements in the numbers between 2002 and 2006 noted in the 'statistical sources' appendix.
16. Cited by Booth and Tatz, *One Eyed*, 216.
17. Shtargot, 'AFL Chief's Broadside at Australia'.
18. A quinella bet picks the first and second horses in one race.
19. Andrew Eddy, 'In the Bag: Punter, 83, wins $509,000'. *The Age*, April 18, 2006, Sport.

References

Adair, Daryl. 'Shooting the Messenger: Australian History's Warmongers'. *Sporting Traditions* 22, no. 2 (May 2006): 49–69

Booth, Douglas, and Colin Tatz. *One eyed: A View of Australian Sport.* Sydney: Allen and
    Unwin, 2000.
Macintyre, Stuart, and Anna Clark. *The History Wars.* Melbourne: Melbourne University
    Press, 2003.

Acknowledgements

I am very grateful to a number of people who made major contributions to this publication. Jen Ward, research assistant across most of its development, tracked down a range of information, as well as providing useful presentation ideas. Ian Spangler debated many of the key arguments, and was continually encouraging throughout the project. Thanks also to Roy Hay, who cheerfully took on the role of editor and provided many insightful and helpful comments.

The publication owes a great debt to the knowledgeable, critical, enthusiastic and very welcoming environment of the Australian Society for Sports History (ASSH). The Melbourne ASSH chapter heard many of the early ideas in three papers to its monthly seminar series. Biannual conferences of ASSH in 2005 and 2007 gave an encouraging and sympathetic hearing to papers trying out some of the arguments. All contributed to making the ideas clearer and stronger.

I have also been lucky in a supportive group of friends, many of whom read pieces and gave helpful comments along the way. Special thanks to Ian Palmer, Andrew Milner and Verity Burgmann. The usual caveats apply.

Research for the publication was greatly assisted by the staff of the St Kilda branch of the Port Phillip Library, and of the State Library, Melbourne. For bringing the publication to fruition, my special thanks to Boria Majumdar, editor of *Sport & Society*, and Melanie Harris, Senior Production Editor, Taylor and Francis.

For my initial interest in history and research projects, as well as encouragement in sport, I am indebted to my parents John and Anne Ward. They also provided an interested and critical sounding board as the publication progressed. For keeping all of those interests going, as well as tolerating the sometimes zany humour, the biggest debt and heartiest thanks go to Gail Ryan. I'd also like to thank Steve Thompson, Associate Editor, and Natalie White, Senior Production Editor, for helping finalise the production of the book.

INDEX

Page numbers in *Italics* represent tables.
Page numbers in **Bold** represent figures.